Post-Holocaust
Jewish–Christian Dialogue

Post-Holocaust
Jewish–Christian Dialogue

After the Flood, before the Rainbow

Edited by Alan L. Berger

LEXINGTON BOOKS
Lanham • Boulder • New York • London

Published by Lexington Books
An imprint of The Rowman & Littlefield Publishing Group, Inc.
4501 Forbes Boulevard, Suite 200, Lanham, Maryland 20706
www.rowman.com

Unit A, Whitacre Mews, 26-34 Stannary Street, London SE11 4AB

British Library Cataloguing in Publication Information Available

Library of Congress Cataloging-in-Publication Data

Post-Holocaust Jewish-Christian dialogue : after the flood, before the rainbow / edited by Alan L.
Berger.
p. cm.
Includes bibliographical references and index.
ISBN 978-0-7391-9900-8 (cloth : alk. paper) — ISBN 978-0-7391-9901-5 (ebook)
1. Judaism—Relations—Christianity—1945- 2. Christianity and other religions—Judaism—1945- I.
Berger, Alan L., 1939- editor.
BM535.P5855 2015
296.3'96—dc23
2014041116

Printed in the United States of America

In memory of Mr. Bernard (Barney) Smith (z"l) and for Mrs. May Smith

Contents

Preface

This volume contains the first ten Annual May Smith Lectures in post-Holocaust Jewish–Christian Dialogue held at Florida Atlantic University. The May Smith Lecture Series was birthed by Bernard and May Smith's passion to seek to improve, mend, or repair the world in so far as this is possible after the devastation wrought by the Shoah. If authentic dialogue can occur between Christians and Jews, after 1900 years of what Jules Isaac termed "the teaching of contempt" for Jews and Judaism, the relationship between the two oldest Abrahamic traditions can possibly become a paradigm for helping to move the world toward peaceful resolution of conflict and away from the ignorance which spawns hatred and mistrust of the Other. The late Mr. Bernard Smith was an inventor and one of America's rocket pioneers. He was a renowned scientist whose work on missiles, including the Sidewinder, earned him many commendations and medals from the United States Department of the Navy. Mr. Smith was also an author and an ardent sailor. His autobiography *Looking Ahead from Way Back* appeared in 1999. In addition, he published several books on sailing, including *The 40 Knott Sailboat*, recently updated as *The 40 Knott Sailboat: Introducing the Aero hydrofoil, a Revolutionary Development in Sailing Craft that Breaks the 5000 year old Speed Barrier*, with line drawings by Barney's daughter Ida (2013). A boat he designed more than four decades earlier recently set a world speed record in its class. Barney was equally concerned with the humanities and the social sciences. He and his wife were voracious readers across the disciplines.

The Smith Lecture Series struck a highly personal chord for both Bernard and May. Mr. Smith confided that for much of his working life he had dealt with the technology of how to destroy other people. The May Smith Lecture, he attested, "is a product of my own extensive dialogue with Dr. Alan L. Berger that redirected my energy toward the opposite goal of seeking to save humanity." May Smith, in whose honor the lecture series is named, has had the experience of being both Christian and Jewish. Born a Christian, Ms. Smith undertook a journey which led her to find spiritual fulfillment as a convert to Judaism. She is indefatigable in her volunteer work on behalf of Jewish causes including support for an orphanage in Israel. She has also volunteered in the Florida public school system. Her life experience as well as her charitable and volunteer work has increased her determination to build bridges of understanding between Christianity and Judaism. The Smith's commitment to hope is based in large measure on the possibility of meaningful interfaith dialogue.

Acknowledgments

I am grateful to the contributors to this volume for their wisdom and generosity. Their commitment to Jewish–Christian Dialogue is exemplary. I also thank my assistant Ms. Bonnie Lander for her expertise and patience in preparing the manuscript for publication. Thanks are due as well to Mr. Dennis Hall for help with the index. The support of the Annual May Smith Lecture in post-Holocaust Jewish–Christian Dialogue Endowment and the FAU Foundation helped bring this project to fruition. Finally, I want to acknowledge my gratitude for the wisdom I was privileged to receive from many conversations held over the years with Barney Smith who died three months shy of his 100th birthday. He was one of the most remarkable human beings I have ever met.

I thank the *Journal of Ecumenical Studies* for permission to reprint my essay "Vatican II, *The Passion of the Christ*, and the Future of Catholic-Jewish Dialogue" which appeared in volume 43, number 1, winter, 2008.

Introduction

Contemporary Jewish–Christian dialogue takes place against the ominous background of the indelible moral stain of the Holocaust. As Professor John Connelly writes in *From Enemies to Brothers* "Once Christians began talking to Jews about theology . . . they began to realize how obscene much of their teaching sounded when spoken in the shadow of the [Shoah's] crimes."[1] The very idea of an authentic dialogue between the two Abrahamic traditions is a new development in the nearly two-thousand-year relationship between Christians and Jews. Previously, while individual Christians could and did have Jewish friends, this relationship was marked by debate and a Christian eschatology which viewed the Jews as theologically doomed. Dialogue, as opposed to debate, entails a vastly different view of the Other. Rabbi Jonathan Sacks meaningfully distinguishes between debate and conversation. Conversation, he emphasizes, "makes space for another deeply held belief [and] is the moral form of a world governed by the "dignity of difference."[2] Furthermore, Rabbi Sacks proposes a test of [true] faith: "Can I make space for difference," he asks. "Can I recognize God's image in someone who is not in my image, whose language, faith, ideals are different from mine?"[3] Failing this, Sacks perceptively notes, "I have made God in *my* image instead of allowing him to remake me in his."[4]

The essays in this volume address the issue of post-Holocaust Jewish–Christian dialogue from a variety of perspectives: cultural; eschatological, historical, linguistic, philosophical, and theological. Moreover, the lines between these perspectives are fluid; their implications frequently blending one into the other. In addition, these essays need to be read with the recognition of monumental change in the Catholic Church and in the Jewish world. Not since the issuance of the watershed 1965 document, *Nostra Aetate* (*N.A.*), along with its subsequent implementing documents, and the statement

We Remember: A Reflection on the Shoah (1998), has the Church been at such a momentous cultural and theological crossroads. What comes immediately to mind is the first papal resignation in over 400 years (Benedict XVI); the election of the first non-European pope (Francis); and the emergence of a strong conservative backlash against liberalizing the church and its relations with the Jewish people.

On the Jewish side there is both hope and caution concerning the dialogue. For the first time in 1,900 years Jews have found a willing dialogue partner. *Dabru Emet* (Speaking truth), a Jewish response to *N.A.*m, and the consequent positive theology of the Jewish people on the part of the church are noteworthy events. Furthermore, the emergence of significant biblical scholarship which sheds new light on vital issues such as Messiah, eschatology, and the initial relationship between the two faith communities has helped in keeping open the dialogical door. Popes John XXIII and John Paul II were instrumental in stressing the Jewish roots of Christianity and in condemning anti-Semitism. In addition, by learning in the presence of the Other, members of interfaith dialogue groups have enriched their understanding of their own faith and deepened their knowledge of the faith of the Other.

Nevertheless, problem areas persist and many issues remain unresolved. Ours is an age where history itself is a contested arena. Many contemporaries are either unaware of *N.A.* or misunderstand its intent. Nor was *N.A.* completely successful in its goal. The late Cardinal Avery Dulles insisted that Paul's *Letter to the Hebrews*, the blueprint for supercessionary theology, rather than the apostle's *Epistle to the Romans*, reflects what the cardinal viewed as the normative (pre–Vatican II) Christian theology of Judaism. There is also the issue of how, or whether, official church doctrine gets implemented on the local level. The persistence in certain quarters of missionizing the Jews remains an intolerable obstacle to authentic dialogue. The divinity of Jesus is another problem area. In 2000, the Vatican issued *Dominus Jesus,* a document that presumed that universal salvation comes only through Jesus Christ and that the Church is the sole modality for the salvation of humanity.

The Church's movement toward canonization of Pius XII—prior to examining the Vatican's wartime archives and while Holocaust survivors are still alive—is offensive to many Jews and Christians. Broadly speaking, the Vatican has yet to meaningfully and significantly address the relationship between its "teaching of contempt" for Jews and Judaism prior to the Holocaust, and Nazi racial anti-Semitism. Moreover, although the Vatican under Pope John Paul II extended diplomatic recognition to Israel, the Jewish State frequently serves as a lightning rod in interfaith matters. Antisemitism remains deeply embedded in certain Christian quarters. Finally, the fact remains that the Vatican is not a monolithic institution. Change takes time and, compounding the situation, not infrequently, the Holy See adopts contradictory positions.

The Smith Lectures are simultaneously an overview of post-Holocaust Jewish–Christian dialogue to date even as they point a way forward, suggesting how the dialogue may possibly aid in achieving a less violent and more peaceful world. The essays share a hope for the future and a determination that the dialogue continue. Elie Wiesel's meditation on hope singles out interfaith dialogue from other domains of engagement such as the political, as a cause for hope. The Nobel Peace Laureate writes: "never before have Jewish–Christian relations been as good or as fruitful as they seem to be now." Citing both Pope John XXIII and John Paul II, Wiesel notes the former's expunging of anti-Semitic elements from Catholic liturgy, and the latter's going even further in the same direction: journeying to Israel; officially commemorating the Holocaust in the Vatican; visiting Rome's main synagogue, all of which "produced a healthy atmosphere of dialogue and mutual respect." Wiesel distinguishes between the hope of the Just and that of the wicked. The just person's hope is inclusive and is shared with the Other. The wicked one, however, believes solely in his own hope, his is an exclusive view which shuns and degrades the Other. Finally, Wiesel views hope in terms of a mission: ". . . it is incumbent upon our contemporaries," he asserts, to invoke and create hope where there is none."

CHRISTIAN SCHOLARS' PERSPECTIVES ON THE DIALOGUE

Four of the essays in this volume deal with the Catholic Church and the role of religion. James Carroll writes of the ambiguous role of religion in the post-9/11 world and why it is vital to confront this ambiguity. Moreover, he attests to the necessity of self-critical reflection and learning to live in a religiously plural world. What Carroll terms "religious fascism" is responsible for the violence and terror plaguing much of the globe. Building on Hans Küng's position, Carroll argues that in order to renew the rational element of religion, the "capacity of each religion to engage in self-criticism and correction" is crucial. Extending the dialogue to include Islam is vital. But the devout face a difficult challenge; how can they "think critically about what they believe"? Specifically concerning the Vatican, Carroll points to the separation of the Church, as the *Sinless Bride of Christ* from crimes committed in the name of the Church. This furthers the "deadly refusal" to confront how religion can "prompt inhuman behavior" such as the Crusades and the Inquisition. The trialogue needs to affirm the principle of interreligious dialogue: each religion must define itself on its own terms. While the West has much to learn about Islam, Islam itself needs to engage in religious self-criticism. "Religious people," he concludes, engage in "self-criticism in the presence of

the Other" [because] "there is simply no other way to fulfill the commandment that binds us all—to honor God by loving our neighbors as ourselves."

John T. Pawlikowski assesses what the Catholic Church did and did not
do during the Shoah. Placing the Church's response against the century-long
war waged by the church against liberalism and human rights, a battle which
only ended with the Second Vatican Council's promulgation of *N.A.* and
Pope John XXIII's encyclical *Pacem in Terris*, which, Pawlikowski attests,
"made a major contribution to the [Church's] about-face." Pawlikowski
urges Catholic leadership to continue to explore Pius XII's wartime record as
well as examining the role of the church as a whole during that time of
unprecedented barbarism. Among the contemporary lessons of the Holocaust, he contends, the church can learn the danger of violent religious language, e.g., "the anti-Semitic rhetoric of classical Christian faith expression
[that] can 'soften' a society for genocide." Furthermore, by continued study
of the Holocaust the church can engage in a "refined self-definition" that will
permit it to "stand at the forefront of a defense of human dignity that escaped
it during the dark night of the Holocaust."

Mary C. Boys wants to reclaim the sacrality of sacred texts. Focusing on
"problem passages," especially the Christian passion narratives, Boys dis-
cerns five types of tellings of these narratives: "A Trembling Telling; A
Troubling Telling; A Tragic Telling; A Transformed Telling; and A Transforming, Trembling Telling." Each telling has consequences, some of which
are positive and others which are quite troubling. Not the least of the latter is
the advocacy of Christian triumphal theology and contempt for Judaism.
Boys argues for a transforming, trembling telling by which she means the
necessity for Christians learning to tell their story "in ways that do justice to
its complex history." This, in turn, entails acknowledging how Christianity
used the crucifixion "against the Jews." This history, she attests, must give
"us [Christians] pause." The sacrilegious uses "to which we have put the
story of the death of Jesus [should] cause us to tremble, tremble." Redeeming
the Christian stories means comprehending that they are connected to a "Way
of Life in the following of Jesus that saves us from excessive self-absorption,
fear, and enslavement to the destructiveness of sin." "Striving to love our
enemies," she concludes, "we lessen the world's violence and the violence
within our own being."

Donald J. Dietrich discusses human dignity as the bedrock of Jewish–Christian relations. Dietrich is keenly aware of the mixed signals sent by
the Vatican concerning the uneasy relationship between Christological
claims and religious pluralism. Nonetheless, he stresses the position of Johann Baptist Metz who argues that post-Holocaust Jewish–Christian dialogue involves a revision of Christianity itself. Dietrich is of course aware
of the skepticism of postmodernity. Nonetheless, he posits that "some Christian philosophers and theologians think that there is considerable evi-

dence . . . of a common human morality . . . uncovered through an ongoing dialogue concerning God and the human condition." This dialogue has the potential to "lead to a universal authentication of the common good." Moreover, "Conscience itself," he continues, "relies on the moral questioning [occurring] in the communities, to which men and women belong." Extrapolating from this, Dietrich attests that Jewish–Christian relations can form such a community.

John K. Roth takes a different tack in writing about how one can-and should-wrestle with the sixth commandment—"You shall not murder"—in light of the Jewish–Christian dialogue. Roth is a Protestant philosopher/theologian whose work has concentrated for nearly four decades "on the Holocaust . . . and on other genocides as well." He asks several questions including, When is killing murder and what constitutes murder? Responding, he analyzes the biblical account of Cain slaying Abel; Nazi Germany's Holocaust of the Jewish People; and post-Holocaust genocides, among them Bosnia, Rwanda, Kosovo, and Darfur. Homicide is wrong. Consequently, genocide and democide are equally wrong, attests Roth. He also enquires about God's relation to murder. God is guilty, not by being a murderer but by "failing to intervene against murderers." The deity is, consequently, a guilty bystander. Roth argues that the sixth commandment reveals that God "takes human accountibility far more seriously than men and women are likely to do." Roth approvingly cites the Jewish philosopher Emanuel Levinas: 'You shall not murder' means nothing less than 'you shall defend the life of the other.'" Jewish–Christian dialogue needs to make Levinas's twin imperatives its "key responsibility."

JEWISH SCHOLARS' PERSPECTIVES ON THE DIALOGUE

Irving (Yitz) Greenberg boldly proposes a positive Jewish theology of Christianity. Modernity offers a second chance for Judaism and Christianity to reconfigure their relationship: pluralism enables one to believe that God's truth is not exclusively the property of one's own religion; the Holocaust compels the question; "Have I self-criticized and self-purified so that my faith will never countenance another possible Shoah?" Greenberg advances three "guiding principles of a positive Jewish theology of Christianity." From the universal Noahide covenant which seeks to perfect the world, stems the command to pursue justice and the warning against killing an image of God. This gave rise to a "series of particular covenants . . . the Jewish covenant, the Christian covenant, Islamic, etc., are [all] permanent." Second, Judaism and Christianity share the central story of creation and redemption. The difference lies in Christianity's emphasis on God's grace, whereas Judaism stresses that "God will work with human mediators." God need not, attests

Judaism, become human to "close [the] gap." The two religions illustrate "the principle of pluralism. . . . God employs both religions for the purpose of *tikkun olam.*" God's grace, and human responsibility, "supplement and correct each other." Even the disagreements are arguments "for the sake of heaven" and advance the covenant. Third, "Judaism and Christianity must shape the emerging pluralism and model how to overcome the forces of aggression and triumphalism . . . still present in every religion." Urgent action is necessary for three reasons: The world needs redemption; Islam is in crisis, moderates must be supported to combat virulent anti-Semitism. Christians can say what Jews cannot say, "we made that mistake . . . [of spreading] hatred in the name of God against Jews. We are deeply ashamed of [it]. . . . Do not make [our] mistake . . . correct yourself now." Thirdly, the Shoah revealed that concentrated power is absolutely corrupting. Religion based on pluralism, freedom and mutual respect will perform at the highest levels of morality and religion. The deepest truth, asserts Greenberg, "is that much of Judaism's accomplishments were made through Christianity and its impact on humanity."

Alan L. Berger responds to the controversial film *The Passion of the Christ* in light of Vatican II and assesses the possible impact of the film on the future of Jewish–Christian dialogue. He discusses the tension between the post-Holocaust bridges of understanding built between the two faith communities and the reassertion of pre-modern Catholic theological thought which embraced the deicide canard and a historically uncritical reading of the Gospels. Mel Gibson's film was based not only on an erroneous reading of the Gospels, but also on the visions of Anne Catherine Emerich, a nineteenth-century German Augustinian nun, who claimed to be an "eyewitness" to the lives of Mary and Jesus. Insisting on sending mixed signals, the Vatican beatified Emerich in October 2004. While both Jews and Christians viewed *The Passion,* they did not necessarily see the same film; Christians saw the passion of Jesus, Jews saw themselves being indicted for his crucifixion. Moreover, neither the Vatican nor the United States Council of Bishops denounced the film, preferring to remain silent. Nevertheless, Berger attests that *Nostra Aetate* has accomplished a great deal in terms of building trust and studying in the presence of the religious Other. Gibson's film, as odious as it was, does present a "teaching moment" for the Church and for those engaged in interfaith dialogue. The persistence of anti-Semitism reveals the urgency of continuing the dialogue.

David Patterson reflects on the meaning of redemption and the Messiah, noting both similarities and differences between Judaism and Christianity. Each faith community embraces the notion that redemption and messianic waiting have a *here and now,* as well as an eschatological significance. Furthermore, each tradition attests to the idea that "some sort of redemption [will occur] after some sort of tribulation." There are, however, differences between the two faith communities. Patterson discusses four key concepts which illuminate the situation: "The Awaited One"; "The Faith Demanded by the Wait"; "The Endless Wait for Redemption"; and "The Meaning of the Messiah in our Time." Patterson contends that both traditions are addressed by, and address, the theological question of the possibility of faith after the Holocaust. He contends that "holy disbelief" necessitates "outrage in the midst of faith." Both Christians and Jews "bear a new wound as the sign of the Covenant." The task of post-Holocaust humanity is "to transform the darkness of Auschwitz into light" by rolling up "our sleeves and mend[ing] the piece of creation entrusted to our care." Extrapolating from the teachings of Emanuel Levinas, Patterson attests that "Precisely because the other may be the Messiah, I must be for the other what the Messiah is for me."

Amy Jill Levine addresses the complexity of the major issues confronting Jews and Christians in dialogue about the Middle East. These issues include both the language each tradition uses in terms of geographic references to biblical sites: Jews speak of *Eretz Yisrael* and *Yerushalayim* Many of the author's Christian friends refer to "The Holy Land" and "Jerusalem," her Muslim colleagues reference "Palestine" and "Al Quds." She also notes that the Bible itself employs various names for the land. Exacerbating the situation is the fact that *within* the Jewish and Christian communities differences exist concerning Israel. Religious Jews differ from secularists. Both in turn oppose ultra-orthodox groups such as the Naturei Karta (Guardians of the City) who contend the Jewish State is illegitimate because it was established by human rather than messianic means. Adding to the complications is the fact that there exist different bibles, liturgies and points of view among the traditions. For instance, God's promise to Abraham "To your offspring I will give this land" begs the question, "Which offspring?" Levine concludes by observing that despite the difficulties, Jews, Christians, and Muslims share a "dominant desire" for peace and each has "deep resources" compelling their followers to "work for peace," which consists of "more than condemning only one side, or pushing only one agenda."

Interfaith dialogue is increasingly recognized as an underexplored potential vehicle for peace-making. Focusing on the post-Holocaust Jewish–Christian dialogical model, one observes how dialogue can bring together even those with long-standing enmity. Each tradition speaks of the end times, eschatology for Christianity involves the second coming of the Messiah, and the *teiku* passages in the Talmud. *Teiku* is an acronym standing for *Tishbi yetrez kushyot veibbayot*. The Tishbite—Elijah—will at the end of days answer all difficulties and problems which currently appear unsolvable. Elijah the prophet is closely associated with the Messiah. The contributors to this volume reveal that after the flood, interfaith dialogue constitutes an active learning and waiting together while mutually seeking a *tikkun* (repair or restoration) of the world in so far as possible after the Shoah. This may possibly help achieve the elusive rainbow which will be a sign that peace and tranquility can reign in the human as well as the divine sphere.

NOTES

1. John Connelly. *From Enemy to Brother: The Revolution in Catholic Teaching on the Jews 1933-1965* (Cambridge: Harvard University Press, 2012), p. 176.
2. Jonathan Sacks. *The Dignity of Difference: How to Avoid the Clash of Civilizations* (London: Continuum, 2003), p. 84.
3. Op. cit., p.201.
4. Ibid.

Chapter One

A Meditation on Hope

Elie Wiesel

This lecture is meant to be an appeal for hope both as concept and program. One speaks about it with great trepidation. No subject seems to me more urgent nor more elusive. An essential element of the human condition everywhere, hope is often stumbling on seemingly insurmountable obstacles.

The twentieth century, the most violent in recorded history according to Hannah Arendt, was shaped by two totalitarian ideologies that promised limitless hope to their nations—and all others. But it was a false hope, based on deceit, unprecedented cruelty and mass murder. False idols and corrupt ideals dominated too many minds. Old theories fell apart, numerous structures collapsed. Then came victory. Fascism was defeated, Nazism vanquished, imperialism, colonialism and racism relegated to the ruins of the past. Apartheid was replaced by democracy, communism by openness and freedom.

We could breathe easier. As students of History we felt that the world had learned vital lessons from its errors. Never again will there be large-scale persecutions of minorities. Never again will there be anti-Semitism. Never again will violence become a language used to solve problems.

As a Jew, I felt comfort in initiatives taken to bring Jews and Christians closer together. Following Pope John XXIII's decision to expunge anti-Semitic elements from Catholic liturgy, Pope John-Paul II went farther in the same direction. His journey to Israel, his official commemoration of the Holocaust in the Vatican, his visit to the Synagogue of Rome, his conversations with Jewish visitors: all these events produced a healthy atmosphere of dialogue and mutual respect. One may say that never before have Jewish–Christian relations been as good or as fruitful as they seem to be now. Rabbis and priests, Jewish and Christian theologians and students frequently meet and discuss ways to defeat intolerance and discrimination. Thus hope was permitted and encouraging.

However, in other domains, our confidence was soon mitigated. Wars, more wars. Vietnam, Bosnia, Rwanda, Kashmir, Sudan, the Middle East. Fanaticism rose in the world of religion and politics alike. Everywhere parents asked: when will the senseless bloodshed come to an end? And we answered: it will end with the century. The next one will be and must be celebrated for its humanity—for its victory over hatred and war.

Who could have foreseen September 11 and the necessary war against international terrorism? Who could have imagined the outrageous attacks on defenseless innocent civilians by suicide terrorists on the ground and air-hijackers? Oh yes, we did expect for the twenty-first century a different beginning.

Where then is hope to be found today? Who among us will rise to proclaim our indispensable conviction that it is not too late to avoid further catastrophes, that the train is not running to the abyss, that humankind does have a future, that hope is possible and justified, especially now: on the bottom of Pandora's box, filled with curses, lies, hope. In other words: it is conceivable that one must go through ultimate suffering and despair to discover hope. Still, a moral question arises: How are we to avoid turning one man's hope into another man's despair?

Hope implies an act of faith—faith in God—if one is a believer, that He listens, that He cares, that He is involved in human History. Faith in human capacities if one is an agnostic: that man can be free and compassionate, capable of generosity and truth.

Is faith enough?

Both in medicine and psychology it has been established that just as the body and the brain cannot live without dreams, the mind and the soul cannot endure without faith and hope. The death of hope is the death of all generous impulses in me. It is the end of all possibilities, options, inquiries, renewals of redemption.

In ancient Greece, tragedies were linked to if not caused by the notion that the hero's fate had been sealed. Prometheus' punishment was preordained, as was Hector's death. Creon had power but not hope, Antigone had hope but not power: she chose death over fear because of her helplessness. As for Socrates, he preferred death to exile for the same reason. Senecca understood that the future of the mighty Roman Empire was hopeless, when he realized that the morality of the vanquished was superior to that of the victor.

But what is hope? For the religious person, it is a divine gift born in the most obscure realm of one's being, blossoming at the paradoxical moment when its absence is stronger than its presence.

For the non-believer, hope represents an affirmation of Man's right to impose meaning on Creation and his triumph in the name of reason.

Hope has its own architecture, its own mysterious trajectory. The whole idea of redemption is rooted in the principle of anticipation, of expectation, of waiting. What is messianism if not hope brought to its incandescent climax?

Hope has a variety of aspects and responds to many needs. There is the hope of the Just and that of the wicked: the first is inclusive whereas the second is not. The Just shares his or her hope with others whereas the wicked believes in his alone.

Hope is one of the foundations of religion—of all religions. Without hope, they vanish. In philosophy, hope represents challenge. Aristotle was the first to make a distinction between simple anticipation and "Euelpis" or true hope. One of Emmanuel Kant's four questions Man faces is: "What is my hope?"

Hope is a transcendental act which accompanies us all in our endeavors and allows us to go beyond our limits so as to enter an uncertain future where dream and desire have the force of memory. Where, under which sky, would we be if we were deserted by hope? We would no longer sense the fragrance of dawn or the nocturnal breath coming from an open window. We would be rendered superfluous, withered branches left behind by the wind. Nothing would elicit our interest because no goal would await us. Hope being the key to freedom, with it life itself would become a prison.

In conclusion, following Albert Camus we ought to consider Sisyphus happy. Created in the image of Him who has no image, it is incumbent upon our contemporaries to invoke and create hope where there is none.

For just as only human beings can push me to despair, only they can help me vanquish it and call it hope.

Chapter Two

The Case for a Positive Jewish Theology of Christianity

Irving Greenberg

The time for Jewry to develop "a positive theology of Christianity" is long past due.[1]

There is a personal story which has led me to explore what is arguably the most positive theology of Christianity written by a believing Jew—but the issue is far beyond the personal. I believe that developing positive affirmations of each other's religions (thus paving the way for a joint partnership and outreach to the world) would be doing God's will—at last. Here I offer global arguments for undertaking the task.

I offer this case although I believe that a religion that validates hatred of Jews or spreads blood libels about them is not a fit covenant partner—for God or for Judaism. Christianity has engaged in such vile behavior for much of its almost two thousand years' existence. However, in a remarkable way, the bulk of Christian churches in the West have turned away from this theology in the past century. The Catholic Church and the mainstream Protestant movements have repudiated anti-Semitism, rejected the charge of deicide, and explored the Jewishness of Jesus. They have moved to affirmation of Judaism's ongoing validity.

Nevertheless, I am aware that the sincerity of the repentance has come into question for some—and not without some justification. In the past two decades we had seen a renewal of some of the worst patterns of the past. The mainstream liberal Protestant Churches in the West have become increasingly supportive of the delegitimation of the State of Israel. It is not a matter of criticizing Israel's treatment of the Palestinians or the growth of Jewish settlements in the West Bank since 1967 in the area designated for an Arab state in 1947. One may legitimately disagree with Israel's policies. I think that

Israel has offered generous terms for peace and for establishing a Palestinian state but has been rebuffed by an Arab leadership that does not want to recognize Israel's right to exist. Despite having to impose hardships on the Palestinians due to the need to protect the security and safety of Israelis, Israel has exercised great restraint in the face of constant terrorism and warfare on its citizens. Yet the institutional leadership in liberal Christian churches has adopted or tolerated the teaching of a most one-sided narrative of this conflict. This version portrays the Jewish state as an inhumane oppressor, as a nation uniquely so immoral as to forfeit its right to exist. This is a blatant falsification of history that ignores that Israel captured these lands in a war of self-defense and offered in vain to turn them back to the nascent Palestinian nationalism in return for a true peace. This also constitutes direct support for an unrepentant hatred that would expel the Jews from Israel, or wipe them out directly. This constitutes the exercise of a flagrant double standard. No other nations in the world—even totalitarian murderous tyrannies, no matter how bad their behavior—are denied their right to exist. This suggests an underlying bias, if not hatred that summons up the old Christian demonization of Jews.

In recent years, mainstream denominations like the Presbyterians and the United Church of Christ have come within a whisker of a majority of voting to boycott and divest from companies dealing with Israel—as if it were an apartheid state (which is a synonym for having no right to exist). Although the Arabs living in Israel are a minority, they have the most freedom and political rights of any Arab (majority) population in the world. Nor is the fact acknowledged that if Israel were disarmed, its Jewish population would be despoiled and murdered. These Churches have given—or accepted without proper cross examination—false witness that Israel is to blame for the decline of Christian populations in the Middle East. The truth is that only in Israel are Christian populations treated so well (and feel so secure) that they have grown. Throughout the region, under Moslem rule (including the West Bank and Gaza) Christians are so disadvantaged that they are emigrating as fast as they can. Their emptying out follows by sixty years or so the expulsion of Jewish populations from Arab lands—and for the same reason. The surge of Arab nationalism and/or Islamic fundamentalism has made life unsustainable for faiths other than the dominant form of Islam. Instead of acknowledging and confronting this development which is perverting mainstream Islam, the churches turn to anti-Zionism and to blaming Israel.

Anti-Zionism—the caricatured portrayal of Jewish nationalism as beyond the pale, politically and morally, is a revived and cosmetically prettified version of the old anti-Semitism. (Such Arab Christian fronts as the Christian Liberation Center of Naim Ateek have openly invoked the old Christian anti-Semitic tropes in anti-Zionist garb and have gotten away with it.) There can be no doubt that the receptivity to such distortions grows in the soil of the old

Christian hatred of Jews and Judaism—now driven underground. After extensive dialogue, liberal groups openly repudiated the teachings of contempt which "validated" the old doctrinal claims of supersession. Both the claim that Jews were doomed to be forever wanderers without a homeland and that Jews were satanic and guilty of blood thirsty behavior were disowned. I find it devastating that the liberal Churches now have revived these claims and given them currency in their new malevolent albeit disguised forms. These assertions put the dignity and safety of millions of Jews at risk.

By contrast, the evangelicals—who theologically have not revised their views that Judaism is superseded and that there is no salvation outside of Christ—nevertheless, have stepped up to become the backbone of American support for the Jewish state and its right to exist. They have managed to internalize American values of loving the other and respecting one's opponents and thus remove the taint of Jew hatred from Christian claims. True, this difference at least in part reflects the more conservative political culture of the evangelists. Much of the erosion in Israel's standing has been in the circles of the left that glorify ex-colonials and treat their behaviors, however violent and oppressive, as beyond criticism. This left also faults American foreign policy behaviors while romanticizing Arab and third world groups. Israel is "guilty" of being Western and modern. Still it is a sobering reminder of the limits of theological dialogue that mainstream churches fall prey to this "kosherized" anti-Semitism while evangelicals are guided by their decency and American values into appreciating Israel's democratic, entrepreneurial and pluralistic culture, whatever its flaws.

In light of all that, I acknowledge that my continuing pursuit of a positive theology is an act of faith—not fully based on the reality of the situation—that Christianity's better nature will win out. I believe that the turn to anti-Zionism (the politically correct form of anti-Semitism) will be checked—as it has been decisively in the Catholic Church and in the more traditional Western Protestant churches.

It is not that the Catholic Church is without sin. In 2004, Mel Gibson's *The Passion* movie received widespread showing, thereby the film became the most successful Passion Play of all time. Gibson took the medieval Passion Play script—with all its hateful, distorting ugly portraits of Jews and broadcast it worldwide to incredible numbers. This act was in flagrant violation of *Nostra Aetate,* the 1965 declaration of the Vatican II Council of the Catholic Church of new approaches to other faiths (and of new respect for Judaism). *Nostra Aetate* specifically stated that due to the origins of Christianity within Judaism and the charged portrait of Jews in classic Christian theology that "the Jews should not be presented as rejected or cursed by God as if this followed from the Holy Scripture." The Passion of Jesus "should not be blamed on the Jews living then or even now." Yet the Vatican and the American Bishops failed to condemn the film. They should have spoken out as follows. "We cannot stop you, the faithful Catholics, from seeing the film. Still we must state clearly that it is a disgrace to evoke such hateful images of Jews. This film is a direct violation of the proclamation of the Church." That was not done. Apparently, the traditional authorities feel so embattled culturally that they grasped at the straw of this film—unwilling to denounce its anti-Semitism lest that offset the positive effect of a powerful traditional retelling of the death of Jesus. They were willing to overlook the anti-Jewish message as secondary and only likely to yield minor damage to Jewish–Christian relations. Still, I judge this failure to be a lapse, not a negative turning point.

Let me acknowledge also that the weakness in yielding to past stereotypes is not a one-sided problem. In the recent past American presidential elections (especially 2004 and 2012) Jews showed their continuing fear and almost instinctive suspicion toward Christianity in the presidential vote. You will recall that in 2004, 75 percent of the Jews voted for the Democratic challenger. Clearly a major reason for that vote, although not the only reason, was this embedded, historic Jewish feeling that if President Bush was a religious Christian it was probably not good for Jews. (For most of Jewish history, if the ruler was a religious Christian it was not good for the Jews.) Yet Bush had supported Israel to the hilt and reached out to Jews by including them in his highest and closest circle. Similarly, Jews voted more than two to one for President Obama against Romney. While the dominant American Jewish political liberalism was the main reason for this one-sided result, a second factor was that Romney is a devout Mormon who was strongly supported by evangelicals. This raised Jewish fears of being excluded or mistreated if such groups would attain political power. Yet here is my conclusion: despite the questions that can be raised about the goodwill and respect toward the Other on both sides, I remain convinced that the emerging possibility is that respect will win out. This will lead to genuine partnership. Therefore the legacy of distrust and rejection between the two faiths must be overcome—for God's sake and for humans'.

A PERSONAL JOURNEY

Until 1961, my conception of Christianity was pretty much like that of any other liberal Jew. I did not have any strong animus against it. I had a recollection that the faith has generally not been nice to the Jewish people, but I had no strong feeling about that—and no strong interest in it either. I sort of knew that Jesus was Jewish. You know the old Jewish joke: How do we know Jesus was Jewish? Because at the age of 33 he was still living at home with his parents; because he went into his father's business; and because his mother thought that he was God! In any event that was pretty much my sense of Christianity.

In 1961, a trip to Israel transformed my life. At the time, I was an American historian trying to make it in America. There I encountered the Holocaust. During the Holocaust I was lucky enough to be a child growing up blissfully on the streets of Brooklyn and I had no clue what was happening. After the War, I discovered that four of my mother's six brothers had remained in Poland. They and their entire families were wiped out. There was not a single first cousin survivor. Furthermore, two of my father's sisters, whom he had left behind, were exterminated along with their families. Still I knew not the Holocaust. Almost two decades later, I came in contact with the event—and the experience overwhelmed me. I spent that year—90 to 95 percent of my time—in Yad Vashem reading, immersed in and devastated by this shattering encounter.[2] By the end of the year I came to the conclusion that official Christianity did not support or even want the Holocaust to occur, and the Nazis hated Christianity too. Still, the bottom line was that in the course of the 2,000-year relationship between the two religions, Christianity had spread a circle of hatred and of degradation around the Jewish people. It portrayed Jews as an uncanny, strange, dangerous, and evil minority that deserved to be ghettoized and persecuted and worse. This set up the Jews, as it were, for the mutated, i.e., racial anti-Semitism that turned the hatred into a total assault. Many Christians were horrified by this murderous attack—but frankly many Christians did not resist very much either. Apparently, they felt in their heart that Jews somehow deserved it, didn't they?

What was even more shocking to me was the thought that these images of a people that one saw in the Mel Gibson film—Pontius Pilate as a nice guy wishing to spare Jesus, the Jews as so cruel that they insist that he die, the Jews seeking to torture him—were congruent with the New Testament portrait. Later, as the hatred intensified, Christians taught that this people cut children's throats to take their blood for the ritual bread, matzah. What else could Jews be capable of? You could only imagine. The images are spread throughout Western literature and art. I came to realize that many of these same images were still being spread by Christianity. This was a threat to me and to my family. (Our first child had just been born.) I kept thinking: what violence would my future children, and grandchildren, be exposed to in a world in which this tradition was being taught worldwide? My wife and I both decided that we would go back to the United States and join the Jewish–Christian dialogue. In all honesty, my main purpose in joining was to say: please stop teaching hatred about my people. Please stop spreading these ugly images because they are very dangerous and very damaging.

When I joined the dialogue, I met Christians on a deep and intense level, for the first time in my life. To my surprise they were amazing people. First of all the ones who joined the dialogue, particularly when motivated by the

Shoah, had a passion; they were true Christians. They were determined that this religion should stop being a source of hatred for Jews, once and for all. They truly wanted Christianity to be a gospel of love; that is its primary teaching. The Christian dialogicians were determined to repent and to renew their religion. That discovery stunned me. After a while, it inspired me. I came to see that any religion that can generate its own intense self-criticism and its own purification is a great religion. Note: I had come to teach Christians that, for twenty centuries they had misused the fact that the Jewish prophets were so critical of Judaism. Based on the prophetic writings— Christians taught that the Jews were a terrible people. After all, their own prophets "proved that point." I tried to get Christians to see that the prophetic critiques were the measure of the high standards of the Jewish people. Behavior that any other people would have accepted and admired, the prophets denounced as failing the test of morality. In the same way I came to see that Christianity (or any religion) that could generate such honest, unsparing self-criticism, such genuine repentance, such a willingness to transform some of its most basic traditions in order to do justice to the Jewish people, had to be respected—even honored. The prophetic tradition lived!—in these people.

I also came to see the sacrificial level of love that Christianity engendered in its true believers. One example: In the 1970s, I was invited to a World Council of Churches Conference in Sri Lanka. When I arrived, I learned there what I had never realized. If you have a religion you believe in strongly, you should invite other religions' believers in and learn from them. They invited me as a deeply believing Jew. They also invited Buddhists, Hindus, Muslims, members of the greatest world religions. It had never occurred to me that you should invite people from a different religion and listen to them respectfully; that in itself was life transforming. During the break on the second day, they took us for a little trip into the backwoods of Sri Lanka. We drove for hours and hours until we arrived at a little children's village run by a group of Norwegian Christians. It turned out that the leader of the group had been a television news anchorman—the Walter Cronkite of Norway. He was the lead anchor on the leading Norwegian television network. At the peak of his career, he made a decision. As a true follower of Christ, how could he sit in Oslo, amidst all this celebrity, and live a life of ease and material welfare? He gave it all up because there was a suffering humanity out there. As a true Christian, he concluded that in such a world, he should suffer as God suffers, along with humanity. He decided to take up the cross and went off to the backwoods of Sri Lanka to create this children's village.

When we went through the village I realized its youngsters were not normal children. These were brain damaged children. Sri Lanka was a poor country, a very poor country then. Plagued by poverty, many parents had great trouble taking care of their healthy children. The truth is that most brain damaged children were abandoned, sooner or later. Many of them died of hunger and neglect. This man created a village to take in such children. His group would adopt them and take care of them. Instead of living a life of luxury and ease back in Norway, these Christians, as disciples of Christ, came to Sri Lanka. For 24 hours a day, 7 days a week, they took care of these children. When we walked through the dormitory, most of the children were so brain damaged that they barely responded; they barely acknowledged passers-by. Some of them had no bowel control and some of them had no physical control; others had no emotional or mental control. After you cleaned up, fed and took care of a child for a day, if you were lucky the child would give you a grunt. That was your recognition and your reward. They were genuine Christians. They loved God by following Jesus and loving God's children—even the least of them—by dedicating their lives to their service. Then I grasped that the faith had been a gospel of love for millions and for hundreds of millions; it just had only been a gospel of hatred for the Jews.

What flashed through my mind at that moment? I thought: how many times in my life, without thinking, I had made this simple comparison, flattering to Judaism, unflattering to Christianity. I am a rabbi and I am proud of the fact. In Catholic Christianity if you want to be a priest or a senior religious figure, you have to be celibate. One must give up family and sexual life to serve God. Often I would tell students: look at the difference between our two faiths. Christianity makes demands for heroic religiosity. I did not dismiss Christianity—but I put it down—as a religion that demands devotion beyond normal human capacity—to the point where it becomes almost "inhuman." It asks people to give up family, to give up sex, to give up relationships for the sake of God. I was proud of the fact that Judaism is much more "human" in its religiosity. It was much more willing to allow the religious figure to enjoy normal family affection and human life. (I have to say: that was in the early days of my marriage. I came to realize later that I am not sure which is more heroic, to be celibate or to be a good husband and a kind, patient father for decades? But that is not the point.) In Sri Lanka, I suddenly realized my easy victory, my subtle up-with-Judaism and down-with-Christianity comparison, was simply self-flattery. It did not do justice to the reality of the power of Christianity. This religion was capable of evoking self-sacrifice out of love of God in a way that I had never imagined—let alone asked for—in my community.

As our involvement with dialogue went on, my wife and I came to know Sister Rose Thering, a Catholic nun who did an important study of Catholic textbooks, showing how Christian textbooks portrayed Jews poorly or negatively represented Judaism. She not only went to work cleaning up those textbooks: for the next 40 years she campaigned to end Christian misrepresentation of Judaism. She worked to protect Jews. She rallied for Israel and for Soviet Jewry. She was a woman who went to protest Kurt Waldheim's

election as President of Austria when he had a record of service in the Nazi
military machine. To humiliate her, the Austrian police not only stopped her
and arrested her, they also strip-searched her, although she was a nun. She
was unfazed. She confronted any authority—including her own bishop, who
denied the dignity and equality of Jews (and others). When you truly meet
such people, you suddenly find your stereotypes shattered and your religious
conceptions transformed. The only thing I can give myself credit for was that
I was open enough and honest enough at that point to admit that Christianity
was a powerful and extraordinary religion.

After fifteen or more years, I got through writing many articles describing
how Christianity had to change, how it had to stop the stereotyping, how it
had to recognize that it did not replace Judaism, how it could learn from
many aspects of Judaism including every day religious activities. (I do not
back away from those writings, they are in my book.) Then I began to ask
myself: as a Jew did I have nothing more to say about Christianity? or did I
not in some way have to appreciate what a remarkable religion it is and
reclaim it as a sibling and partner of Judaism. This is my personal story that
led me to acknowledge that Jews need a positive theology of Christianity.

DOING GOD'S WILL

Nevertheless, as said earlier, the issue far transcends my personal journey.
Why do I believe that such a religious re-thinking would be doing God's
will? Looking back now, I would argue that we are being given a second
chance. Very rarely does any group get a second chance in history. One must
be alert and take advantage of such an opening. If Judaism gave birth to a
religion that did so much for the world—that taught billions about a loving
God and a covenant to perfect the world—how shall Jews understand that
today? I believe that it was God's intention that Christianity develop out of
Judaism and become another religion. It was meant to be a covenantal religion, parallel to Judaism with a message of *tikkun olam*—that God wishes to
partner with humans to repair and perfect the world. Such a religion could
have been born only inside Judaism for that was Judaism's core message.
Then I believed that it was God's will that the new faith spread—not among
Jews, because they had their own, highly meaningful covenant. The Israelites
lived by their religion, long before Christianity was born and they continued
to live by it. In fact, after Christians separated from Judaism, Judaism went
through one of its great renewals, the flowering which we call rabbinic Judaism. Christianity was intended to separate at the biblical stage and bring this
message of God and of hope and of redemption to the gentiles. Only a
religion less ethnically Jewish and with less distinctive observances could
have spread so far.

Today, both religions have a second chance to correct the errors made in the first parting of the ways. Both sides misunderstood and misinterpreted what happened. Christians claimed that God had repudiated and replaced Judaism. Jews claimed that Christianity was a false Messianism, a religion corrupted by human error into worshipping a man. As a Jew I start with correcting the Jewish response. For the record, there are one billion seven hundred million Christians in the world. Jews should stop and ask themselves: why is that so? Is this all a triumph of human misunderstanding? Sometimes I think that the Jews tacitly believe that Christianity is literally unbelievable. Consider: virgin birth, Immaculate Conception, God becomes flesh. This is something only a *goyishe kopf* could really, really believe in. Historically, Jews questioned how a highly developed intellectual could really take those beliefs seriously. Some concluded that for the rest of the world, Christianity is acceptable because the gentiles are not smart enough to critique a fairy tale. But is that the only thing we can say about Christianity? Is that the only explanation for its vast spread? Or is the very accomplishment of bringing a message of faith and ethics to hundreds of millions who never would have met a Jew, of bearing witness to nations who never would have heard about the God of Israel were it not through Christianity, is this role not to be taken seriously?

What then was the cause of the misinterpretation between the two faiths? Much of the responsibility remains with those Christians who went out to teach this teaching and succeeded greatly among gentiles but not much among Jews. These Christians could not imagine that God wanted these two religions side by side. (To be fair, the ancient world—including Jewish culture—had little sense of pluralism.) Therefore, they said Christianity is the child born of Jewish faith. They used the metaphor: parents die and the child takes over. They interpreted Christianity to be the religion that superseded, i.e., replaced Judaism in God's economy. If that narrow conception of God's revelation were not bad enough, they compounded the problem. Having succeeded to convert vast numbers of gentiles, Christians were nevertheless troubled. Why are the Jews still alive? They offered an evil explanation of the persistence of the Jews. Instead of understanding that God sustained them and wanted them to grow, the answer they gave was that Jews were not really alive. They were being kept alive by the Devil. (That theme already shows up in the New Testament.) In later developments, they explained that Judaism only appeared to exist—because it was fossilized and frozen. In still later development; Jewish worship was portrayed as the synagogue of Satan, it lived off the blood of Christians, etc. Thus a theology which started with a claim of replacement, followed through with teachings of increasing degradation of the Mother faith. This led to a need to isolate the Jews and turn them into pariahs. This would convince Christians—if not Jews—that the practitioners of the covenant of Sinai were actually dead spiritually. Alternatively, if Jews were totally segregated then they would be spiritually pushed out of Gentiles' religious lives. Sometimes these ideas led to policies whereby Jews were expelled and/or killed.

The Jewish mirror interpretation is understandable but, in retrospect, was no less a misinterpretation. If Christianity says that Jews are dead, then it must be a lie! because we know that we are alive. If Christianity claims that Jesus is the true Messiah and therefore we have no right to go on living as Jews, then clearly he must be a false Messiah. We feel our own vitality. We see clearly that the world is unredeemed—then Christianity can only be a false faith. Since it is preaching hatred of Jews, it is a gospel of hatred. In Christian lands, the Jews defined the dominant faith as the lowest of the low. Since Christians say that God became human and they worship this human, that is idolatry. After all the heart of monotheism, the heart of Jewish teaching is that there is only one God. Therefore this dominating, persecuting religion must be the ultimate religious misunderstanding: idolatry. Idolatry had no redeeming features and deserves only extirpation. We cannot do it—but God will. Thus negation of the other was the dominant view on both sides.

What followed also was inevitable: Rejection, hatred, disrespect and conflict. Both sides paid a very heavy price. Judaism turned more insular, more tribal, more disrespectful of other religions. Note: I do not equate the two religions in this matter of behavior. Jews paid a much heavier price because they were a small minority. They were abused. They were actively persecuted. Ultimately, this Christian triumphalist self-understanding had a negative impact on other peoples and faiths. Christianity's claim to have replaced Judaism enabled it to make the claim that it was the only true religion—and therefore *the* absolutely true religion. Therefore no other religion should exist in its presence. Therefore there can be no salvation outside the Church. There can be no savior other than Jesus. If you do not come to Christ then you go to Hell. You will never be accepted by God. That teaching led to Christian misbehavior not just toward Jews but toward Islam—as in the Crusades. In the nineteenth century, Christianity felt that it had religious superiority and the moral right to proselytize and suppress religions in the Far East. Thus it came on the back of Imperialism and lent its imprimatur to white colonialism.

Think of how frustrating this history has been to God who sought to reach out to the nations through a less ethnic and less culturally Jewish religion. Think of the Divine suffering, when God sought to move into a more active covenantal relationship with Jews in rabbinic Judaism, only to experience the persecution and isolation of God's chosen. Think of God's pain as the human covenant communities spent their energies in attack and defense, in rejection and mutual degradation—instead of in partnership to reach out to all of humanity. Now, our chance to end God's pain in this matter is at hand.

PLURALISM: OUR SECOND CHANCE

We are living in one of these remarkable eras where we are given that opportunity to reconfigure our relationship. This new age begins first of all with modernity. One can say many negative things about modernity and its solvent effect on religions and values. Still I submit that thanks to its dynamism and openness, it brings people of every stripe and religious faith together. This leads us to the discovery of the image of the God of the Other. The central Jewish teaching is that every human being is an image of God. Every image of God is intrinsically of infinite value. Every human being, because they are an image of God, should be seen, recognized and treated like an equal. After all, there is no preferred image of God. Each image of God is unique—one of a kind. This central teaching of the core human dignities—infinite value, equality, uniqueness, is embedded in the heart of Judaism and Christianity—has been obscured for thousands of years by religious teachings of contempt. When you teach that Jews are degraded or that Jews are cunning or whatever stereotype, you deny their uniqueness. When you persecute them, you deny their equal dignity; you deny their value. For millennia, most religions in every culture taught this way about outsiders. The most powerful thing about modernity is that it has brought people all together. If they are not your next door neighbor, then you see them on television. You see the other faiths in the media. You see other religious ways in film. For the first time in history others are not "Chinks" or "Japs" or "gooks"; they are not "goyim" or "kikes" or whatever degrading images with which we have grown up. Now they are unmistakably recognized as living human beings, with all the uniqueness and infinite value and preciousness of human beings.

Take the case of women. For much of human history they were self-evidently the second sex, less valued in their life than men, existing to serve men. Through the power of modern culture, they were brought forward and recognized as, each one, an image of God, unique, equal, of infinite value. That has happened across the board to people of color, of different sexual orientation, of different faiths. In the case of Jewry, non-Jewish lay people took the lead to discover that the Jew was not someone with horns. The Jew was not somebody in some way morally or spiritually degraded but a neighbor, a friend, a human being with all the dignity of a human being. Jews made the same discovery about the Other. Once a person discovers this truth about the Other, then he/she becomes uncomfortable with the negative stereotypes that his/her religion has of the other faith. All the subtle ways that we put the Other down become unacceptable. In time, this led to liberalism, to tolerance, to dropping the old antagonisms. This process went particularly far in America which is the scene of the most democratic encounter of Jews and non-Jews. In time, this opened the door to a reconsideration, by theologians and religious leaders, of the relationship of the two traditions. This gave us our second chance.

Taking the new opportunities to develop a pluralist understanding of the Other and of God's plan for humanity is essential. The alternative is a polarization that can endanger our civilization. Why is this so? Over time, the process of debunking stereotypes and self-evident assumptions of superiority had more drastic effects. As the process went on, the older, more fundamental positive values in religion were also being undermined. Some people reasoned that the issue was not really liberalism or modification of religion. This situation—where claims of superiority did not stand up because the Other was present and impressive—led some to the practice of relativism. They judged that in the false portrait of the Other, one saw the weakness and the lack of credibility of *all* religious claims. They concluded that no religion had the right to make any claims of authority. This was not an isolated occurrence. In all liberalizing religions, a crisis of relativism has arisen. One outcome is that throughout the culture, there is a growing feeling that tolerance leads to moral immobilization—a situation in which you cannot make judgments. As many people have accepted this conclusion, relativism has grown. On the other hand, many responded with an opposite reaction—as we are seeing worldwide. This is reflected in the rise of fundamentalism, particularly of the radical kind. When people become concerned that in this exposure to each other, all traditional values are undermined, when they become convinced that family itself is at risk, that all statements of right and wrong are becoming unacceptable—or even just vulnerable—this leads to an extreme reaction. Some people say: we must give up choice. We have to use force to uphold right and wrong. Once you get women out of the house, once they get educated, they will never choose to stay home and build family. They will never choose to be mothers again. Therefore, we have to violently and forcibly prevent women from going to university. Put them back behind that chador, put them back in the kitchen—and the family will be saved. These views are surging not just in Islam. In Christianity and in Judaism we are seeing a major strengthening of fundamentalism.

What is the alternative? We start with the breakthrough of modernity's incredible achievement as making us see the Other as fully human. This leads us to feel that if the others are fully human, then their religion cannot be any less dignified or any less respected than mine. That makes the new relationship possible. Since we had not worked out the full details of how unstereotyped faiths relate to each other, the initial impact of full exposure was the growth of relativism and the backlash of fundamentalism. But those who believe that religion's rock is God—and not the inferiority of the Other—will explore an alternative relationship. We seek a way that is affirming of the Other but self-respecting at the same time, i.e., pluralism. Achieving this relationship is the great spiritual challenge of our generation. This is the alternative to the classic absolutism of the past. Absolutism meant that each religion insists that it has the whole truth. Every word of the Torah is dictated by God, every word of interpretation of the New Testament and of the Koran is Divinely revealed. Therefore every religion portrayed the other faith as inferior or superseded. That was the absolutism that undergirded the finest of religions for the past 2,000 years. This position is steadily eroding in the presence of the Other. Yet in the alternative of relativism, the cost is too high. When we cannot really judge the Other, then no faith carries norms or values. Then one is left in a world of "preferences" in which the good is easily vanquished by the forceful or the trendy. Neither of these options does justice to the real opportunity. The real opportunity lies in pluralism.

Let me emphasize the difference between pluralism and relativism as many remain confused on this issue. In my own community, the Orthodox Jewish community, pluralism is still generally rejected. People feel that one cannot uphold the authority of the tradition once one admits that another tradition also has authority. But this view misses precisely the heart of pluralism. In relativism, you can uphold all religions because all judgments of right and wrong are ruled out. By contrast, pluralism grows out of affirmation. I believe absolutely in my own faith. I affirm revelation from God. I am able to contradict or reject doctrines of other groups because I am defined and committed by my faith. A pluralist may well say that I affirm the fullness of my own faith's claims. However, I understand the *limits* of my absolute faith. *Pluralism is about limits.*

There are many versions of the limits. Even if it is the word of God, my faith is not intended to be accepted by every other religion and every other community. As I argue in my book, Judaism was intended by God to speak to—to guide the lives of—Jews. The other religion, Christianity, was intended to bring a Divine message to Gentiles and so on and so forth. Another variant: My claims—and the others' as well—are absolute but not all encompassing. They have limits; they leave room for others' faiths. I can also say that I believe my tradition has much Divine truth in it—but it has not exhausted God's truth. God has more truth and can share it with other people in different forms and religions. Or: I affirm that my religion has great values and much truth in it—but my understanding does not exhaust its truth. Therefore someone with a different viewpoint, with a different understanding— even a contradictory one—should be treated with respect. The other interpretation should be learned from and should be understood so that we can maximize the understanding. Or: my religion may be both Divine and flawed because it must participate in human life and culture with those built in limits. Or: my faith may be Divine, yet include flaws. God has intended that those flaws be corrected or checked by other religions.

This is the great spiritual challenge of our time. Is there a stable form known as pluralism which without giving up traditional values, without giving up the authority of religion is nevertheless able to make room for the infinite revelation of God? Can we develop a boundless love of God, that is not exhausted or monopolized by one religion, by one people, by one understanding? Only such a faith/love/revelation can retain its credibility in the presence of other powerful religions, lived by images of God—without deteriorating into relativism. Once we recognize the great stake all religions have in developing pluralism, we are prepared to reach out to learn from and partner with the other faith. We also recognize that we need the efforts of both biblical faiths to achieve this goal. We welcome mutual loving help and criticism. We need to learn from each other. We need to constitute ourselves—our two communities of faith—as the laboratory for overcoming the past and creating a genuine pluralism.

THE HOLOCAUST

The second driving force for our second chance is the Shoah, the Holocaust. The central point is that this event was so shattering, so tragic, so horrifying that people of goodwill in every religion come to realize that one cannot go on with the hatred or the past put downs and stereotypes. We now understand that however well-intentioned to uphold the authority of one's own faith, in the end caricatures can lead to the most terrible and terrifying, morally destructive outcomes. In this age, there is a lot more power in the hands of potential evil doers than ever before. We cannot be as accepting of the petty degradations, of the minor stereotypes, because one denial leads to another. Eventually we build religious structures in which the other person is outside of my moral universe. Whatever religion I am in, the other religion is outside. This leads to a weakening of solidarity and moral responsibility. This creates a morally solipsistic faith which allows (or encourages) the abandonment of others in danger. Then this can lead to another Holocaust. Upon encounter with the Nazi Holocaust, every decent person, every faith that is still rooted in life, becomes determined not to let this happen. After the Holocaust this reconnection for the sake of solidarity is the healthiest and most encouraging response, whether it is among Christians or Jews. This reaction has been the driving force for a new encounter—and a new mutual affirmation—between Jews and Christians.

It is now sixty years since the end of the Holocaust. In these six decades—starting with Roman Catholicism and *Nostra Aetate*—the new view has spread. Take the case of Pope John Paul II. He was a conservative pope who wished to restore some of the past tradition which Vatican II had marginalized. Nevertheless, he continued the pattern of revising Christian doctrine about Judaism and of correcting Christian teaching. He was the first pope in history who went to a synagogue and spoke there. He was the first to say that Judaism, the original valid covenant, was ongoing and never repudi-ated. He affirmed that it was a religion that is still valid today. This statement has been made by the leading denominations of Protestantism also, particu-larly in the West. These revisions were made possible by a great deal of self-criticism, which included open apologies for enabling the Holocaust and repentance for past evils inflicted. In this extraordinary response, the Holo-caust becomes a force for repentance, for responsibility, for love. This devel-opment is a remarkable statement of the capacity of human understanding to turn past hatred into affirmation by the alchemy of human love.

Therefore, after all the legitimate criticisms of Christianity are made in light of the Holocaust, every Jew must ask him/herself a simple question: Have we applied this principle of correcting every stereotype in our own tradition? Have we challenged every negative image of the Other because we understand where it can lead? Every person must ask: Have I applied this discovery of the image of God in the Other to my own religion, to my own community, to my own religious thinking? Have I self-criticized and self-purified so that my faith will never countenance another possible Shoah? In Judaism, we honestly would have to answer: no. Each one of us must say to one's self—is there anything in my tradition that in any way makes another person less than equal? This question got me in trouble inside the Orthodox Jewish community because, as my wife pointed out in her writings, women are not quite equal in my own tradition.[3] Still this issue itself must be gener-alized. If there is anything in my tradition that makes another human being less than equal, anything that makes another faith less than respected and dignified, then it has to be confronted and corrected. That is the will of God. In the same way, I found that I could not go on speaking of Christianity as idolatry. I could not go on tolerating images of contempt on the Jewish side, any more than I wanted Christians to go on with theirs.[4]

A POSITIVE JEWISH THEOLOGY OF CHRISTIANITY

What would be the guiding principles of a positive Jewish theology of Chris-tianity? I would suggest three fundamentals: First, the original covenant, the original partnership of God and humanity is not Judaism, any more than it is Christianity. The original covenant described in our own Torah—a Bible that is shared by Jews and Christians—is the Noahide Covenant. God enters into a partnership with Noah—that is to say, with a human being.[5] (There were no Jews before Abraham.) Noah is the ancestor of all of humanity. The covenant is a covenant of *tikkun olam*, of perfecting the world, of filling the world with life.[6] The Noahide Covenant incorporates the commitment of God to work with humans and humans to work with God, to overcome poverty, hunger, oppression and war. The goal is to overcome death itself by creating life and by working for the elevation of the dignity of every form of life—not just human. According to the Noahide Covenant, for example, all humans (not just Jews) are commanded not to eat blood. Even if one kills an animal to eat it, humans are not to eat blood—as a sign of respect for the life even of animals. In the seven Noahide laws as portrayed in Jewish tradition, all humans are commanded to set up courts and provide justice between humans. All humans are warned against killing an image of God, etc. All subsequent religions—particularly the covenantal faiths—are called to work for this very goal. Since achieving the task is very difficult, all must seek out partners—viz, all other religions—to accomplish the goal.

The heart of all religion, at least from this Jewish understanding, is the covenant, the partnership of God and humanity, to perfect the world. Our common goal is to make sure that human life is treated with all the dignity of a life that is of infinite value; that is equal and unique. Abraham's covenant, i.e., the beginning of Judaism or Sinai, the covenant of the Jewish people, is just a particular application of the general principle. Through Abraham and through Exodus and Sinai God brings Jews into this partnership. This is but the first of many partnerships. What is the role of the partnership group? To serve as teachers, to teach these ideas to the world, to serve as role models, to create and show a living community that lives by these values. That is what the Jews have been in history, teachers and role models. In our time, we realize that we are also co-workers. We cannot accomplish the goal by ourselves. Later religions—and I start now with Christianity, which was born 1,800 years after Judaism—take up the same unfinished task.

In my book I argue that Jewry needed 1,800 years before the Jews internalized the covenant. Only then could Judaism develop the next outreach— Christianity. I believe that Buddhism, Hinduism, Islam—any other religions—even those that are not covenantal in structure—are (or can become) valid expressions of the Noahide covenant. In the words of Isaiah, the Noahide Covenant has never been repealed, or superseded (Isaiah 54:9–10). That is the assurance given to all by God—that the Lord does not abandon God's promises unfulfilled. Just as the Noahide Covenant is still valid, so are the later iterations. Just as the Noahide Covenant was never replaced but was turned from one universal covenant into a series of particular covenants, so the Jewish covenant, the Christian covenant, Islamic, etc., are permanent. That pact with God is the fundamental authorization behind all religions—all religions that work for life and for human dignity. All religions that work to perfect the world should be treated as valid religions—to be shown the greatest respect even if one disagrees with them.

The second fundamental is: Of all these religions Judaism and Christianity are the two which are closest to each other. (In the Orthodox community, the standard joke is: what is the nearest living religion to Judaism? The answer is: Lubavitch.) But the closest living religion to Judaism is, in fact,

Christianity. The central story of Judaism is Creation. This is not a world generated by a cosmic accident. It is a world created by God, intended to become perfect. That is why Creation will eventually end up in redemption. Both religions promise that there will be a Messianic Age, when the world is made perfect. Then humans (together with God) will overcome war and poverty and hunger and oppression and sickness. That is the Jewish story and Christianity offers the same narrative. How are we going to get there? Through a covenant, through a partnership of God and humanity in which both our ritual as well as our ethical behaviors are intended to repair and build a perfect world. Christianity affirms the very same process and out-come. According to Christianity, this is a Creation, a world brought into being by a creative God, who intends it to be perfect. This planet will end in a Messianic Age when it is perfect. We will get there by a covenantal partner-ship of God and humanity. All this we have in common.

Of course there are striking differences between the two religions. We differ on how the covenant works and whether God or humans lead the bridging activity; we disagree on a variety of ritual practices and even wheth-er one needs rituals. There are a vast number of differences, even contradic-tions between the two faiths. Still there are no other two religions that share such a common core in such a fundamental way. Let no one confuse that I mean to deny the substantial differences. How does this partnership between God and humanity finally accomplish its goal? Christianity believes that humans became so degraded and so intrinsically evil that humans could not save themselves in this partnership. Therefore God had to become human to reconcile the ideal and the reality to bring humans back to God. That is what Jesus does. God becomes human and sacrifices himself to bring people up from their unworthy sinful nature to the level where they can be forgiven and carry out this partnership. The Jewish response is not to underestimate the gap and not to underestimate the human capacity for evil. Nevertheless as a religion we teach that God will work with human mediators. People like Moses, and other prophets, are mediators. God will send us instruction, the word of God, Torah. In the end God does not have to become human to close that gap.

That God becomes human in the flesh is shocking to traditional Jewish monotheism. That claim constitutes a fundamental difference between the two faiths. Do not misunderstand me. I uphold the Jewish side of that dis-agreement. Still, this disagreement is an argument as to how the covenant works. It is not a denial from either side that there is a Creation whose goal is redemption. Nor does either faith deny that humans have a central role to play to perfect the world through their covenantal activities. Where we differ, we differ. Christians will criticize our positions or disagree and we will disagree with theirs. But the principle of pluralism allows us to acknowledge that God employs both religions for the purpose of *tikkun olam*. I further affirm that both religions, side by side, can accomplish much more in their difference than if they were identical or if one won out over the other.

For example: most of mainstream Christianity teaches that the primary source of forgiveness is God's grace. One cannot earn forgiveness; humans are intrinsically unworthy. Atonement is God's pure gift. Judaism argues otherwise. As Christians thought about the issue, some realized that a sole emphasis on grace is too one-sided. Therefore there are many Christians who affirm that there is room for works and good deeds as part of that process of forgiveness. On the Jewish side the affirmation is that forgiveness comes from God's grace—but humans have to play a more active role "in evoking grace." They have to be more responsible, they have to do more *mitzvot* and more good deeds. However, many Jewish classic sources and thinkers stress that there are moments of forgiveness that are pure Divine Grace. Which primary emphasis is correct? Should we stress God's grace or human responsibility? Which side is right? I would argue that both are right. The truth is you can reach more people by using both these two approaches. Furthermore, both views supplement and correct each other. Both faiths also nuance their primary assertion—with the contradictory principle. This fulfills the famous rabbinic story: that both claimants are right—yet the one who objects that this is a contradiction is also right.

Does God come closer through a mediator as Jesus? Obviously a billion people think so. Does God come closer through revelation and personal contact? Millions of Jews for thousands of years have upheld that principle. Judaism is the longest living religion of the three major monotheistic religions. I would argue that both answers together bring God and redemption to more people.

Which is more important, the genetic birth continuity of Judaism or the born again fellowship of Christianity? Here again it is not either/or. Both religions incorporate the other's primary element. The answer to reaching more people, again, lies in offering both options.

In short the two religions can do more of God's work when they work side by side. The differences will not go away. The differences between monotheism and trinitarianism are fundamental. (Still, Jews and Moslems should stop polemically denigrating Trinitarianism as idolatry because in the end Christians teach that Jesus brings people to God, the God of Israel, the God that we all worship who is the one and only God.) In the end I believe that the disagreement between us is a *machloket lishem shamayin,* an argument for the sake of Heaven.[7] If the Christians had not chosen their revisionist path (undoubtedly influenced by Hellenism's models) they might have been tempted to stay inside Judaism. If they stayed inside Judaism, there would have been one of two bad outcomes: The younger faith would have taken over Judaism which God did not want because Judaism has its unfinished mission. Or Christianity could have stayed so Jewish ethnically and behaviorally that it would not have been accepted by the Gentiles. This would have frustrated God's desire to reach out. Thus the outcome of the disagreement between us is the advancement of the covenant. We need to train ourselves to see the disagreement not from our vantage point of a contradiction or as a threat to our integrity—but to uphold the controversy from God's perspective. I would argue for one more application. Not only are these the two closest religions. In a way Jews and Christians are members of the same family. We are not in the same immediate family, maybe call us second cousins. Note: The whole of humanity are cousins. We are all the children of Adam and Eve—that is classic Jewish teaching. But these two communities are closer relatives because both identify as children of Abraham. To be a child of Abraham is to feel like a second cousin. An anthropologist pointed out that the current science attesting that all humans are descended from an African Adam and Eve means that all *homo sapiens* alive are a maximum eighty-second cousin to each other. Then the consciousness of being second cousins is a powerful connector between us; it represents a distinctively close bond. (At the same time, the image of a maximum of eightieth+ cousins reminds us that all humans—however disconnected from each other now—are, in fact, members of one larger human family.)

The deepest truth is that much of Judaism's own insights made Christianity possible. Christians should bless God every day that Judaism existed, and exists. That religion made them and many of their accomplishments possible. The deepest truth is that much of Judaism's accomplishments were made through Christianity and its impact on humanity. This Christian religion also insisted that Judaism was at the center of God's concern (however this was twisted to evil effect). Jews should bless God every day that Christianity existed and exists. The core of our own self-image is that Judaism was intended to be and has been a blessing for the world. Many of those blessings, that message of love, that message of God's care, that message of *tikkun olam* came through Christianity to hundreds of millions who never would have heard it otherwise. Ergo, we would have been much less influential but for Christianity.

True, the persecution and the killing of the past was a great tragedy. Much of it grew out of the human need to be right. (Therefore when I am right the other must be wrong.) This concept—that only I/my side can be right—must be repudiated. If I am the object of God's love, if I feel, and I do feel, that the Jews are the Chosen people, then how can I affirm that others form covenantal communities? What does chosenness mean? Chosenness means I experience God's love, I experience being singled out. I experience being redeemed, helped, saved, as in the Exodus. That is a real experience, why deny it? But by the same token Christians are a chosen people. They have enjoyed God's love; they have benefitted from God's concern. They have experienced God's saving power through their Christianity, through Jesus, through their own religious life. (All this can be applied to Islam, etc.) Then why do I need to insist that God chose only one group? We have to affirm that God does choose—but God practices multiple choice. God has infinite love; that is not exhausted by saving one people or by loving one community; God's love overflows and continues to seek out human communities to sustain them—and to inspire them to work for *tikkun olam.*

Let me add a third reason that leads me to believe that now is the time to affirm these pluralist principles. Judaism and Christianity must shape the emerging pluralism and model how to overcome the forces of aggression and triumphalism which are still present in every religion. I say this—even though I freely confess that I am concerned about a loss of boundaries between religions. Sometimes in speaking so positively of Christianity, I fear there are Christians out there who are still trying to convert Jews. This is a violation of the integrity and the respect that Jews are entitled to. I even fear that some missionaries may exploit my ideas of closeness of the two faiths to persuade Jews to join them. I understand the risks, but there are urgent reasons to push ahead now. One is: the world needs redemption. The key to our religion, Judaism, and the key to Christianity—is the belief in *tikkun olam.* Look around. The world still suffers from hatred, war, poverty, suffering, oppression. Any religion that believes in *tikkun olam* should welcome every ally. We do not have excess energy to fight each other anymore. That fighting disgraced God's name. Killing in the name of religion today desecrates God's name; it has to stop. Cooperation is desperately needed because religion must recover its own credibility. Secondly, we need all the help we can get to perfect the world. There was a time when I really thought that Judaism was the only religion and it was going save the whole world. Sometimes I looked up and said: my God, there are only twelve million of us. Twelve million Jews are going to lift this whole world to perfection? (My God, I am going to get a hernia!) Thanks to the dialogue and encounter with other religious communities, I discovered (with great relief and joy) that we are not alone. There are a billion nine hundred million Christians who are trying to lift this world with the Jews. That there are a billion one hundred million Moslems whose ideal seeks to raise the world to a Messianic level. (Islam must tame its radicals, purge its stereotypes and violence toward others to do so, but it has an opportunity to do so.) There are hundreds of millions of others that are trying to lift up the world. We should feel grateful for every partner and seek to work together.

There is another reason. Here I focus on Jewish–Christian relations in particular. Right now Islam is going through one of the great crises of its history. There is a tragic and heartbreaking scene in Moslem religion today. Violence and hatred are spreading in its mainstream. This is partly because Islam never went through modernity, unlike Judaism and Christianity. Note that I am not claiming that Judaism and Christianity are superior religions—

intrinsically more peaceful. Rather, I suggest that Islam never went through the modern period. Parts of its mainstream have not discovered yet, the fullness of humanity of all non-Muslims. Islam has not internalized yet the critique of religion that modern culture developed so powerfully. Moslems are much less prepared to live in this open world. In addition, Arab Moslems are frustrated because they have not solved the problems of the modern economy or of the operations of democracy. As a result, there is a breakdown within Islam. The most radical form of fundamentalism is operating in the Moslem world. Jihadism has spread beyond a radical fringe of 5 or 10 percent that resorts freely to violence. The dangerous development is that the mainstream is now being dragged down. The spread of anti-Semitism, in its ugliest forms, is a symptom of this sickness. Syrian television and Tehran now broadcast images of Jews baking matzahs with blood. It is no coincidence that Holocaust denial finds hospitality in these countries. The raging hatred and teaching of contempt is the worst form of repetition of the past excesses. Now there is a struggle for the soul of Islam. If Islam goes all the way down this path, this way leads people to attempt genocide. Indeed there are "devout" Muslims already who threaten destruction of Israel or who plan genocide of the Jews.

At such a time it is critical that Jews and Christians together confront this evil tendency. I use the word confront in the best sense. This is not a call for a showdown or a shootout. Both faiths, together, must work with Moslem moderates to try to regain control. Earlier I spoke of Jews and Christians as second cousins. In Jewish tradition close family members have a special responsibility for each other. Christians can make an indispensable contribution to this process. Christians have to say to jihadists: you think there are five million Israelis or twelve million Jews; therefore you can fantasize wiping them all out. In fact, you are dealing with a billion plus people who are not going to stand by, so there is no hope of achieving resolution that way. Do not repeat the past errors and sins of Christianity. Do not go down that road. Christians can say what Jews cannot say: we made that mistake. For one and two thousand years we spread hatred in the name of God against Jews. We are now deeply ashamed of that tradition. We now understand that to save our souls, we must repudiate that part of our tradition. Do not make that same mistake, learn from our errors; correct yourself now.

There is a third reason why we have to speak up now. After the Shoah, pluralism is not just the word and the will of God. One primary lesson we learned in the Shoah is that concentrated power, absolute power, is absolutely corrupting. Concentrated power enabled Nazism to carry out the most horrific genocide of all time. We have to welcome every form of pluralism, every mode of breaking up power. Whether it is democracy that breaks up political power or whether it is pluralism that breaks up religious power, everyone who is committed to "Never Again" must practice a thoroughgoing and wide ranging pluralism. Jews should not want to be the dominant or only religion in any country. That is why I believe that the Orthodox monopoly in Israel must be ended. I think Christians have to understand that in America and everywhere else, their leadership role should not be pushed toward dominance or turned into dismissal of others. Those Christians who seek to reassert the Christian roots of American culture must simultaneously consciously strive to avoid turning this into a reach for monopoly. Achieving pluralism is something which we morally, culturally and educationally can only do together.

A FINAL NOTE: THE POWER OF FREEDOM AND CHOICE

I want to end positively with a word of hope. Many Jews are afraid that if religions give up their claims of superiority—or if they drop the negative stereotypes—this will lead to intermarriage and to assimilation. They fear that openness will result in the loss of the Jewish people. Many Christians are worried in the same way; the Evangelicals particularly have had trouble coming to grips with the idea that there can be some salvation outside and beyond, not just through, Jesus. They worry these new ideas will weaken the power of their own faith, or undermine their own commitments. The record of the recent past suggests the opposite. The great lesson in the last two hundred years is that freedom/choice exercised in the presence of the Other is the most committed, the most productive, the most powerful form of behavior. In the last one hundred and fifty years compare the performance of free economies, marked by decentralization and free choice, and by the presence of the Other as competitor. They have far out produced centrally controlled economies, as in socialism or communism. In the last one hundred and fifty years we have seen that same record in the military. Which armies have fought most effectively? Not the dictators' armies. Those people who understood choice, those who understood that I do not claim total authority so that I now have the right to totally destroy my enemy; those who did not believe that they were divinely commanded under orders to kill all who oppose them; those who understood in a democratic way the value of life and the respect of the Other—even if I have to fight them—won. If free armies can outclass dictatorships, if free economies can out produce rigidly controlled ones, why should we not believe that free religions cannot compete? Religions not based on disrespect, do better. A Judaism not sustained by the assumption that Christianity is bizarre (and I cannot respect it) will attract more. A Christianity not presuming that Judaism is so inferior (that I could not respect it) will receive more people. Why should we not have the confidence to believe that religions based on freedom, on pluralism, on mutual respect, will in fact perform at the highest levels of morality and of religion?

Testing this principle is the calling of this generation for Jews and for Christians. We can drop the easy victories and simple put downs, the inherited dismissals, and together work for *tikkun olam*. The world needs this approach. This must be our choice to truly consecrate God's name. Together the two religions—backed by the extraordinary explosion of democratic values and a yearning for freedom can bring us much closer to the dreamed of Messianic age.

A CLOSING QUESTION: WHAT IF WE BRING THE MESSIAH?

Now, what happens if—thanks to the wide ranging cooperation I am proposing, in fact we bring the Messiah? At the end of all this, we would be back to the question: who was right? After all, the big difference between our two faiths is that Christians say the Messiah came already while Jews say the Messiah has not come yet. So what happens when we bring the Messiah?

Let me say first of all that the binary opposition of the two faiths on this issue is an exaggeration. Although Christians say the Messiah came already they also admit that the Messiah must come back in a second coming. In that doctrine, is the Christian admission that the Jews are not so wrong. The Jews know what they are talking about when they insist that the world is not redeemed. On the other hand, Jews who say the Messiah has not come yet still affirm and live the Shabbat. What is Shabbat? For a day, Jews act *as if the Messiah has come*. On Shabbat, there is no war and no work. There is nothing to do because we act as if it is a perfect world. Shabbat is the Jewish admission, it is not so *meshugah* for Christians to say that even if the whole world is not redeemed you can experience that the Messiah is here. Here again Judaism and Christianity incorporate much more of each other's views than they acknowledge to each other or to themselves.

This brings us back to the question: if the Messiah comes thanks to our joint efforts, then is this the first or second coming? When I first joined the dialogue and spoke to fellow Jews and fellow Christians, I said let us not argue about this. Let us just perfect the world. When the Messiah comes we will ask the Messiah: is this the first or second coming? We will get the answer then. There is no need to fight over this now. I confess that in my heart of hearts I believed that when the Messiah came and was asked this question, he/she would say it is my first coming. Then I would say: a-hah, the Jews were right all along. I talked to a Christian friend once and confessed this secret. He acknowledged to me: you know what, in my heart of hearts I am convinced he will come and say this is the second time, so Christians will have been right all along.

Challenged by this exchange, I thought about it a lot and came to the following conclusion. If we get together and truly partner, we will perfect the world—thus we will bring the Messiah. When the Messiah finally arrives, they will call a press conference. The first question the reporters are going to ask the Messiah is: "Is this your first coming or your second coming?" The Messiah will smile and say, "God told me to answer: no comment." Then we will all realize that the true fulfillment we sought was not to be right—it was to be there at the achievement of *tikkun olam.*

NOTES

1. A fuller theology with more specific treatments of various issues between Judaism and Christianity is spelled out in greater detail in my book, *For the Sake of Heaven and Earth: The New Encounter Between Judaism and Christianity.* (Philadelphia: Jewish Publication Society, 2004).

2. I describe the experience in my book so I will not go through all the details in this article. See *For the Sake of Heaven and Earth: The New Encounter Between Judaism and Christianity*, pp. 4–26.

3. Blu Greenberg, *On Women and Judaism: A View from Tradition* (Philadelphia: Jewish Publication Society, 1982).

4. For an example of continuing dismissal of Christianity in the traditional (Orthodox) community which has not participated in the Jewish–Christian dialogue, see J. David Bleich, "Entering a non-Jewish House of Worship," in his Survey of Recent Halachic Literature, *Tradition*, vol. 44, no. 2 (2011), pp. 73–102. To be fair, Bleich insists that rejection of the other religion need not/should not be translated in negative attitudes or behaviors toward the other person. For a counter voice, a positive theology toward Christianity after engaging in dialogue, see Eugene B. Korn, "The People Israel, Christianity and the Covenantal Responsibility to History," in Robert Jensen and Eugene Korn, editors, *Covenant and Hope: Christian and Jewish Reflections*, (Grand Rapids: Eerdmans, 2012), pp. 145–172.

5. The text indicates that the covenant is with *all* living things. Genesis 9:9–10. Presumably, however, only humans can consciously partner with God.

6. The summary Divine instruction of the requirements of the covenant are: "Be fertile and increase; abound on the earth and increase in it." Genesis 9:7.

7. The Talmud states that "Every argument for the sake of Heaven will have an enduring [positive] outcome." Pirkei Avot, ch. 5, m. 20.

Chapter Three

Vatican II, *The Passion of the Christ,* and the Future of Catholic–Jewish Dialogue

Alan L. Berger

The Second Vatican Council was one of the most important religious events of the twentieth century.[1] Given impetus by the horrors of the Shoah, the courage of Pope John XXIII, about whom Hans Küng observed "in 5 years he renewed the Catholic Church more than his predecessors had in 500 years," the work of Jules Isaac in identifying and refuting what he termed "the Teaching of Contempt," and the determination of Cardinal Augustin Bea Vatican II meant the Church can no longer ignore the world.[2] Convened initially in order to deal with liturgical reform and ecumenism, the Council issued *Nostra Aetate* (*N.A.*, "In Our Time"), a paradigm-shattering document, especially in note four which committed the Church to reassess its theology of Judaism. *Nostra Aetate,* although by and for the Church has a dramatically universal resonance. It can be understood within the context of what Judaism terms *Hesbon ha-Nefesh*, a reckoning of the soul.

Now that forty years—a biblical generation—have passed it is clear that this document *was the key which opened the door of possibility* for meaningful Catholic–Jewish dialogue. Rabbi A. James Rudin attests that because of *N.A.* "there have been more positive [Catholic–Jewish] encounters since 1965 than there were in the first 1900 years of the church."[3] One small measure of this turnabout is the fact that a conference such as this dealing with the impact of *N.A.* on the new era of interreligious relationships—and others like it being held in various venues, including Jerusalem—would have been impossible even forty years ago.

Yet unresolved and, perhaps, unresolvable issues remain which pose at least two questions: what do each of the faith communities perceive as a dialogue, and what are its anticipated outcomes? I shall return to these questions later. Many in the Jewish community wonder about the meaning of Church apologetics. Mindful of the plethora of positive developments in the dialogue and the growing areas of joint study and social justice efforts, a fundamental question remains about the relationship of Church proclamations in the way they inform the dialogue on three issues: anti-Semitism, the Shoah, and the role of Israel. The controversy surrounding Mel Gibson's 2004 film *The Passion of the Christ*—intentionally released on Ash Wednesday—and the enthusiastic response among many in the Christian, although by no means exclusively Catholic community, reveals that the issue of anti-Semitism and the Shoah still separate the two faith communities. In what follows I shall argue that while we live after the Flood, we still have not been granted a full vision of the Rainbow.

ANTI-SEMITISM

Addressing the persistent and pernicious issue of anti-Semitism on the twentieth anniversary of *Nostra Aetate*, Edward H. Flannery inquired how a dialogue could prosper in the face of two unspoken questions each partner implicitly raises. One partner wonders *Why are they so persecution-minded and concentrated on their troubles?* The other partner wonders *Why are they so indifferent and callous about the persecution of my people?*[4] In view of the trauma to Catholic–Jewish relations induced by reactions to *The Passion of the Christ,* Flannery's inquiry assumes added urgency twenty years after he first posed it. Mr. Gibson may or may not be an anti-Semite, (his 2006 anti-Semitic tirade in Los Angeles following his arrest for drunk driving leaves little doubt about his attitude toward Jews), but one thing is certain: this film would not be made by an individual interested in fostering any of the dimensions of the 1974 Implementing Guidelines issued by the Vatican relating to *N.A.*, particularly those concerning its declaration of the special relationship between Christianity and Judaism and the recognition that genuine dialogue demands the legitimacy of self-definition.

Rabbi Irving Greenberg notes that the Second Vatican Council hinted that the Jews never forfeited their election, and moreover, the Council Fathers combined this with a call or promise to teach the Gospels in a way that would not present Jews as reprobate. This choice had the advantage of leaving Gospel authority untouched.[5] But note four, following the example of Paul's Letter to the Romans, 9–11, upon which it is based, and which committed the Church to re-examine its theology of Judaism, exemplifies the perils of theological ambiguity. Thus, while acknowledging the "spiritual ties which link the people of the New Covenant to the stock of Abraham," the statement then attests that "the Church is the new people of God. . . ." Rabbi Riccardo Di

Segni, Chief Rabbi of the Jewish Community of Rome, wonders if this is in a sense a reprise of the *Adversos Israel* position.[6] He astutely enquires, "whether the existence of a 'new' people of God means that the old one can no longer be considered as such, or whether the old and the new people are both called to play a role in the history of salvation."[7] This re-raises the ongoing covenantal questions, is there a single or a double covenant. In addition, it brings to the forefront what should be the appropriate image for Catholic–Jewish relations: siblings, fraternal twins, co-emergent religious communities.[8]

Gibson's film exploited the weaknesses and ambiguities of *N.A.* Vatican II, unfortunately, left open the option for traditionalists who reject both the teachings of the Council itself, and the legitimacy of all Popes after Pius XII to utilize the Gospels in an historically uncritical fashion. Further, the abiding image of the Jewish people according to this reading is one of Christ-killers. The deicide charge has followed the Jewish people since its appearance in the Gospel of Matthew. Ironically, Matthew is viewed as the most "friendly" of the Gospels concerning the linkage of Jesus to his Jewish milieu, even tracing his lineage to King David. Yet it contains the infamous declaration: "His blood be upon us and our children" *(MT 27:24–25)*. When coupled with the advent of passion plays this curse has historically led to violence against the Jewish people.

In this context, it is instructive to compare two responses to *The Passion*. Mr. William Donahue, President of the Catholic League for Religious and Civil Rights, is a spokesperson for traditional Catholicism. In an open letter to the Jewish community, he described the Gibson film as "magnificent beyond words." Directly addressing the deicide charge leveled against the film, Donahue had this to say: "Anyone who believes in collective guilt or believes that today's Jews are responsible for the behavior of some Jews two thousand years ago is demented."[9] Donahue's intemperate use of the word "demented," aside, Richard Rubenstein—who is assuredly not demented—on the other hand, writes that he "saw Jesus' sufferings, presented graphically on the screen, as foreshadowing all the agonies my people had endured because of the deicide accusation and the Jews' 'inability' to share in the 'good news' of Christ's promise of salvation."[10] The charge of deicide against Jews," Rubenstein continues, "places *unbelieving* Jews squarely in the camp of Satan, as does the Gibson film."[11] Clearly the film exposed a major fault line separating Judaism and Christianity.

VATICAN II AND ITS LEGACY

Viewing the official statements, promulgations and responses of the Church concerning anti-Semitism during the past 40 years, one notes an impressive and constructive series of documents which portend great promise for Catholic–Jewish dialogue. To mention the more prominent among them one need point only to the documentary legacy of *Nostra Aetate* which was promulgated in the sixties. *The Implementing Guidelines* to the document appeared in the seventies. The *Guidelines* in turn, were followed a decade later by two important documents; *Notes on the Correct Way to Present Jews and Judaism in Preaching and Catechesis in the Roman Catholic Church* and *The Bishops Criteria for Evaluation of Dramatization of the Passion.* In the nineties a variety of proclamations appeared including statements by the Polish, French, and Belgium episcopates. The far better known, but more controversial *We Remember: A Reflection on the Shoah* was published in 1998, followed two years later by *Dabru Emet*, a Jewish acknowledgement of the theological change manifest in the Catholic Church. At the beginning of the twenty-first century the Vatican issued *The Jewish People and Their Sacred Scripture*. This was followed by *Walking God's Paths*, a DVD which features Jews and Christians in conversation. The dialogue thus appeared well-launched to mutually face the challenges presented by a new century that had begun in a spasm of religious fanaticism.

With all of these positive developments, certain critics began to enquire, why cannot the Jews take "yes" for an answer? The Church may well begin to wonder what it is the Jews want, why are we the ones constantly prodded? A major issue is the Church's own insistence on sending mixed signals. For example, *We Remember* aroused a storm of controversy over two issues, its distancing of the teaching of contempt from Nazi race-based Jew hatred and its defense of Pope Pius XII. Further, at the same time that he beatified Pope John XXIII, Pope John Paul II also bestowed that status on Pope Pius IX. While it is true that the Church is free to beatify anyone it chooses, it is also the case that the Church sends a universal message with beatification; this person's life, thoughts and deeds are worthy of emulation. It encourages the faithful member of the Catholic Church to look at the example and follow the way of those whom the Church beatifies.

Advocating reconciliation and memory is antithetical to the actions which occurred during the pontificate of Pius IX. In the words of Gerhart Riegner, "the beatification of Pope Pius IX was a terrible shock for us." How, Riegner asks:

> Is it possible to comprehend, after a solemn expression of repentance and asking pardon for all wrongdoings against Jews throughout history [*We Remember*], the beatification of somebody who more than anyone else personified the most authoritarian and closed attitude in the Church and who strongly condemned all modern movements? How hold up as an example for veneration a person who re-established the ghetto of Rome, who renewed all the discriminations of which the Jews were victims in the state and in the church, and who concealed and defended the clandestine conversion and abduction of

a Jewish child and his elevation to the priesthood? Are these acts indicative of "unconditional fidelity to revealed truth?" [John Paul II utilized this phrase in describing Pius IX.].[12]

Dialogue requires a commitment to move forward together on the basis of trust. Yet the Church, perhaps unwittingly, appears torn between moving forward and looking backwards. In May 2001, I shared a platform with Archbishop Joseph Zycinski, who had been appointed by Pope John Paul II, in Lublin, Poland. The topic was "Christian–Jewish Relations in the 21st Century." Archbishop Zycinski greeted the audience—nearly three hundred college and university students from around the globe, most of whom were not Jewish, with the same words Pope John XXIII used in welcoming a Jewish delegation to the Vatican, "I am Joseph your brother." He then told a story of two young Jewish boys who were sheltered during the Holocaust by Polish Christians. The dénouement of the tale was that both boys had subsequently become priests. This story, perhaps meant as inspirational, was in fact theologically jarring and smacked of triumphalism.

MEL GIBSON AND *THE PASSION OF THE CHRIST*

A plethora of books, articles, and opinion pieces have appeared dealing with the Gibson film. I do not intend to rehash their arguments here.[13] Rather, I simply state two points. First, Gibson's film is the most widely watched passion play in history. It reopens in a spectacular and violent manner old and never fully healed theological wounds. Like its predecessors, this passion play embraces a Manichaean worldview. Jesus and his followers—none of whom is identified as a Jew—are the sons of light. Jews are sons of darkness mysteriously in league with the devil. Further, Jews have committed the unpardonable crime of deicide leaving them eternally reprobate. The deicide charge, muted in *N.A.*'s note four, although the word "deicide" is not explicitly mentioned, lies at the core of Gibson's film.

Second, the interview the filmmaker had with Diane Sawyer stated positions which many in the Christian community hold deeply.[14] Gibson made three basic points. His film is based on Gospel accounts of the crucifixion. Thus, his film is, literally, the Gospel truth. Consequently, even Christians who criticize the film are, by Gibson's definition, not only anti-Catholic but, more crucially, anti-Gospel truth. Second, this film is a statement of his belief as an authentic confessing Catholic. In fact, Gibson contends that the Holy Spirit worked through him to direct the film. If this is the case, one is hard put to reconcile it with Gibson's response to Frank Rich's criticism of *The Passion*—"I want to kill his dog." Gibson's third stated reason for making the film is of a piece with his claim of authenticity. *The Passion*, he told Ms. Sawyer, is "penance" for many years of living a life devoid of spiritual meaning. He attests that he was on the verge of suicide before being saved in order to make this film. In short, Gibson implies that he, like the apostle Paul, had a conversion experience which altered, and saved, his life.

This may well be the case. But Gibson's film does not appear in a historical vacuum. It comes at a time in the post-Auschwitz world when crucial questions are being raised about the role of religion in aiding extremism, the ugly resurgence of anti-Semitism in Europe and its intensification in the Arab Middle East, the call of Pope John Paul II for the Church to repent of its sin of the teaching of contempt, an intense discussion about the responsibility of the artist toward history, and the role of film as an art form shaping reality in the post-Modern world, defined by an increasingly polarizing culture war. Perhaps most significantly, *The Passion* appears at a crucial moment in the post-Holocaust history of Jewish–Christian dialogue, coming on the heels of the controversy over access to Vatican documents dealing with the wartime record of Pius XII, the revelations about the killing of Jews by poles in Jadwabne during the Shoah, the Convent and Crosses controversy at Auschwitz, and the canonization of Edith Stein. The fresh winds blowing through the post–Vatican Church are being threatened by a gale force howling in the opposite direction.

Erroneously claiming to portray the biblical account of Jesus's passion, Gibson's film—in a best case scenario—raises fundamental historical and theological questions. For example, how should one read the Gospels? What is the relationship between historical truth and biblical parable? James Carroll refers to this phenomenon as "history remembered" as opposed to "prophecy historicized." Where does Gibson's film leave the dialogue? Will the dialogue of historical and textual scholars with those in their own faith community have a transforming effect on the laity? Can interfaith dialogue weather the twin threats of fundamentalism, on the one hand, and secular cultural forces, on the other. How these questions are pursued will go a long way in determining the success of the dialogue.

To return to *The Passion,* we take note that Gibson, not content with his idiosyncratic Gospel reading, relies heavily on extra-biblical scenes and events. For example, he extensively utilizes the visions of Anne Catherine Emmerich [1774–1824], a German Augustinian nun whose "eyewitness" accounts of the lives of Mary and Jesus appeared in a book edited by Clemens Brentano. Nine years after Emmerich's death, Brentano published *The Dolorous Passion of our Lord Jesus Christ After the Meditations of Anne Catherine Emmerich*. From this alleged "eyewitness" to the crucifixion, Gibson takes his androgynous devil figure, the emphasis on Jesus' scourging, a weak-willed and indecisive Pontius Pilate, and a single-minded determination to blame "the Jews" for crucifying Jesus. Furthermore, in Gibson's cinematic representation, there is no indication that Jesus, his Mother, and the apostles were Jews. In Gibson's cinematic "gospel" Christianity emerged full blown with the appearance of Jesus when, in fact, this great religious tradition only began assuming a distinctive theological form some two centuries afterwards.

Insisting on its practice of sending mixed signals on the matter of Catholic–Jewish dialogue, the Vatican beatified Anne Catherine Emmerich in October of 2004. Despite official statements that the case for her beatification rests on the basis of her virtues and not what she has written, this act will be taken as Vatican approval of Emmerich's views. Consequently, the beatification of a nineteenth-century nun with anti-Semitic views assumes its place alongside the beatification of Pius IX as an act which may cause many in the Jewish community to question the Church's understanding of Jewish sensitivities and the meaning of dialogue while simultaneously reinforcing a still prominent feeling of uncertainty about the Church's intentions.

Gibson's film is both "anti and ante" Vatican II. James Carroll portrays the issue in far grimmer terms than *merely* a rejection of Modernism. He contends that the film's aim is to "remove the Holocaust as a defining point of moral reference." Furthermore, Carroll observes that Gibson's message is "You want to see what real suffering looks like, check out the flayed Christ. And, by the way, look who caused his misery."[15] Thus, Mr. Gibson is simultaneously engaged in the fruitless and sterile exercise of comparative suffering as well as in advancing anti-Semitic stereotyping. *Nostra Aetate* rightly condemned both of these practices.

An interfaith Scholars Committee whose members worked independently of one another critiqued Gibson's script. Appointed by Dr. Eugene Fisher, Secretariat for Catholic–Jewish Relations of the United States Conference of Catholic Bishops, the Committee noted that the script was deficient in several areas. It ignored completely the evidence of scientific historical scholarship concerning the composition of the Gospels. Further, the script accepts uncritically the alleged visions of Anne Catherine Emmerich, substituting her "eye-witness" and bogus account of the crucifixion for the Gospel versions. The scholars also noted the film's linguistic difficulties, e.g., the Gospel accounts are in Greek rather than the Aramaic and Latin spoken by the actors. Finally, the scholars all cited the film's potential for instigating anti-Semitism. The final script was marginally corrected. But the major response by Icon, Gibson's production company, was two-fold, a threat to sue the Committee members, and an attempt to impugn the scholars' reputations.

Father John Pawlikowski, a scholar long involved in Catholic–Jewish dialogue, and a member of the above mentioned Scholars Committee, utilizes medical terminology in discussing the Church's pre-Vatican anti-Judaism. He advocates "spiritual chemotherapy" be administered against the cancer of Jew-hatred. Moreover, extending the metaphor, he views Gibson's film as a "relapse." The disease has returned with, pardon the pun, a passion. Unlike cancer, however, anti-Semitism is contagious. A Pew poll taken shortly after the film's release reported a slight rise of 9 percent in the number of people who believe that the Jewish people are responsible for the death of Jesus.

As a Jew, I do not feel it proper or responsible to comment on what Christians believe. Pawlikowski observes, however, that Gibson's portrayal of Jesus omits his role as a savior. The message of love is obliterated and the film offers only a glimpse of the resurrection. Pawlikowski—and not he alone—wonders what kind of God would demand this type of violence in order to send a message to humanity. Gibson's emphasis is not on living a religious life, but rather on the medieval ideal of enduring unbearable agony, the true contemporary *imitatio dei.* The director may in fact have been interested in countering other recent artistic images of Jesus as rock star (*Jesus Christ, Superstar*) or as homosexual (*Corpus Christi*). Gibson's Jesus is a one-dimensional macho figure evidently either above or indifferent to the entire bloody episode.

CATHOLIC–JEWISH DIALOGUE

I believe that in assessing the state of post-*Passion* Catholic–Jewish dialogue it is necessary to distinguish between short and long-term prospects. Although it seems counter-intuitive, I am fairly optimistic about the short term, but far less certain concerning the long-term outlook.

The Ba'al Shem Tov (1698–1760), founder of the Hasidic movement in Judaism, contended that evil could be the footstool of good. We live at a time of great change in the post–Vatican II history of Catholic–Jewish dialogue. Much attention, effort, and thought have been, and are being, devoted by both sides to ensure that the dialogue not only continues, but matures. This means that disagreements do not derail interfaith relations. Quite the contrary is the case. Disputes may, as the *Guidelines* suggest, serve to deepen and enrich one's understanding of the faith of others as well as one's own beliefs.

The uproar caused by Gibson's film has—intentionally or otherwise—caused many people to reflect on their own views of religion and to re-read sacred texts. Moreover, the light of critical scholarship is being shone on the socio-religious world of antiquity. Crucial archaeological evidence helps contemporary discussion of ancient texts. The fact that the interfaith Scholar's Committee recognized the dangers of the deeply flawed *Passion* script is just one sign of the deepened trust developing between Catholic and Jewish intellectuals; good theology cannot rest firmly on a historically faulty foundation. As noted above, a plethora of scholarly anthologies dealing with issues raised by the Gibson film have appeared. These works critique the film's shortcomings and draw attention to its outright falsifications. Moreover, people are being encouraged to ask questions and to study sources in an ecumenical environment. All of this activity is in the spirit of *Nostra Aetate*'s vision of the Church engaged with the world.

Long term, however, the prospect appears to me far less certain. As the notorious Henry Ford once observed, "History is more or less bunk." Clearly, we never know what the future will bring. This of course does not absolve us from the right and the obligation of thinking ahead. In terms of Catholic–Jewish dialogue several key questions arise. Will succeeding popes have the same degree of personal commitment to the enterprise as did John Paul II and Pope Benedict XVI? If not, will the effort be put on the ecumenical back burner? Jewish history records what happened when a new pharaoh arose who did not know Joseph. [16]

Further, Americans increasingly receive their knowledge of history not by reading books, but by watching films. This means that whatever "learning" occurs does so by means of passive receptivity which promotes neither critical thinking nor the life of the mind. "Already many—if not most—mainline Protestants and Catholics," as Mary Boys of Union Theological Seminary observes, "are at best only dimly aware of the substantial rethinking of the past thirty-five years. Anti-Judaism remains alive and all too well within the Church." [17] Moreover, in times of cultural stress and uncertainty there is a strong tendency to fall back on stereotypes which give false assurance by demonizing the Other.

In this context it is significant to note that the DVD version of *The Passion of the Christ* was released in September 2004. *Experiencing the Passion of Jesus*, a study guide to the film published by Zondervan, continues the anti-historical view of first-century-C.E. religious life in ancient Palestine, while manipulating the reader into an "either/or" view of Jesus as the Christ. In other words, one is either on the side of the true believers—Jesus is the son of God—or one is a sinner. The text seeks to explain neither historical complexities nor theological nuance. It does not take a great deal of imagination to realize that this "study guide" will fuel negative stereotyping of Judaism.

The challenge confronting the post–Vatican II Church is how to respond to such assaults. The record to date is itself ambiguous. Rabbi DiSegni astutely observes that there is a sad impression in the Jewish world that:

> When confronted with strong mystical experiences and huge interests of a pastoral nature, but also other types, the problem of the correct relationship with the Jews seems to be the last thing to worry the church, which then thinks that a generic reference to the official documents [contradicted by the facts] is sufficient to patch up the damage. [18]

The ongoing issue therefore is one of *implementation*. The church has demonstrated its admirable capacity for theological formulation. What we now

need is deeds rather than creeds. The Hebrew Union College Historian Michael Cook puts the matter in perspective by commenting that when faced
with this discrepancy, the Church resorts to "saturation bombing" or re-
printed Vatican II documents.[19] Moreover, the Sydney, Australia, *Morning
Herald* reports that Gibson has been invited to re-create the crucifixion of
Jesus in the streets of Sydney if the city is chosen to host the Catholic
Church's 2008 World Youth Day.

The Church dare not allow a second institutional moral failure of silence
after Auschwitz. The controversy generated by Gibson's film is at the same
time an unparalleled "teaching moment" for the Vatican. I note as an aside
that until now there has been no official comment on the Gibson film from
either Hollywood, which represents secularism par excellence, or from the
Vatican. The late John Paul II was silent after *The Passion,* as he was when
Syrian President Bashir Assad greeted him in Damascus (May 8, 2001) with
a vicious anti-Semitic statement accusing the Jews of deicide. Silence never
helps the victim. Rather it indicates either approval or apathy. Furthermore,
the flurry of contradictory statements attributed to the Vatican following
Gibson's film did nothing to assuage the concerns of Jews and others about
the theological and historical errors of the work. If faith is what makes us
human, observes Rabbi Jonathan Sacks, then those who do not share my faith
are less than fully human. From this absolutist position, great human catastrophe—typically perpetrated in the name of God—Crusades, Inquisitions,
Jihads, and Genocides have ensued.[20]

SEPARATED BY A COMMON LANGUAGE

One of the fundamental issues separating Jews and Christians in the dialogue
is that we are divided by a common language. A brief look at the issue of
repentance and forgiveness illustrates this point. Judaism teaches that there
are two types of transgression, that between one individual and another (*beyn
adam leAdam*), and that committed by humans against God (*beyn adam
leMakom*). The person sinned against is the only one who may properly
forgive the sinner. There is no corporate forgiveness in Judaism. Further,
only God can forgive transgressions against the deity. There is, as Professor
David Blumenthal notes, "no spiritual or halakhic mechanism in Judaism by
which Jews can formally 'forgive' the Catholic Church, or the community of
Catholics, for the centuries of injurious teaching and persecution of Jews
culminating in the *Shoah.*"[21]

This leaves the notion of *mechila*, the act of "forgiving the other's indebt-
edness" which can be granted only if deserved. *Mechila* requires that "the
offended party has sure grounds to think that the offending party has done
teshuva" (genuinely turned away from that which is evil or hateful and

turned toward that which is righteous). In the context of Catholic–Jewish dialogue, notes Blumenthal, this requires three conditions be met.

> First, desisting from the sin of persecuting Jews, including desisting from teaching doctrines and supporting popular attitudes that encourage or even tolerate the persecution of Jews; second, making appropriate restitution where there are material claims that can be compensated; and, third, the reform of character through intellectual-moral analysis, remorse, and confession. [22]

The Church can demonstrate the authenticity of its teshuva through deeds, not creeds. Consequently, how it deals with anti-Semitism, terrorist incidents, the Church's historical record dealing with the Shoah, unreturned Judaica, e.g., manuscripts and art, relations with Israel, the nature of Catholic mission, Church teachings about Jews and Judaism, and relations with local Jewish communities are, attests Blumenthal, "action-yardsticks" which measure the nature of Catholic teshuva. [23] Thus far, it appears that this teshuva is stronger in certain areas than in others. In any case, the ebb and flow of dialogue is closely linked with such efforts.

CONCLUSION

Amidst the controversy over the Gibson film, it is important to note the appearance of another, far better, historically accurate, and inspirational passion film. *Sister Rose's Passion*, winner in the 2005 Best Documentary Short category, tells the story of Sister Rose Thering, a Domincan nun. [24] Fifty years ago, a young Sister Rose exposed and critiqued the Christian Teaching of Contempt which was thoroughly embedded in Sunday school texts, catechisms, and other educational material. Sister Rose who as a doctoral student at St. Louis University was told by that city's archbishop "don't hang out (the Church's) dirty laundry," proceeded to do exactly that in exposing the widespread prevalence of negative stereotypes in Catholic educational material such as the blood libel and the deicide accusation.

Sister Rose's dissertation on this topic greatly influenced Cardinal Bea, Director of the Secretariat for Christian Unity whose commission worked on the several drafts of *Nostra Aetae*. It is no exaggeration to state that her work, and her consistent struggle against an entrenched Church theological conservatism were important factors in helping the Council Fathers to understand the role of the Church in fomenting the teaching of contempt for the Jewish people. *Nostra Aetate,* while having faced numerous obstacles in getting passed, bears the stamp of Rose Thering's pioneering efforts, especially in underscoring the fact that the Romans, not the Jews, crucified Jesus. Furthermore, Sister Rose continued to labor tirelessly to convince congregations and parishioners to adopt the Church's new stand. One hopes that this story will be heard far and wide.

Returning to the questions asked at the beginning: how do the communities define the dialogue, and what are the anticipated outcomes? At least three notions are significant here. Each party must respect the integrity of the other. The dialogue is an important opportunity for one's own growth in terms of understanding the Other. Further, this understanding applies equally to the opportunity of deepening and enriching one's understanding of one's own tradition. The anticipated outcomes, are however, perhaps more ambiguous. For Jews the issue is at least two-fold. On a primary level, in the post-Auschwitz world where anti-Semitism is still rampant the concern is physical safety. This concern is reinforced by the vitriolic anti-Semitic outbursts of Iranian president Mahmoud Ahmadinejad a Holocaust denier, who has recently proclaimed that "Israel should be wiped off the map" and that Israelis should return to Europe and establish a nation there. As Saul Bellow notes in *To Jerusalem and Back*, not even the creation of a Jewish state has changed a basic fact of Jewish life, ". . . the Jews, because they are Jews, have never been able to take the right to live as a natural right."[25]

Jews in the dialogue also utilize the opportunity of teaching the facts about Jewish history and religious practices. For example, although the Vatican has accorded political recognition to the State of Israel, it is less clear whether the Church understands the role of Israel in relationship to Jewish Peoplehood. The Jewish State is obviously a political fact of life. But it also impacts directly on Jewish identity. If the Church restricts its understanding of Israel solely to the political arena, it misses a central defining characteristic of post-Holocaust Jewish identity. Michael Kotzin notes the troubling dimension of what he terms as the Vatican's "two track approach, relating to Jews as a religion through dialogue while seeing its relations with Israel purely in a political framework."[26]

For Christian partners in dialogue, the process of theological self-critique is aided immeasurably by seeking to understand Judaism on its own terms rather than by means of negative stereotypes. Certainly one lesson for Christianity is that Jews, in rejecting the Messiahship of Jesus are simultaneously affirming their own tradition. Consequently, Catholic–Jewish dialogue can reduce the temptation to embrace supercessionism and to deny the credibility of attempts to convert the Jews. Christians can also affirm the danger of resurgent anti-Semitism and embrace the teachings of the Second Vatican Council that one cannot be a Christian and an anti-Semite. The longer term outcome of the dialogue on Christianity is uncertain and the questions about the theological and demographical asymmetry between Christianity and Judaism remain.

What is the next step for Catholic–Jewish dialogue? Both faith communities live in a world where neither is in the majority. Religious pluralism is a fact of twenty-first century life. *Nostra Aetate* hinted at this in its comments on non-Christian religions. But the dialogue has the potential to model a way of ethical and moral existence in a world where religiously sanctioned mass murder and terror has become an inescapable fact of life. And death. The question arises whether the dialogue can be a moderating voice amidst a chorus of violence. Can the dialogue point beyond itself? Reflecting on issues such as covenant, the role of the Other in God's plan for salvation, and how to achieve a world of justice suggest that the dialogue can have universal implications.

Nostra Aetate, and its documentary legacy, illustrates on the one hand, how far the dialogue has come. For instance, after Auschwitz there is unprecedented openness between the two traditions, a building of trust, the beginnings of theological reflections which portend profound transformation, a fraternal reading of the Bible, the scholarly quest for origins, the fruitfulness of civil discourse, and the emergence of dialogical groups on the international, national, and local levels. On the other hand, the persistence of anti-Semitism, the temptation to triumphalism, the fundamental theological asymmetry, the recognition that we are different in basic ways, the lack of fully comprehending the meaning of Israel, and language itself—Judaism lacks the word "theology," speaking instead of "fear of heaven (*yirat Shemayim*), point to the urgent necessity to continue the important discourse engendered by *N.A.*

NOTES

1. An earlier version of this essay was read in Rome at the Conference "Nostra Aetate Today: Reflections 40 Years After the Call for Interreligious Relationships." Pontificia Universita Gregoriana. September, 2005. I am grateful for comments of Professor Asher Z. Milbauer and Rabbi A. James Rudin on subsequent drafts.

2. Hans Kung, *Reforming the Church Today: Keeping Hope Alive* (London: T. & T. Clark, 2000), pp. 66–67.

3. A. James Rudin, *Twenty Years of Jewish-Catholic Relations*. Edited by Eugene J. Fisher, A. James Rudin, and Marc H. Tanenbaum (New York: Paulist Press, 1986), p.15. It should at the same time be noted however that *Nostra Aetate* fails specifically to mention "deicide," the Holocaust, or the State of Israel.

4. Edward Flannery, "Seminaries, Classrooms, Pulpits, Streets: Where We Have to Go," in *Unanswered Questions: Theological Views of Jewish-Catholic Relations*. Edited by Roger Brooks (Notre Dame: University of Notre Dame Press, 1988), p. 140.

5. Irving Greenberg, "Anti-Semitism in 'The Passion,'" in *Commonweal* (New York), May 7, 2004, p. 12.

6. Riccardo DiSegni, "Steps Taken and Questions Remaining in Jewish-Christian Relations Today" Paper read in the series "The Catholic Church and the Jewish People from Vatican II to Today." Pontifical Gregorian University, October 19, 2004, p.3. Available online at http://www.bc.edu/research/cjl/meta-elements/texts/conferences/Bea_Centre_C-J-Relatio. . . 11/112004.

7. Ibid.

8. John Pawlikowski raised this question in his plenary address at the "Nostra Aetate Today: Reflections 40 Years After Its Call for a New Era of Interreligious Relations" Conference. Rome, Pontifical Gregorian University, September 25, 2005.

9. Donohue's remarks are cited by David Berger, "Jews, Christians, and 'The Passion,'" in *Commentary* (New York), vol. 117, n. 5, May, 2004, p.30.

10. Richard L. Rubenstein, "The Exposed Fault Line," in *After the Passion is Gone: American Religious Consequences*. Edited by J. Shawn Landres and Michael Berenbaum (Walnut Creek: Altamira Press, 2004), p. 207.

11. Ibid.

12. Gerhart M. Riegner, Letter to the Editors, *SIDIC* (Rome), vol. XXXIII, no. 3, 2000, p. 15.

13. See the following representative works: *After the Passion is Gone: American Religious Consequences; Jesus and Mel Gibson's The Passion of The Christ: The Film, The Gospels and the Claims of History*. Edited by Kathleen E. Corley and Robert L. Webb (London: Continuum, 2004); *Pondering the Passion: What's At Stake for Christians and Jews?* Edited by Philip A. Cuningham (Lanham: Rowman & Littlefield Publishers, Inc., 2004); and *Re-Viewing the Passion: Mel Gibson's Film and its Critics*. Edited by S. Brent Plate (New York: Palgrave Macmillan, 2004).

14. Diane Sawyer, Interview with Mel Gibson, ABC, February, 2004.

15. James Carroll "Additional Perspectives on *Passion of the Christ*," in "Kill Jesus," by Amy Hollywood, *Harvard Divinity Bulletin*, (Cambridge), Summer, 2004, p. 34. It is significant to note that in early December, 2005 an announcement was made that Gibson plans a made-for-television (ABC) mini-series about a Holocaust rescuer. It takes no great leap of imagination to ponder the possibility that Mr. Gibson will distort the message in a way that absolves the Christian teaching of contempt for Judaism as sewing the seedbed of the Shoah.

16. This is not to equate present and future popes with an ancient Egyptian king. However, it is conceivable that the Church's increasing concern with its African and Asian constituents, for whom Jewish–Christian dialogue is not a vital matter, and where there are insignificant numbers of Jews, will relegate such dialogue to the theological backburner.

17. Eric Geller cites Mary Boys, *Has God Only One Blessing?* in his paper "Our Race Against Time," which is available online at http://www.bc.edu/research/cjl/meta-elements/texts/topics/NA/Geller/.htm

18. DiSegni. Ibid., p. 5.

19. Michael Cook, "The Mel Gibson Ordeal: An Insider's Account," in *The Chronicle: Hebrew Union College-Jewish Institute of Religion* (Cincinnati), Issue 63, 2004, p. 15.

20. Jonathan Sacks, *The Dignity of Difference: How to Avoid the Clash of Civilizations*. (New York: Continuum, 2003), p.46.

21. David Blumenthal. "Repentance and Forgiveness," in *Cross Currents* (New York), 48, no.1 Spring, 1998, p. 80.

22. Ibid., p.81.

23. Ibid.

24. *Sister Rose's Passion* Film by Oren Jacoby. New Jersey Studios, LLC, 2004.

25. Saul Bellow, *To Jerusalem and Back* (New York: Viking Press, 1976), p. 26.

26. Michael Kotzkin, "Facing the Unresolved Issue in Interfaith Dialogue," *Forward Forum* (New York), October 28, 2005, p. 11. At the *Nostra Aetate* Today Conference, several delegates referred to the Church's lack of attention to the intimate connection between the State of Israel and the Jewish People. This point was made with great eloquence by Professor Ruth Langer of Boston College in her conference plenary address.

Chapter Four

Though the Messiah May Tarry

A Reflection on Redemption in Our Time

David Patterson

A question that burned in the souls of the Jews during the dark night of the Shoah is: if this horrific evil does not bring the Messiah, then what will? After all, the Talmud teaches that the Messiah will come either in a time of great goodness or in a time of great evil (*Sanhedrin* 98a), and how much greater can the evil be? The question continues to burn, along with other questions, both ancient and new: How long shall we wait? Have we had enough of waiting? What must we do to bring redemption so long overdue? What is at stake in waiting and working for the coming of the Messiah? Is the price for his coming too high?

Among the Thirteen Principles of Faith outlined by Maimonides the twelfth is an affirmation of *Ani maamin*: "I believe with complete faith in the coming of the Messiah; even though he may tarry, no matter what, I shall await his coming every day." That is, I believe despite the evidence of the eyes. I believe no matter how foolish the belief. Not only shall I "await" his coming, but I shall "expect" it, which is another meaning of *achakeh*, the verb translated as "await," as if he might come at any instant, with the performance of *this* mitzvah, this commandment—even and especially in a post-Shoah world. For Christians and Jews, the wait for the Messiah is a wait for something real, on all levels, no matter how long it may take; otherwise the wait itself is unreal and pointless, no matter how persistent it may be. Just as Jewish and Christian traditions are rooted in the conviction that something real transpired at Mount Sinai, so do those traditions live in a movement toward something real that will transpire in a messianic age. Each has its own eschatology—that is, its own vision of the Last Days—but there are variations both between and within the traditions. One difference is that many

Christian teachings envision a final separation of the righteous from the wicked, with the latter consigned to eternal damnation; most Jewish teachings, however, envision an elevation of all souls to the level of righteousness. In both cases there is some sort of redemption after some sort of tribulation.

Martin Buber maintains that redemption means the realization of "the true community," so that the Messiah is he who makes it possible for God and humanity to dwell in *this* world,[1] and not the one who leads us into a "heavenly" world. For Jewish consciousness, in contrast to most Christian thinking, the longing for God is not a longing to enter His kingdom; rather it is a longing to enable Him to enter *this* kingdom. The flesh-and-blood reality of *this* world is what makes both the wait for the Messiah and the advent of the Messiah something as concrete as human community.

Two things, says Buber, are required for the creation of a true community: each member of the community must live in a relation to a transcendent center, and each must live in a relation to the Other that is expressive of the higher relation.[2] The failed utopian movements of history have shown that neither the vertical nor the horizontal relation can stand on its own; each requires the Other. Emil Fackenheim has rightly asserted that "the 'brotherhood of man,' unless it is part of a messianic hope, is a romantic illusion."[3] For Judaism and Christianity "the brotherhood of man" is no illusion. That is what makes both traditions messianic to the core, despite the differences in how the two think about the Messiah and the ultimate redemption.

And there *are* differences in how the two traditions understand the Messiah and redemption, as well as in their understanding of the related matters of faith and covenant. These are the key concepts that we shall consider here: the Messiah, faith, covenant, and redemption. The context for these reflections—what I refer to as "our time"—is a post-Holocaust world in which Jews and Christians have for the first time entered into a serious dialogue. It is a world in which these fundamental concepts that shape the two traditions have been radically challenged; it is a world, therefore, in which the two traditions themselves face radical challenges. The future of both traditions is at stake in how we confront these challenges. Let us begin, then, with the most basic of the categories common to the two traditions: the Messiah.

THE AWAITED ONE: SOME DIFFERENCES BETWEEN CHRISTIANS AND JEWS

The one whom the Jews await bears little resemblance to the one who, the Christians believe, has come. Briefly stated, according to traditional Christian doctrine, each of us has inherited the taint of Adam's sin, so that each of us is in need of redemption through a sacrificial offering. Because the stain we bear is part of our essence, the one offered up must be pure in essence.

And only God—or the Son of God—is pure in essence. The Redeemer whose sacrifice purifies us of our sin, then, is the Divine incarnation of God, born of a woman who was herself immaculately conceived, since his vessel, too, must be pure. Because sin is definitively tied to death, the Messiah not only redeems our sin through his crucifixion, but he also triumphs over death through his resurrection. He is the necessary mediator between an inherently sinful humanity and an infinitely holy divinity, as it is written: "No one comes to the Father except through me" (John 14:6). The ultimate separation of the righteous from the wicked, according to most Christian scenarios, amounts to a separation of those who accept Jesus as their Savior from those who reject him. Of course, there is some argument as to what "accepting" Jesus amounts to. Does it lie in belief or in actions? Most Christians maintain that it lies in both: each is as essential as the other.

Although in Judaism there are many different views on the Messiah,[4] a few things are clear. The one whom the Jews await is not the son of God any more than any other human being is a child of the Holy One. Nor do we view his resurrection from death as part of what defines him; the Midrash, in fact, speaks of his death without resurrection, saying that when the Messiah dies, the World to Come will be ushered in (*Tanchuma Ekev* 7). Further, he is not born of a virgin, who in turn would require an immaculate conception. From a Jewish perspective, the conception of any human being can be "immaculate," since the marital union that produces a child is itself holy, as is the one born from that union. Hence the dual meaning of *kiddushin*: it translates both as "holiness" and as "marriage." Because we do not inherit Adam's sin, we are born innocent and untainted, as we affirm each morning in our prayers, declaring to God, "The soul You have placed within me is pure." Hence there is no need for a human and Divine sacrifice to atone for our sins. Indeed, only we, and no other, can atone for our sins.

The one whom we await, then, is not one whose blood will cleanse us of our inherently sinful being; rather, he will return us, body and soul, to the inherently holy relation to God and to one another, precisely in this world, and not another: Jesus' statement, "My kingdom is not of this world" (John 18:36) is alien to Jewish teaching about the Anointed One. As we have seen, Jewishly speaking, the Messiah's kingdom is *in* this world and *of* this world. Therefore the Messiah comes not to deliver us *from* the world but to draw Torah *into* the world, so transparently that the word of the Holy One will become part of every human heart (Jeremiah 31:33), and justice and righteousness will reign throughout this world (Isaiah 9:6). Swords will be beaten into plowshares, and "nation will not lift up sword against nation" (Micah 4:3). The Jewish wait for the Messiah is a preparation for such a world. With regard to other unfulfilled prophecies of the Messiah, the most prevalent of all is that the Jews will be returned from their exile. Various prophets invoke various signs of the coming of the Messiah, but almost all of them invoke this one.[5]

Beyond that, the teachings are less clear and more mysterious. In the Talmud, for example, it is written, "Know that there exists on high a substance called 'body' [*guf*] in which are found all the souls destined for life. The son of David will not come before all the souls which are in the *guf* have completed their descent to the earth" (*Yevamot* 63b). According to other traditions, Gog and Magog will launch three wars against the Messiah in the winter month of Tevet; this is a motif that one also finds in Christian eschatology. Messiah ben Joseph will fight those wars; Rashi says he will be killed and then followed by Messiah ben David, who will usher in the everlasting age of peace (see Rashi's commentary on Talmud tractate *Sotah* 51). It is written that, if the Torah is black fire on white fire (*Devarim Rabbah* 3:12), as stated in the Midrash, then the Messiah will reveal the meaning of the white fire. Perhaps he will also reveal the meaning of other flames. Whether the one who tarries is the Nazarene or Messiah ben David, those flames that consumed two-thirds of the Jews of Europe may at times put a strain on our faith. But here too, in the matter of what faith means, there are differences between Jewish and Christian understanding.

THE FAITH DEMANDED BY THE WAIT

Whereas Christian understandings of faith often emphasize belief in a creed, in Judaism belief is not a defining aspect of faith. "Faith" or *emunah* entails much more than the acceptance of a doctrine. It is not reducible to an "assent of the understanding to what is believed," as Thomas Aquinas defines faith,[6] or to the passion that Kierkegaard defines as faith.[7] Nor is it precisely "the substance of things hoped for, the evidence of things not seen," as it is written in the Christian Scriptures (Hebrews 11:1). In addition to "faith," *emunah* means "conscientiousness," "honesty," and "trust." Looking at other dimensions of emunah, we note that the cognate verb *aman* is to "foster" or "bring up"; *neeman* is to "be found true" or "trustworthy," and the adjective *amun* means both "faithful" and "educated." In a word, faith is not the opposite of disbelief. Rather, faith is opposite of folly and irresponsibility, the complete reversal of our deadly isolation within the illusory ego.

Thus Abraham Joshua Heschel writes, "Faith is the beginning of the end of egocentricity. 'To have faith is *to disregard self-regard*'. . . . 'I believe in God' does not mean that *I* accept the fact of *His* existence. It does not signify that *I* come first, then *God*, as the syntax of the sentence implies. The opposite is true. Because God exists, I am able to believe."[8] Which means: I do not "believe" in God, as someone might believe in the tooth fairy. Rather, God "believes" in me—and through me. Torah enters the world through me, as an *event*. Faith means imparting flesh and blood to our teaching of Torah through deeds of Torah. Faith is an unfolding, an overflowing of sanctity into the world, both from within and from beyond the world.

Having faith, then, is not a matter of affirming, "I believe in God," but of declaring, "Here am I, Your servant, ready to serve," ready to enter a service that is the opposite of servitude. Stated differently, to have faith is to live in a "covenant," which is a meaning of the cognate *amanah*, and to live in a covenant is to live according to the commandments and thus enter into a partnership with God to create a world where the Messiah may become manifest. Understood in terms of covenant, faith becomes an issue for God as well. In the psalms, for example, we declare that God accomplishes His works *beemunah*, "through faith" (Psalms 33:4), and that He judges the nations *beemunato*, "in His faith" or, as it is often translated, "in His truth" (Psalms 96:13). Each morning upon waking we affirm in the *Modeh Ani* God's "great faith" in us for returning us to life and sending us on the day's mission. Jewishly understood, faith entails truth, relation, understanding, partnership, readiness, judgment, and more. Such a view of faith does not necessarily contradict a Christian understanding of faith. Indeed, it may well enhance the understanding of the Pauline dictum that we are "justified by faith" alone (Romans 5:1).

But where does all of this leave us, living as we do in the shadows of Birkenau? If, despite our faith, the body of Israel was consumed in the flames of the crematoria, has faith proven to be meaningless? Eliezer Berkovits has one response to this question: "In the presence of the holy faith of the crematoria, the ready faith of those who were not there is vulgarity. But the disbelief of the sophisticated intellectual in the midst of an affluent society—in the light of the holy disbelief of the crematoria—is obscenity."[9] Disbelief can be holy because, as we have seen, faith is not reducible to belief. It can be holy when, insisting on the truth of what Jewish tradition places in our care, it insists on the fidelity of the One who summons us to faith. Here holy disbelief is not so much an absence of faith as it is the presence of outrage in the midst of faith. Indeed, in this case, acceptance would be the opposite of faith. Whereas traditional Christianity may have regarded questioning God as a weakening of faith, in Judaism it happens that precisely the man of faith is the one who questions God.

After Auschwitz the wait for the Messiah is an impatient wait, an outraged wait, a wait made not only of doing but also of questioning. That is where we encounter God: in the question, in the *shelah*, at the center of which is *el*, or "God:" God is alive in the question. A question concerning what? Not the truth of Torah. No, it is a question put to the God of the Covenant precisely in the name of Torah; it is a confrontation with the One who—if one dares to speak such words—seems to have abandoned His Torah. Remaining within the Covenant, we remain within the relation, and we have good reason for our outcry; abandoning the Covenant, we have no grounds for complaining, which, outside of the Covenant, amounts to little more than pretentious whining. If we abandon the Torah—if we abandon the wait, even though the Messiah may tarry—then the outrage and the question become vain self-indulgence, as does everything else. Only when we adhere to Torah are we in a position to argue with God, as the Torah commands us to do.

A teaching from the Book of Deuteronomy, a Scripture shared by Christians and Jews, is pertinent here. It concerns the discovery of the body of a murder victim "lying in the field" (21:1) and whose murderer is unknown. In such a case the elders of the nearest Jewish community must come out and say to God, "Our hands have not shed this blood. . . . Suffer not innocent blood to remain in the midst of Your people Israel" (21:7–8). That is, the hands with which we perform the commandments of Torah have not brought this about—how, then, God, can You stand silently by? Similarly, Jewish law states that if we find someone who has been murdered, his body and clothing bloodied, and there is no prospect of identifying the murderer, then we must bury that person just as we found him (*Kitsur Shulchan Arukh* 197:9). The point? To put it in God's face, as if to say, "Behold what has become of Your creation! What are You going to do about it?"

To "believe" *beemunah shlemah*, in "complete faith," is to draw both the question and the care into our thoughts, words, and deeds. This *shlemah*, this "completeness" or "wholeness" of faith, is the *shalom*, the "peace" that we seek in the Messiah. It is not a state of contentment, which may characterize a state of blissful indifference. Rather, it is about maintaining the tension of the longing and the intensity of the care. In our own time it is about a strife of the spirit, a post-Shoah wounding, without which we are not whole. In the *afterward* of the Shoah both Christians and Jews bear a new wound as the sign of the Covenant, without which there is no redemption. Does this new wound make it a New Covenant? If so, how so? What exactly are the messianic dimensions of the Covenant in our time, a post-Holocaust time?

MESSIANIC DIMENSIONS OF THE COVENANT
AFTER THE HOLOCAUST

Both Christians and Jews would agree, I think, that living in faith, the human being expresses the covenantal relation to God through a care for the other human being, as when Abraham rushed out to greet the three strangers approaching his tent (Genesis 18:2)—his first action after sealing the Covenant of Circumcision. And his second action? It was to enter into an argument with God (Genesis 18:25). In the first Jew, then, we see two basic dimensions of the covenantal task in the post-Holocaust era: care and outrage. This is where there may be some disagreement between the two traditions. "Covenant" is not just *brit*: it is *brit milah*, which means both a "covenant of circumcision" and a "covenant of the word." As manifestations of a relation with the Creator of heaven and earth, both harbor a revelation of meaning in our midst.

To be *mul* or "circumcised" is also to be "facing" or "confronting" another, both human and Divine. Therefore to enter into the Covenant is to become accountable for another, for the sake of another, even for the sake of the one whom we might oppose, both human and Divine. The belief in the coming of the Messiah with *complete* faith lies in the wholeness attained in the bond between human and human, between human and Holy One, as articulated in the two tablets of the Covenant of Torah. Why does God give Moses two tablets, and not one? Not because He cannot write small enough to get it on one tablet. No, it is to articulate the "between space" of two realms of relation: the first tablet pertains to the relation between human and God and the second to the relation between human and human. And yet *there is only one relation.*

What makes the wait for the Messiah interminable is not just that *he* tarries. It is that *we* tarry, especially in the postmodern, post-Shoah era, when so many of us throw up our hands and declare that we cannot go on as if it were business as usual, with the implication that the Jewish testimony slated for annihilation is now meaningless. It is true that the "business" of Judaism and Christianity is no longer "as usual." But if we are to transform the darkness of Auschwitz into light, rather than throw up our hands, we must roll up our sleeves and mend the piece of creation entrusted to our care. Here, Fackenheim realizes, faith means viewing history as a "dialectic of the doing of man and the doing of God," in such a way that the messianic wait is not just our waiting for the Messiah—it is his waiting for us: in Fackenheim's words, he is "waiting for man to perfect the world" or "waiting for him to ruin it."[10] If each of us possesses a messianic spark, it ignites a fire that can either save or destroy. If each living creature possesses a spark of the Messiah, then the *other* human being bears a trace of the Messiah. Contrary to the utterance on the cross, it is not quite finished; or, at the very least, the meaning of the utterance bears reconsideration in a post-Holocaust world.

Here we have an enlargement upon the point that, in his many disguises, the Messiah might be *anyone*. Listen to a tale:

> There was once a Rosh Yeshiva, the head of a religious school, whose students treated each other with terrible rudeness. He tried everything to solve the problem, but everything failed. Finally, the Rosh consulted a rabbi known for his wisdom. After listening to his story, the sage told him, "I cannot tell you exactly what to do, but it occurs to me that one of your students may be the Messiah."

The Rosh Yeshiva returned to the school and declared to his students, "One of you may be the Messiah." After that they treated each other with great courtesy.

In a similar vein, the Talmud teaches that two times are destined for the coming of the Messiah: now and the appointed time (*Sanhedrin* 98a). This teaching is based on the words from the prophet Isaiah: "I Hashem will hasten it in its time" (Isaiah 60:22); that is, I will either hasten it to make it now, or it will be in its appointed time. *Now*, if we treat others with the loving kindness we would show the Messiah himself. In other words, now *is* the appointed time. "Messianism," says Emmanuel Lévinas, "is therefore not the certainty of the coming of a man who stops History. It is my power to bear the suffering of all. It is the moment when I recognize this power and my universal responsibility."[11] So what about the literal meaning of the Messiah, the scion of David, whose coming we pray for three times a day? According to Lévinas, it is all too literal, more literal than we care to think: *I* am the one who must take upon myself the messianic task and testimony— literally. *I* am the one who bears responsibility for creation and humanity— literally. Precisely because the Other may be the Messiah, I must be for the Other what the Messiah is for me.

Which means: even though the Messiah may tarry, I must not tarry. I must study, even though I do not understand; I must pray, even though I hear no reply; I must treat my fellow human being with kindness, even though I see no point or profit. Even though—or especially because—there can be no resolution. Here we come to a most crucial realization: the Messiah is by definition *the one who tarries*, signifying a redemption that is *always yet to be*, always future, because what we do now is never *enough*. "The line of the horizon vanishes as one approaches it," says André Neher, "but the Jew knows that even if the horizon vanishes, in its vanishing it turns toward a vertical position. The point of turning towards the vertical is the 'maybe' of the Messiah."[12] This "maybe" that constitutes the future derives from the "certainty" that constitutes the past. It is as certain as the commandment that the Covenant summons us to follow. A commandment to do what? Not to serve by waiting but to wait by serving. Now we see why the ego is the primary obstacle to the coming of the Messiah. For the ego always insists upon being served, rather than serving. How, then, may we understand the redemption that comes upon the abrogation of the ego, in the light of the wait that seems endless?

THE ENDLESS WAIT FOR REDEMPTION

Turning to the matter of redemption, we return to a point of difference between Jewish and Christian traditions raised earlier. The word *faith* appears in the Christian Scriptures one hundred times more frequently than in the Hebrew Bible, and the Hebrew Bible is about six times longer than the Christian Scriptures. Because of this accent on the faith of the individual, Christians generally view redemption in terms of a *personal* salvation, so that salvation belongs to the individual believer. And it rests at least as much upon the content of belief—on accepting Jesus as the Savior in accordance with John 3:16—as it does upon the actions of the believer. This is not to say that from a Christian standpoint actions are meaningless; rather, it is to say that belief is essential.

In Judaism, belief is not so essential, at least not in the same way. Hence in Judaism we have the concept of the Righteous Among the Nations, people who are near to God, even though they are not followers of Judaism. Because the Jewish accent is on living in such a way as to assume responsibility even for the actions of others, redemption is a matter that concerns the community. Because redemption is not about *me*—because it means serving others in spite of myself—it requires getting rid of the one thing most precious to me: my ego. Perhaps here lies the key to waiting and working for redemption, both for Christians and for Jews. Here too lies one key to the animosity that both face in the effort to bring about the redemption of humanity, from left-wing intellectualism to Islamic Jihadism.

On September 23, 2008, Mahmoud Ahmadinejad was given a podium at the United Nations. From that place of distinction he spewed forth a diatribe against the Jews that the Führer himself could have delivered from the balconies of Berlin. And—with the admirable exception of the United States and Israel—the nations of the world . . . *applauded*. Viewing this Jew hatred in the contexts of the Jewish wait for the Messiah, we discover the essence of anti-Semitism: it is an anti-messianism. The "wandering" Jew turns out to be the waiting Jew and therefore the hated Jew, for the Jew's wait unsettles those who would have things settled through the totalitarian rule of one worldview. The presence of the Jew is a constant reminder that we are forever in debt and that no payment will do, because payment is always due. And so among the anti-Semites it is a truism that the Jews control the ledgers of the world. The hatred of the Jews is the oldest hatred, because the challenge from the Jews is the oldest challenge to the ego that would curl up in the comfort of looking out for Number One. Both the religious and the ideological forms of anti-Semitism seek a final solution in the matter of redemption. In their totalitarian appropriation of the Other, both would either assimilate or annihilate the Jew, whose *very existence* disturbs their sleep with the insistence that the wait for the Messiah is an interminable service to the other person.

The opposite of the totalitarian rule over all humanity is the redemption that includes "all the nations of the earth," for whose sake God enters into the Covenant with Abraham (Genesis 12:3). Contrary to certain forms of religious fanaticism, for Judaism there is no dividing the world into the damned and the saved on the basis of belief. This point is made most perfectly in the story of Jonah. For many forms of religious and ideological fanaticism, to bring the people of Nineveh to God would mean converting them to the –ism in question; for the Jew Jonah, it does not mean converting them to Judaism—it means leading them to realize that their treatment of one another is an expression of their relation to God, the Creator of heaven and earth, without whom life has no meaning. And so in his wait for the time of redemption, the Jew waits not for the world to adopt a certain creed but for the world to take on a certain character. One thing is clear, at least from a Jewish standpoint: the matter of redemption is not settled. What is clear to Judaism, however, may create some confusion in Christianity, where, according to traditional understanding, the redemption was accomplished with the Resurrection. Where redemption is concerned, most Christians believe there is nothing to wait for.

But the Jews insist upon the wait. How long shall we wait? According to the *Pesikta Rabbati* (compiled in the ninth century), we have another 365,000 years of waiting (1:7). Which is to say: the wait is infinite. Thus in the Talmud it is written, "Cursed be the bones of those who calculate the end. For they would say, since the predetermined time has come, and yet the Messiah has not come, he will never come. Nevertheless, wait for him" (*Sanhedrin* 97b). In that *nevertheless* lies the endlessness not only of the wait but of the work: do not calculate the "end"—hasten it. Indeed, in the Talmud it is written that there will be no Messiah for Israel, because those days have already passed, in the time of Hezekiah (*Sanhedrin* 99a); the point is not to put an end to the wait and the expectation but to underscore its endless duration. The Talmud also maintains that all the dates for the ultimate redemption have passed (*Sanhedrin* 97b). Once again, the teaching is not that we should leave off with waiting; rather, it is that now only *we* can bring the Messiah, for only *we* can wait infinitely, through the continual effort to meet an infinite responsibility to and for the other person. Only we can wait, and not God, because only we operate within the narrow confines of time. Time is the tarrying of the Messiah; that the Messiah tarries is what gives meaning to life, for the dimension of meaning is the dimension of time.

The Messiah, therefore, does not end history; rather, the endless wait for the Messiah even though he may tarry, *is* history. Here time is understood as the never-ending movement toward the Holy One, seeking a closeness that can never be close enough. My endless wait must consist of this endless movement toward God, which is a movement toward the one created in His image and likeness, a movement into human relation in the post-Shoah aftermath of a radical assault on human relation. Recall what was declared to Elie Wiesel in Buchenwald: "Here, there are no fathers, no brothers, no friends. Everyone lives and dies for himself alone."[13] Redemption lies in the endless task of creating a realm in which there are fathers, brothers, and friends—mothers, daughters, and sisters—a realm in which the Messiah will feel at home. A realm is which he is no longer needed.

THE MEANING OF THE MESSIAH IN OUR TIME

In Judaism the coming of the Messiah is the advent of dwelling in the world, and not the separation of the saved from the damned, as it is sometimes understood in Christianity. Whereas for most Christians, the redemption that the Messiah brings is not tied to a specific place, for most Jews it is tied to a return to the Land of Israel. Many Christians see the return of the Jews to the Holy Land as a prelude to the return of the Messiah, but they do not see their own return to the land as a defining feature of redemption. Still, this post-Holocaust return of the Jews to the center stage of history has sent theological tremors throughout the Jewish and Christian worlds.

Fackenheim once declared that if *"the messianic hope died during the Holocaust . . . the post-Holocaust State of Israel has resurrected it,"*[14] not because the Jews have been instilled with a new faith but because they have been renewed with a new historical mission, a messianic mission. This is the meaning of Israel's national anthem *Hatikvah*. Significantly, *tikvah* means not only "hope" but also "cord" or "thread." The messianic hope revived through the Jewish return to Jerusalem is a messianic tie to history, to God, and to humanity. It is a return to a living link both to the sacred tradition and to the messianic future.

In the Midrash it is written that in the messianic age all prayers will cease except the prayers of thanksgiving (*Midrash Tehillim* 2:56:4). This thanksgiving is also essential to ushering in the messianic age. It is not a thanksgiving for what has befallen us or for what we have received. Rather, it is a gratitude for having been commanded and thus entrusted with a mission, no matter how impossible the mission may seem. It is a gratitude for the meaning of the Messiah and for the strife of the spirit that the endless wait entails. This gratitude may be a much more profound common ground between Christians and Jews than any creed.

Because the one who waits is grateful for the strife of the spirit, it is something in which he or she can rejoice. Madness? Perhaps. But remember the parable from the Baal Shem Tov. There was once a house in which people were having a wedding festival. The musicians played, the guests danced, and the house was filled with joy. But a deaf man passing by stopped to look in through the window. He saw the people whirling about the room, leaping, and throwing about their arms. "This house is filled with madmen!" he cried. For he could not hear the music.[15] Working to make way for the Messiah is often compared to making preparations for a wedding festival. As part of the preparation for redemption, the wait for the one who tarries must appear very strange indeed to those who do not hear the Voice of revelation that summons the wait. And in the post-Holocaust world, a dance of joy and thanksgiving must appear to be as impossible as it is absurd. This joy, too, may provide a common ground between Christians and Jews, however absurd it may seem—if only we can hear the music.

The Chasidic master Moshe Leib of Sassov once said, "When someone asks the impossible of me, I know what I must do: I must dance!"[16] The dance is most crucial when gravity most weighs us down. That is when our joy can take on substance. And joy is essential to the advent of the Messiah. Hence the teaching from Maimonides: "The highest peaks of faith, truth, and devotion are reached only through joy."[17] In the joy that Maimonides invokes lies the meaning of the Messiah in our time. To believe in the coming of the Messiah with complete faith is to cry out, "Yes," to the Divine pronunciation that creation is good, worthwhile, and meaningful. *Yes* to the interminable wait for the Messiah. *Yes* to the summons to rejoice.

This *Yes* bespeaks the Holy Name without uttering the Name. And it sustains the wait without the coming. Here the wait becomes a way of serving Him and thus hastening the redemption that is eternally immanent—if only we may *act* on our wait. Which brings me to one last tale, a tale of the Messiah. One day, as they were walking near the gates of Rome, deep in discussion, the talmudic sage Rabbi Yehoshua ben Levi asked Elijah when the Messiah would come. The prophet pointed him toward a leper sitting outside the gates, saying, "He's right over there. Ask him yourself." So Rabbi Yehoshua went over and asked the Messiah, "When will you come?" And the Messiah answered, "Today"—that is, "Today, if you heed the Voice of Hashem" (*Sanhedrin* 98a). In the light of what has been said, perhaps we realize one more possibility: had Rabbi Yehoshua helped the leper with his wounds, perhaps the Messiah would have revealed himself—and we, both Christians and Jews, would be engaging in these reflections with the Messiah himself.

NOTES

1. Martin Buber, *On Judaism*, trans. Eva Jospe, ed. Nahum N. Glatzer (New York: Schocken Books, 1967), pp. 110–11.

2. Martin Buber, *I and Thou*, trans. Walter Kaufmann (New York: Charles Scribner's Sons, 1970), p. 94.

3. Emil L. Fackenheim, *What Is Judaism?* (New York: Macmillan, 1987), p. 170.

4. The best anthology of Jewish teachings on the Messiah is Raphael Patai's *The Messiah Texts* (New York: Avon, 1979).

5. For example: Isaiah 11:11–12; Jeremiah 23:3, 29:14, 32:44, 33:7; Ezekiel 39:25; Joel 4:1; Zephaniah 3:20; Zechariah 10:8–10.

6. See Thomas Aquinas, *On Faith*, trans. Mark D. Jordan (Notre Dame, IN: University of Notre Dame Press, 1990), p. 39.

7. See Søren Kierkegaard, *Fear and Trembling*, trans. Alastair Hannay (New York: Penguin Books, 1985), p. 95.

8. Abraham Joshua Heschel, *A Passion for Truth* (New York: Farrar, Straus and Giroux, 1973), pp. 189–90.

9. Eliezer Berkovits, *Faith after the Holocaust* (New York: Ktav, 1973), p. 5.

10. Emil L. Fackenheim, *Quest for Past and Future: Essays in Jewish Theology* (Bloomington: Indiana University Press, 1968), p. 90.

11. Emmanuel Lévinas, *Difficult Freedom: Essays on Judaism*, trans. Sean Hand (Baltimore: The Johns Hopkins University Press, 1990), p. 90.

12. André Neher, *They Made Their Souls Anew*, trans. David Maisel (Albany: SUNY Press, 1990), pp. 61–62.

13. Elie Wiesel, *Night*, trans. Stella Rodway (New York: Bantam, 1982), p. 105.

14. Fackenheim, *What Is Judaism?* pp. 268–69.

15. From Meyer Levin, *Hassidic Stories* (Tel-Aviv: Greenfield, 1975), p. 86.

16. See Elie Wiesel, *Somewhere a Master*, trans. Marion Wiesel (New York: Summit Books, 1982), p. 110.

17. Maimonides, *The Commandments*, Vol. 1, trans. Charles B. Chavel (New York: Soncino, 1967), p. 286.

Chapter Five

Speaking of the Middle East

Jews and Christians in Dialogue and Dispute

Amy-Jill Levine

The Middle East is in the news. The Middle East is always in the news. There can be political revolutions in Africa, killer tornados in Massachusetts, major scientific breakthroughs at Florida Atlantic, and—aside from details about sports or Lady Gaga—the Middle East will still claim the headlines.

The rhetoric is often heated and one sided. Reporting about the Middle East from the Christian Broadcasting Network or the Fox Network is distinct from the same coverage on National Public Radio or Al Jazeera-English. Jews hear about rocket attacks against the citizens of Sderot, threats against Israel by Iran's premier, Palestinian television programming that encourages children to blow up Israelis, dancing in the streets of Gaza on Sept. 11, 2001, homicide bombers hailed as martyrs and role models, and mourning in Gaza for Osama Bin Laden. Christian groups in the United States and Western Europe who have had long associations with churches in the Middle East hear reports from fellow Lutherans in Gaza or Presbyterians in the West Bank or Catholics in Jerusalem about the loss of their homes and the destruction of their vineyards, imprisonment of Palestinian peace activists, illegal activity by illegal settlers with the Israeli government ignoring violations, Israeli military incursions into their neighborhoods, humiliating treatment by Israeli soldiers, and denial of basic human rights. Christians worry about their dwindling numbers in the Middle East and blame Israeli policy for the exodus; Jews note, "Israel is the only place in the Middle East where the Christian population has grown over the last 60 years."[1]

Distinct and often heated rhetoric is found both between and within Jewish and Christian communities. Jewish–Christian dialogue groups disband as Christian participants condemn Israel's settlement expansion, the security

57

barrier, failure to grant the Palestinians political autonomy, and incursions into Gaza, while regretting but excusing acts of terror against Israeli citizens. Jews do not understand why their Christian colleagues cannot see Israel as the only state in the world threatened with delegitimization by the United Nations and threatened with extermination by Iran; they do not understand why their Christian neighbors ignore the Hamas charter which contains comments such as: "For Zionist scheming has no end. . . . Their scheme has been laid out in the *Protocols of the Elders of Zion*, and their present [conduct] is the best proof of what is said there" and "There is no solution to the Palestinian problem except by Jihad. The initiatives, proposals and International Conferences are but a waste of time, an exercise in futility."[2]

Jews will sometimes temper their criticisms of Israel given the state's pariah status in blocs of the United Nations[3] and the sense that it needs all the support it can get. As Peter Beinart reports, "On its website, AIPAC celebrates Israel's commitment to 'free speech and minority rights.' The Conference of Presidents of major Jewish organizations declares that 'Israel and the United States share political, moral and intellectual values including democracy, freedom, security and peace.' These groups would never say, as do some in Netanyahu's coalition, that Israeli Arabs don't deserve full citizenship and West Bank Palestinians don't deserve human rights. But in practice, by defending virtually anything any Israeli government does, they make themselves intellectual bodyguards for Israeli leaders who threaten the very liberal values they profess to admire."[4] Christians will sometimes temper their critique of actions grounded in Islamic fundamentalism in order to protect their co-religionists in Islamic states. Perhaps it is this fear that motivated Gregory III Laham, Patriarch of the Church of Antioch and leader of the Melkite Greek Catholic Church, to announce that there was a "Zionist conspiracy against Islam behind al-Qaeda's attack" at Baghdad's Our Lady of Salvation Catholic church this past November (2010).[5]

Christian churches produce statements that advocate for peace in the Middle East; Jewish groups condemn the language of the statements, if not necessarily their intent, as anti-Jewish.[6] Conversation is stopped, distrust grows, and the goal of strategic alliances between Jews and Christians supporting a two-state solution becomes increasingly distant.

As tense as relations have become between Jews and Christians, they are perhaps even more tense within each community. Jews who support J Street or Americans for Peace Now—that is, Jews who support a two-state solution, who find Israeli settlements in Arab East Jerusalem and the West Bank an obstacle to accomplishing that, and who are convinced that for Israel to absorb the West Bank would mean either a demographic end of a Jewish state or the creation of an undemocratic one—disagree with Jews who argue that the entire land was promised to the Jews, those convinced that setting the pre-1967 borders as the starting point for the negotiations of land exchanges will *eo ipso* endanger Israel, and those who insist that no negotiation is possible with the Palestinians given their refusal to recognize Israel, Hamas policy, and insistence on the "right of return." Both groups disagree with Jews of Neturei Karta who argue on talmudic basis (*b. Ket.* 111a) that divine initiative rather than human force will bring about Jewish sovereignty. The Neturei Karta also state, "The true Jews are against dispossessing the Arabs of their land and homes. According to the Torah, the land should be returned to them."[7] A number of secular Jews on the political left would agree with that last point—but little else.

The rhetoric has gotten so heated that members of Jewish peace organizations are called by fellow Jews self-hating and not just anti-Zionist but enemies of Israel. Columnist James Besser recorded in "The Jewish Week" some of the comments he received about J Street, an organization that describes itself as "The political home for pro-Israel, pro-peace Americans,"[8] : "J Streeters are the 'kapos' of the 21st Century. . . . They're the 'Judenrat' of modern times. Their goal is nothing less than the eradication of the Jewish state, just like Hitler tried to destroy Europe's Jews. None of this 'they're wrong, and here's why' stuff for J Street haters, no siree; they're genocidal maniacs, self-hating Jews, Jewish anti-Semites, haters of Israel. They're part of George Soros' plot to bring down Israel and America."[9]

No wonder the Jewish Council for Public Affairs began a "civility campaign" to help the Jewish community, broadly defined, hold conversations among its members over the Middle East without rancor.[10]

Christians are equally divided. Some insist, "The miraculous appearance of the Israeli state just after the darkest moment in Jewish history is hard to interpret outside of a theological framework."[11] Some argue that the foundation of the state fulfills biblical prophecy. The well-known Dispensationalist author Hal Lindsay writes: "The prophet Ezekiel predicted the Israelites would be returned to their ancient land and the nation reborn in the 'last days.' God says: '*For I will take you from the nations, gather you from all the lands and bring you into your own land*' (Ezekiel 36.24). . . . All of this has taken place in living memory. Against impossible odds, Israel was reborn as a nation May 15, 1948. Against all odds, the nation has survived and won five wars that were intended to annihilate it."[12]

Some Christians believe Jews should rule not just Israel as it existed at the 1967 borders, but a wider area, following Genesis 15.18, "the LORD made a covenant with Abram, saying, 'To your descendants I give this land, from the river of Egypt to the great river, the river Euphrates'; others, in a commensurate view, see Israel's trading land for peace and the possibility of dividing Jerusalem as signs of the end-time.[13] Yet still others, including some who self-identify as Evangelical, do not see the realization of biblical promises in the creation of the state of Israel as precluding a Palestinian state.[14]

Other Christians support Israel not only because it is a democracy with strong ties to the United States, but also because, as G-d states to Abraham in Genesis 12.3, "I will bless those who bless you, and the one who curses you I will curse; and in you all the families of the earth shall be blessed." Therefore, they find it to be in America's best interests to support Abraham's descendants wherever they are, including in the land of Israel. Some point out that nations who failed to support Jews—from ancient Persia, Greece, and Rome to fifteenth-century Spain and Portugal to the British Empire, Nazi Germany and the Soviet Union—all lost their power.

Still other Christians (and some Jews as well, such as many within Jewish Voice for Peace) regard Israel as an apartheid state. They support BDS policies (i.e., boycott, divest, and sanction) to pressure Israel economically. These policies range from all Israeli products to divesting from companies doing business with Israel (Caterpillar Inc. is a frequent target because it allegedly profits from the occupation) to full cultural and academic sanctions. Some Christians blame unrest *throughout* the entire Middle East on the Jewish state. For instance, the 2010 British Methodist statement "Justice and Peace for Palestine and Israel"[15] avers: "For this report, the key hindrance to security and a lasting peace for all in the region is the Occupation of Palestinian territory by the State of Israel, now in its fifth decade." Similarly, in his March 1, 2010, letter to Pope Benedict XVI in preparation for the October Vatican Synod for the Middle East: a Message to the People of God,[16] Gregory III Laham, the Damascus-based patriarch of the Church of Antioch and all the East, wrote, "There is a diffuse but sure rise of Islamic extremism, *provoked by the threats of the Israeli government* against Palestinians, Lebanon, Syria, [and Iran], which is spreading throughout all the countries in the region."[17]

Descriptions of Israel as an apartheid state are often supplemented by a theological argument that the covenant of the land is contingent on the behavior of its citizens. According to this approach, since Israel does not manifest "love of neighbor," the state is illegitimate. (Ironically, groups that deny the founding of Israel as the fulfillment of biblical prophecy condemn Israel for failing to follow a biblical standard to which they hold no other country.)

Yet another increasingly popular view is that the state of Israel is theologically misbegotten. This approach sees Israel as the world's response to the Shoah,[18] with Palestinian Arabs paying the price for the sins of the world. Therefore, the world needs to atone for the sin of creating the Jewish state, with the penance including the aforementioned "right to return," reparations paid to Palestinians who were resident in present-day Israel prior to 1948, and a Palestinian state with its capital in Al Quds. (No mention is made of reparations to or the regaining property by the 600,000–800,000 Jews expelled from Arab countries in 1948.)

For many Christians and Jews, some form of sharing Jerusalem between Israel and a Palestinian state is a logical step. For others—especially those Jews who remember being denied access to worship at the Western Wall in Jordanian Jerusalem prior to the six-day war in 1967—the division again of the city is unthinkable.

Blocking conversation within and between groups as well are different definitions of the term "Zionism." The term, first used in 1890 by Nathan Birnbaum, an Austrian Jew, and developed by Theodore Herzl in the later 1890s, had a secular focus: the early Zionists argued not for a divine right to the land; they argued for a Jewish state that would make life safer for Jews facing oppression in Europe. Zionist Jews seek the right for Jews to have a homeland like all other peoples have a homeland. Judaism is a religion, in that one can convert to it. But Jews are also a people—as the French are a people— and Jews often understand "being a people" as involving connection to a land—just as being French involves connection to a particular area of Western Europe. For these early Zionist Jews and many Zionist Jews today, the founding of the state was the fulfillment not of a biblical promise, but of national aspirations. Israel was and is the one place in the world where Jews have the autonomy other national groups have. It was, and is, also a place that welcomes persecuted Jews: from the 600,000–800,000 Mizrahi Jews who were welcomed in 1948 to the exodus of the Falasha from Ethiopia in the 1980s to the Refuseniks of the former USSR and, sadly today, new waves of refugees from France and Argentina, Hungary and the Netherlands.

When we speak of *Christian* Zionism today, however, we are usually speaking about a religious view. Christian Zionists are a large and diverse group. Some argue that God promised the land to the Jews. Others argue that Christians owe support to the Jewish state as part of their atonement for sins earlier Christians committed against Jews. Still others argue that support for the Jewish state is mandated in Scripture. And still others argue that Jews are to be protected because they provided the world the Scriptures of Israel and the Christ "according to the flesh" (Romans 9.5).

In a move that will certainly have implications for Jewish–Christian dialogue, numerous church bodies today are preparing reports that denounce Christian Zionism.[19] The statements tend to treat Christian Zionism as a monolith and tend to frame their arguments against Zionism in any form. Critique of triumphalistic versions of Christian Zionism—e.g., that would deny the Palestinian population any form of self-determination; that anticipate the building of a Third Temple and so the destruction of the Al-Aqsa Mosque—is surely warranted. But the effect of a blanket condemnation is to slip back into the Zionism-equals-racism claims of the U.N., the Durban Conference on Racism, and much anti-Israel rhetoric from throughout the globe.

How then do we have a conversation? One way to engage the question is to look at how Jews and Christians—from the perspectives of Scripture and liturgy rather than of contemporary politics—have understood the Middle East. To understand the present and to plan for the future, it is important that we know our past.

We begin with Scripture, to see not only *where* Jews and Christians have been in dialogue and dispute but also *why*. Since we can only take a few soundings, we'll see what the text says about the name of the land, the covenant with Abraham, and the demands for the holiness of the land as well as the people who live in it. We then turn to the New Testament's revision of the earlier biblical focus and the distinct interpretations of the Tanakh and Christian Bible (Old Testament and New Testament) today. This approach helps explain in part why Christians and Jews, although claiming the same Scriptures, have such different understandings of them.

Finally, on introductory matters, I think it only fair to tell you where I stand on these issues. I am a Jewish Zionist. I believe that Israel has the right as all nations do to exist in security. I see Israel as a Jewish state comparable to the way in which France is a French state and Egypt is an Egyptian state. I see Israel as a representative democracy, where citizenship encompasses Jews, Christians, Muslims, Samaritans, Druze, Baha'is, secularists, etc., who have all of the rights *and* responsibilities citizenship carries. I am, finally, a non-paid consultant for Americans for Peace Now (an independent group that supports and works with the Israeli organization *Shalom Achshav*), for Churches for Middle East Peace (CMEP), and for the Anti-Defamation League. I attended the J Street meeting in February 2011 because I consulted for a panel on Christian responses to the Middle East, but I am not a member of J Street.

WHAT THE BIBLE SAYS

The question "what does the Bible say" is a fraught question. The biblical text is an anthology of different writers addressing different issues in different locations at different times. Further complicating discussion: English-speaking Jews and Christians, lacking requisite skills in Hebrew (for the Tanakh/Old Testament) and Greek (for the Deutero-canonical/Old Testament Apocrypha and New Testament texts), follow different translations (e.g., usually the JPS for Jews; the New International Version or King James Version for Evangelicals; the New Revised Standard Version for Liberal Protestants; the New American Bible or the Jerusalem Bible for Roman Catholics). The Christian Bible is not the same thing as the Jewish Bible; nor do all Christians have the same Bible (the canon of the Catholic and Ortho-dox churches has more books than the canon of Protestant churches). Thus, when we ask, "What does the Bible say?" we have to ask: Whose Bible? Which canon? Which translation? Which edition?

Regardless of translation, however, we know that the land is important to the Bible. In the NRSV (both Old and New Testaments), the word "Israel" is used 2,278 times—much of the time the reference is to the "children of Israel," but the connection between the people and the land is indelible. The term land appears 1,959 times (it is the fourth most used substantive noun), and "land of Israel" 35 times.

NOMENCLATURE

Through the centuries, the land has been known by different names. Many of my Christian friends speak of "the Holy Land" and "Jerusalem"; Muslim friends refer to "Palestine" and "Al Quds"; the people in my synagogue speak of *Eretz Yisroel* and *Yerushalayim*. There is power in naming. As for what the Bible calls the land—it gives us options. The earlier books speak of the *land of Canaan*. Canaan was the son of Ham, the son of Noah. When Ham did something to his father (saw him naked? raped him? castrated him?), Noah responded: "Cursed be Canaan; lowest of slaves shall he be to his brothers. . . . Blessed by the LORD my God be Shem; and let Canaan be his slave" (Genesis 9.25–26). The story is an etiology to explain how Israel became dominant in a land inhabited by, among others, Canaanites.

Land of the Hebrews is only used once, by Joseph, to explain his incarceration in Egypt: "I was stolen out of the land of the Hebrews; and here also I have done nothing that they should have put me into the dungeon" (Genesis 40.15). The designation "Hebrews" typically appears when a person in the Tanakh is talking to non-Hebrews. The term the people of Israel use with one another when they are talking about the land they understand as their homeland is the *land of Israel*. Such distinction in designation is not uncommon; groups often have different forms of self-identification when they speak among each other and when they speak to outsiders. In synagogue worship, we speak not about "Jews" but about the "children of Israel."

Land of Israel starts to appear in 1 Samuel (13.19) during the beginnings of the monarchic period. Following Solomon's reign (ca. 900 B.C.E.), the united monarchy breaks up, leaving the *land of Israel* in the north, and the *land of Judah* in the South. *Land of Judah* appears 46 times (including the Deuterocanonical literature/Old Testament Apocrypha), often in distinction from the *land of Israel* (see, e.g., Amos 7.12). The *land of Judah* appears once in the New Testament, in Matthew's nativity story (2.6), in a quote from the Prophet Micah (5.2): "You, Bethlehem, in the *land of Judah*" will be the place of the messiah's birth. *Land of Israel* also appears in Christian texts. For example, in Matthew's Gospel, an angel tells Joseph, who has taken his family to Egypt, "Get up, take the child and his mother, and go to the *land of Israel* . . ." (2.20). Joseph relocates the family to Nazareth in Galilee, in the *land of Israel.*

Thus, when we speak of the "land of Israel," the definition changes; this point should be considered by anyone stating that today's Israel should consist of "biblical borders." Indeed, no biblical text makes clear the exact borders.

Wider reading in Scripture only adds to this complexity. The Assyrians conquered the *land of Israel* in 722 B.C.E., exiled many Israelites, and resettled the area with people conquered elsewhere in their empire. The combined population group takes its name from the northern kingdom's capital, *Samaria*. Thus there was the Kingdom of *Judah* in the South, and the Kingdom of *Samaria* in the north.

The Assyrian conquest and its aftermath do more than provide information on contemporary, politically loaded terminology. They also provide the origins both of the legend of the "ten lost tribes" and the Jewish messianic hope known as the "ingathering of the exiles." For traditional Judaism, the messianic age is marked by the return of all Israel—including the descendants of the deported population—to the land of Israel. For many Jews as well as Christians, the founding of the modern State of Israel was the beginning of the ingathering of these tribes and so the beginning of the messianic age. The idea of the ingathering of the exiles comes into today's Christianity with organizations like "On Eagle's Wings" that help relocate Jews to Israel.[20]

In 587, Babylon invaded the southern kingdom of *Judah*, destroyed the Temple, and took many of the Judahite people into exile. In 538, Persia conquered Babylon, and King Cyrus, finding it easier to rule his empire by having local elites in his service, invited the Judahite population to return. The place to which they return is now called *Yehud*,[21] a term attested on Persian-period coinage and in the biblical books of Daniel and Ezra.

Starting in 333 with the conquests of Alexander the Great, the land is called *Judea*, as in Matthew 2.1, "Jesus was born in Bethlehem of *Judea*. . . ." Rome first kept the term *Judea*, as seen on the *Judea Capta* ["conquered Judea"] coins, named because of their inscription and minted to commemorate Rome's victory over the Jews in the 66–70 C.E. revolt. In the first century, the entire land (i.e., with the most generous borders) was called *Judea*, although sources also distinguish Judea as the southern area with the capital at Jerusalem, naming Samaria and Galilee as distinct regions (see Judith 1.9; 1 Maccabees 3.10; 10.30, 38; 11.28, 34; 2 Maccabees 15.1; Luke 17.11; John 4; Acts 1.8; 8; 9.31; 15.3). The place-names pile up, layer upon layer, and through the generations, they designate different areas. For example, today people in favor of a two-state resolution will speak of the "West

Bank" or the "[Occupied] Territories"; those in favor of "Greater Israel" refer to this same area as "Judea and Samaria."

Biblical geography only gets more complex. Along with these six ancient designations—*Canaan, land of the Hebrews, land of Israel, Judah* [and *Samaria*], *Yehud*, and *Judea* [and *Samaria*], is *Zion*, mentioned 196 times, such as in the famous Psalm 137.1–2, "By the rivers of Babylon—there we sat down and there we wept, when we remembered Zion. There our captors asked us for songs . . . saying, "Sing us one of the songs of Zion!" The several Gospel uses of this term are typically quotations from the Tanakh, such as John 12.15, "Do not be afraid, daughter of Zion; Look, your king is coming, sitting on a donkey's colt" (cf. Zechariah 9.9). The *land flowing with milk and honey* appears 20 times. Milk and honey are perhaps the only two naturally produced foods that do not require anything to die or be removed from its life-source. *Promised land* is only found in the Epistle to the Hebrews, although the Tanakh frequently speaks of the promise of the land. *Holy land* appears only in Zechariah 2.12 ("The LORD will inherit Judah as his portion in the *holy land*, and will again choose Jerusalem"), Wisdom of Solomon 12.3, and 2 Maccabees 1.7.

Whether the Bible refers to *Palestine* depends on the Bible one uses. The Hebrew text eight times mentions *Pileshet* in reference to the coastal area where the Philistines, a people perhaps originally from Crete, settled; the major cities were Ashkelon, Ashdod, Gaza, Gath, and Ekron. Sargon II of Assyria (722–705) called the region *Palashtu* or *Pilistu*. Genesis 21.34 references "the land of the Philistines (*P'lishtim*). Most English translations render the term *Philistia*. Herodotus, the fifth-century B.C.E. Greek historian, spoke of "a district of Syria called Palastina," which brings us closer to the term "Palestine." *Pileshet* enters the King James Version of the Bible in four instances as "Palestina" (Exodus 15.14; Isaiah 14.29, 31, and Joel 3.4). The New King James Version (NKJV) reads "Philistia" for these references.

Following the Second Jewish revolt (the "Bar Kochba Revolt") in 132–135 C.E., Rome renamed Jerusalem Aelia Capitolina in honor of the god Jupiter, and it called the land *Syria Palaestina* in the attempt to erase Jewish identity. But expressions such as *land of Israel, Judea and Samaria*, and *Palestine* lived on.

The Bible offers no single, clear set of boundaries or even terminology that might be translated by the most literal of readers into a contemporary political reality. When we today select one or the other of these place-names, we, too, are making choices with religious and political significance. To see the potential impact of language on Jewish–Christian relations, we only need look to the terms by which we speak of biblical figures. It is not unusual to hear, in Christian sermons and Bible studies, about Abraham, or David, or Jesus, in their "Palestinian" contexts. Such identification already occurs in Eusebius, the early Christian historian (263–339 C.E.), but it became normative in some North American Protestant settings via the *Scofield Reference Bible* (first printing, 1909),[22] which is, for such settings, comparable to reading "Chumash mit Rashi." The names for the place mattered then, and they matter now.

LAND AND THE COVENANTS

The biblical emphasis on this particular area of land—granting fluid borders—and the attachment of the people variously known as Hebrews, Israelites, Judahites, Yehudim, Judeans, and Jews, to that land are permanent and palpable. The attachment begins with the promises to Abraham.

Genesis locates the land in Abram's future even before he received his divine calling. According to Genesis 11.31, "Terah took his son Abram and his grandson Lot . . . and his daughter-in-law Sarai . . . from Ur of the Chaldeans to go into the land of Canaan; but when they came to Haran, they settled there." There Terah dies. The trip to Canaan is put off, deferred. This deferring becomes a biblical motif. When Pharaoh takes Sarai into his harem, Abram has no exit strategy: G-d has to act. When Jacob resettles with his family in Egypt, he has no exit strategy. G-d had to act.

The Bible is aware of the allure of other lands. Egypt, or Babylon, or Persia—or Boca Raton—all have their allures. Thus it frequently delineates the dangers of living outside Israel. Move to Egypt, and your wife is taken into a harem, or your children are enslaved. Live in Babylon, and you're thrown into a fiery furnace or a lion's den. Move to Persia, and there's a warrant for genocide. The story continues: move to England, Spain, or Portugal, and you'll be expelled. Move to Germany or Russia or Poland. . . . For the Bible, in Diaspora the people can be, should be, "a light to the nations" (Isaiah 42.6; 49.6). However, the general biblical view is that the land of Israel is home.

Abram "passed through the land to the place at Shechem. . . . At that time the Canaanites were in the land. Then the LORD appeared to Abram and said, 'To your offspring I will give this land.' He built there an altar to the LORD . . . " (Genesis 12.6–7; cf. 17.8, "I will give to you, and to your offspring after you, the land where you are now an alien, all the land of Canaan, for a perpetual holding; and I will be their God"). The verse has four notable implications for discussion about the land. First, it suggests that at the time of its composition, Canaanites were no longer in the land. It is a reminder to readers that the earlier population—described without negative terms—should not be forgotten, and it calls readers today to remember the histories of their own communities: the Tequesta, the Jeagas, and the Ais of what is today Palm Beach County; Tennessee's Cherokee; Aboriginal groups in Australia; Canada's First Nations, and many others.

A second implication comes from the reference to Shechem. In Genesis 34, Abram's great-grandchild Dinah is raped, or seduced, by Shechem, prince of Shechem. That encounter leads to a slaughter of the Shechemites and the displacement of Jacob's camp. For Abram, Shechem is a place of peace and stability; for Jacob, it is a place of attack and disruption. How we understand the land is always contingent on how we understand its inhabitants, and those understandings change over time.

Third, the first permanent structure Abram builds—likely the only one, since Abram is a transhumant pastoralist—is an altar. The altar belongs to G-d, as does the land on which it stands. Thus in Leviticus 25.23, G-d commands, "The land shall not be sold in perpetuity, for the land is mine; with me you are but aliens and tenants." As Psalm 24.1 states, "The earth is the Lord's, and all its fullness." The only piece of land Abraham legally purchases is the family burial plot, the cave of Machpelah in Hebron. Whereas the Hittites offer Abraham any place he wants, Abram insists, "I am a stranger and an alien residing among you; give me property among you for a burying place . . . " (Genesis 23.4). The text is insistent on the legality of his purchase: "Abraham weighed out for Ephron the silver that he had named in the hearing of the Hittites, four hundred shekels of silver, according to the weights current among the merchants . . . in the presence of all who went in at the gate of his city."

Finally comes the promise: "To your offspring I will give this land." The point recurs in 13.14–15: "The LORD said to Abram . . . 'Raise your eyes now, and look from the place where you are, northward and southward and eastward and westward; for all the land that you see I will give to you and to your offspring forever.'" These promises are *unconditional* and they are *permanent*. G-d does not say: I'll give you this land *if* you do something for me.

However, Abram has no offspring, and the narrator has already indicated that Abram's wife is infertile. Thus the verse prompts the question: "Which offspring?" The answer will become a dividing point between some Jews and Christians.

The term for "seed" (Hebrew *zera*; Greek *sperma*) is a singular that functions as a collective. For Genesis, it refers to Abraham's physical progeny. G-d tells Isaac: "I . . . will bless you; to you and your seed I will give all these lands, and I will fulfill the oath that I swore to your father Abraham. I will make your seed as numerous as the stars of heaven, and will give to your seed all these lands . . . " (Genesis 26.3–4). Jacob learns, "the land on which you lie I will give to you and to your seed . . . your seed shall be like the dust of the earth, and you shall spread abroad to the west and to the east and to the north and to the south . . . " (Genesis 28.13–14). Jacob tells his son Joseph that "God Almighty" [*el shaddai*] promised, "I will make of you a company of peoples, and will give this land to your seed after you for a perpetual holding" (NRSV, Genesis 48.3–4; cf. Exodus 6.4, 8). The Hebrew *achusat olam* can be translated "eternal possession."

The meaning of the promise changes in the Christian canon. Paul writes in Galatians 3.16, "The promises were made to Abraham and to his off-spring; it does not say, 'And to offsprings,' as of many; but it says, 'And to your offspring,' that is, to one person, who is Christ." Paul reads the collective as a singular and interprets it to refer to Jesus. To replace physical descent—Abraham's biological descendants, the Jews—with a "spiritual descent" already signals an attendant disinterest in the land. In antiquity, land and people were connected: the Egyptians to Egypt, Samaritans to Samaria, Jews to Judea, and so on. The connection was presumed to have its origins in biological descent. On one reading of Galatians, the promises to Abraham are detached from his descendants and the special role for those descendants, the Jews—including the connection to the land—is eliminated. Yet for Paul, Galatians is not the last word. In Romans, a later text, Paul proclaims, "They are Israelites, and to them belong the adoption, the glory, the covenants, the giving of the law, the worship, and the promises . . . as regards election they are beloved, for the sake of their ancestors; for the gifts and the calling of God are irrevocable" (9.3b-4; 11.28b-29).

In their journey through the wilderness, the people receive another covenant, this one mediated by Moses at Mount Sinai. The covenant of the land is permanent. But the Sinaitic covenant states that the people do not always have the right of domicile. According to Leviticus, if the people violate G-d's commandments, "the land will vomit [them] out for defiling it" (18:28). There is, however, no "forever" to exile. Deuteronomy 16.20 announces, "Justice, and only justice, you shall pursue, so that you may live and possess/inherit (*yarashta*) the land that the LORD your God is giving you."

This is a land that is special: it can vomit out its inhabitants; it demands justice. It is the only place where sacrifices to the Lord can be offered. It is the only place that demands sabbatical—letting the land lie fallow every seven years—and jubilee, when alienated property is redeemed.

It is also a land where non-Israelites will live and be loved: Exodus 22.21 mandates, "You shall not wrong or oppress a resident alien, for you were aliens in the land of Egypt." Leviticus 19.33–34 insists, "When an alien resides with you in your land, you shall not oppress the alien. The alien who resides with you shall be to you as the citizen among you; you shall love the alien as yourself, for you were aliens in the land of Egypt." Deuteronomy 10.19 proclaims, "You shall also love the stranger, for you were strangers in the land of Egypt." Moreover, the land will be inherited not just by Jews, but by many peoples. Ezekiel 47.21–23 reads: "'So you shall divide this land among you according to the tribes of Israel. You shall allot it as an inheritance for yourselves and for the aliens who reside among you and have begotten children among you. They shall be to you as citizens of Israel; with you they shall be allotted an inheritance among the tribes of Israel. In whatever tribe aliens reside, there you shall assign them their inheritance,' says the Lord GOD."

According to both the Pentateuch and the Prophets, it was the people's failure to pursue justice and holiness, their trusting foreign nations and foreign gods rather than their covenant, that sent them into exile. When they pay their debt to G-d, G-d returns them to their land. Deuteronomy 30.3–5 tells Israel that following the punishment for its sin, "the LORD your God will restore your fortunes and have compassion on you, gathering you again from all the peoples among whom the LORD your God has scattered you. Even if you are exiled to the ends of the world, from there the LORD your God will gather you, and from there he will bring you back. The LORD your God will bring you into the land that your ancestors possessed, and you will possess it; he will make you more prosperous and numerous than your ancestors." Similarly, Isaiah 60.21 concludes: "Your people shall all be righteous; they shall possess the land forever."

Whether the founding of the State of Israel is the fulfillment of these promises, whether it is the beginning of a process of fulfillment, whether the fulfillment will come at the messianic age, whether the promises have transferred from the Jewish community to the church, or whether all these statements represent only the hopes of ancient writers and have no contemporary political value will depend on the views of the individual providing the answer.

DIFFERENT BIBLES; DIFFERENT LITURGIES, DIFFERENT LENSES

Given this biblical focus on the land, promise, and restoration, the attachment of Jews to the land is understandable. However, the attachment becomes attenuated in Christian circles through select citation, translation, and canon formation. Because Jews and Christians are not reading the same Bibles, they often develop different views concerning the land.

Isaiah, speaking to his exiled community in Babylon, proclaims a word of hope: "Comfort, O comfort my people, says your God; speak tenderly to Jerusalem, and cry to her that she has served her term, that her penalty is paid . . ." (40.1–2). The next verse—"A voice cries out: 'In the wilderness prepare the way of the LORD, make straight in the desert a highway for our God'"—for Isaiah means that the people will return home. The promise of and yearning for the land will both be answered. The New Testament applies the verse to John the Baptist (Mark 1.3), seen as preparing the way of repentance in his wilderness setting, and so deemphasizes the import of the return to the land. This is another instance, like Galatians 3, where the followers of Jesus refocus the importance of the land.

A second example of de-emphasis comes from Matthew's Christmas story. The first evangelist applies the following quotation from the prophet Jeremiah to the children of Bethlehem killed on King Herod's orders:

> Thus says the LORD:
> A voice is heard in Ramah
> lamentation and bitter weeping.
> Rachel is weeping for her children;
> she refuses to be comforted for her children, because they are no more. (2.18)

Matthew cuts the quote off before its end. Jeremiah, in the famous "new covenant" chapter, continues (31.15–17):

> Thus says the LORD:
> Keep your voice from weeping, and your eyes from tears;
> for there is a reward for your work, says the LORD:
> they shall come back from the land of the enemy;
> there is hope for your future, says the LORD:
> your children shall come back to their own country.

This idea of the "ingathering of the exiles" is part of the Jewish liturgy: benediction 10 in the weekday *amidah* states: "sound the great ram's horn for our freedom, raise the banner to assemble our exiles, and gather us together from the four corners of the earth."

Translation also contributed to the early church's increasing disinterest in the land. In the famous "Beatitude" of Matthew 5.5, Jesus states, "Blessed are the meek, for they will inherit the earth" (NRSV). For Christian readers, the focus is universal. Usually unnoticed is that the beatitude draws upon Psalm 37.11: "The meek shall inherit the land, and delight themselves in abundant prosperity" (NRSV). For ancient Israel and first-century Jews, "land" was not the same thing as "earth." "Land" meant first and foremost the land of Israel, the land of the covenant. The Hebrew for "land" is *eretz*; the Septuagint translates the term as *ge*, and that is how it appears in Matthew. Jews in Galilee or Judea who heard this beatitude would have heard the reference to the *land* of Israel.[23]

While Jewish hopes in general remained firmly grounded, early Christians looked not to the earthly promised land but to the heavenly one. Part of this refocusing stemmed from Platonic philosophy: the notion that what is seen on earth is only a shadow of the real. For example, the Epistle to the Hebrews (a New Testament document of unknown origin and date) states, "By faith Abraham obeyed when he was called to set out for a place that he was to receive as an inheritance and he set out, not knowing where he was going. By faith he stayed for a time in the land he had been promised, as in a foreign land, living in tents. . . . For he looked forward to the city that has foundations, whose architect and builder is God" (11.8–11). "Land he had been promised" can be translated as "promised land" (*gen tes epangelias*), but the true "promised land" in this text concerns the city whose architect is G-d. That is the heavenly, not the earthly, Jerusalem.

Distinct emphases are also illustrated in the orders of the Jewish and Christian Scriptures. The Torah ends with Moses on Mt. Nebo, overlooking the promised land: faithful Jews could identify with him, assured that even if they died outside Zion, their children someday would enter. The theme of the yearning for the land resounds at the end of the Tanakh. The Jewish canon follows the Torah with the Prophets (Nevi'im) and ends with the Writings (Ketuvim). The last book in the Ketuvim is 2 Chronicles, which concludes with King Cyrus's edict to the Jews in exile in Babylon: "The LORD, the God of heaven, has given me all the kingdoms of the earth, and he has charged me to build him a house at Jerusalem, which is in Judah. Whoever is among you of all his people, may the LORD his God be with him! Let him go up" (36.23); "let him go up"—in Hebrew, *v'ya'al*, let him make *aliyah*. The Jewish Bible thus ends with the exhortation to return to the land.

This accentuation of the land continues in post-biblical Judaism, which complements its biblical readings with liturgical emphases. Traditional Jews pray facing Jerusalem; synagogues are oriented toward Jerusalem. Jewish prayerbooks, dating as early as the fourteenth century, include in the *amidah* the prayer "Blessed are You . . . who will gather the dispersed of Your people Israel. . . ." Many synagogues recite, with minor shifts in wording, *Tefilah Lim'dinat Yisra'el*, the prayer for the state of Israel (composed in 1948): "Our Father in Heaven, Rock and Redeemer of the people Israel, bless the State of Israel with its promise of redemption/ dawn of deliverance/the beginning of our redemption" (*reishit tzmichat ge'ulateinu*). But this focus on the land ebbs for the New Testament and so for the Christian community. The "Old Testament" places the Writings in the middle and concludes with the Prophets. The last Prophet is Malachi, who predicts the return of Elijah and so the expectation of the messianic age, which arrives in this canon with the next book, the Gospel of Matthew.

The de-emphasis on the land continues in Christian lectionaries (analogous to the weekly Jewish reading, the *parshat ha-shavuah*, of Torah and Haftarah; not all churches follow lectionaries—those that do not may place a greater emphasis on the land). Lectionary readings emphasize the Prophets rather than the Pentateuch, and so the focus on the land is attenuated in Christian worship. Nor are there Christian holidays that focus on the land. Jews still celebrate, although not with pilgrimage to Jerusalem, the Bible's three pilgrimage festivals—Sukkot (Booths), Pesach (Passover), and Shavuot (Weeks). All three have both a salvation historical and a territorial focus. Sukkot commemorates Israel's wandering in the wilderness, Passover celebrates the Exodus from Egypt, and Shavuot recollects the giving of the Torah on Mt. Sinai. But all three are also agricultural and pilgrimage festivals: they all initially had a focus on the land that yields food and on Jerusalem as the site where the offerings were brought. Thus, in the Jewish celebrations, the land is necessarily recalled. The church ignores Booths, replaces Passover with Holy Week (with Jesus as the new Paschal lamb—a symbolism eloquently portrayed in John's Gospel), and replaces Shavuot with Pentecost (see Acts 2), which represents the time the Church claims receipt of the Holy Spirit and so anticipates the gentile mission. Pentecost looks outward from Jerusalem, not toward it.

This steady Christian dissociation with the land is not incidental to the faith; it fits closely with some of the deepest Christian commitments. Worship in antiquity was connected to geographical locations: Isis implied Egypt; Diana was related to Ephesus; Aphrodite to Corinth, and worship of the G-d of Israel necessarily connected a person to the land of Israel. The church eliminated the geographical connection to religion. One is not born a Christian, in the sense that one is born French (that is, to French parents), or a Jew (that is, excepting Jews by choice, to Jewish parents, with Jewish identity determined initially by the paternal line, then following the Second revolt, by the maternal line, and in Reform Judaism today by either parent as long as the child is raised as a Jew). One is "born again" or "born from above" (John 3 *passim*) or "born anew" (1 Peter 1:23) a Christian by water and spirit. Galatians 3.28 states that "in Christ" "there is neither Jew nor Greek." By the second century if not before, Christians considered themselves a "third race" (*genos*), and for these Christians, home was not on earth, but in heaven, as the Epistle to the Hebrews intimates. When the Epistle of James (1.1) and the First Epistle of Peter (1.1) address themselves respectively to the "Twelve tribes of the Diaspora" and "to the exiles of the Diaspora," they are likely thinking of readers as scattered from their heavenly home.

Increasing the sense of distance from the earthly land, some second- and third-century Christians determined that the biblical promises regarding the land were allegories. Church fathers such as Origen and Eusebius claimed that G-d wasn't really talking about the land of Israel but the heavenly Jerusalem. Others asserted that the promises to Abraham were really promises to the Church: "along with Abraham we shall inherit the holy land, when we shall receive the inheritance for an endless eternity, being children of Abraham through the like faith . . . but it is not you [that is, "it is not you Jews"], 'in whom is no faith'" (*Dialogue with Trypho* 119). Today this view is called, in its Protestant manifestations, "replacement theology"; in Catholic and Orthodox settings, it is called "supersessionism."

In yet another permutation, in his *Contra Faustum* St. Augustine suggested that the Jews lost their title to the land and therefore must wander because they crucified Jesus. We see a version of this view in the response of Pope Pius X (1904) to Theodore Herzl, who was seeking Vatican support for a Jewish homeland: "We cannot prevent the Jews from going to Jerusalem— but we could never sanction it . . . the Jews have not recognized our Lord, therefore we cannot recognize the Jewish people." (The Vatican established diplomatic relations with Israel in December 1993.[24])

Such views are recapitulated by some churches today. The 2010 Presbyterian Church USA Report on the Middle East asks: "It appears that during the first century C.E., Christian authors rather fully transferred the locus of God's concrete presence in the world of space and time from the place of Zion—that is, Jerusalem—to the person of Jesus, who had been crucified and raised from the dead just outside Jerusalem. The Roman destruction of Zion—that is, the temple in Jerusalem—in 70 C.E. doubtless hastened that process. So what do Christians make of the claim that a link endures between God's covenant with Abraham and the promise of land?"[25] The question format, in the context of the Report's general condemnation of Israel, leads in one cogent reading to the conclusion that the covenant of the land is at once abrogated, fulfilled, and replaced in the person of Jesus.

Cyril Salim Bustros, who in June 2011 was elected archbishop of the Melkite Greek Catholic Archeparchy of Beirut and Byblos, and who was prior to that the eparch of Newton, MA, announced in a press conference on October 23, 2010, following the Vatican Synod for the Middle East,[26] that "as Christians, we're saying that this promise [of land] was essentially nullified [French, *abolie*] by the presence of Jesus Christ, who then brought about the Kingdom of God. As Christians, we cannot talk about a 'promised land' for the Jews. We talk about a 'promised land' which is the Kingdom of God. That's the promised land, which encompasses the entire earth with a message of peace and justice and equality for all the children of God. . . ."[27]

Former Anglican bishop of Jerusalem Riah Abu el-Assal calls Palestinian Christians "the true Israel" as he asserts, "We are the true Israel . . . no-one can deny me the right to inherit the promises, and after all the promises were first given to Abraham and Abraham is never spoken of in the Bible as a Jew . . . He is the father of the faithful."[28] Fr. George Makhlour of St. George Greek Orthodox Church in Ramallah writes: "What Abraham was promised, Christians now possess because they are Abraham's true spiritual children just as the New Testament teaches."[29]

Different Bibles, different lectionaries and holidays, different emphases all combine with different political agendas and sources of information and definitions. We cannot begin to have a conversation until we can learn to hear with each other's ears, and until we become familiar with each other's texts, histories, and practices.

FINAL THOUGHTS

Today, Jews are heirs of a Bible that stresses in language, in canon, and in quantity as well as quality a concern for the land of Israel. Christians have a different Bible, with a different order, different translations, and different emphases. We are products of our past, and we read those pasts selectively. But we are shapers of the present, and we are responsible for the future. The impasse has to be broken; civility is essential; conversation is necessary. How then might we proceed?

To be pro-Israeli need not and should not make one anti-Palestinian, and vice versa. The Bible itself speaks of shared land, and it insists on justice above all. Moreover, the covenant with Abraham is broad enough to be shared: not only among Jews and Christians, but with those who claim descent from Abraham's son Ishmael, with Muslims as well.

Israel today should be understood as a state, a nation like all other nations, and therefore it should be held to the same standards as every other state. Israel should not be given a free pass for actions that would be judged to be illegal or immoral if they had been done by other nations. And Israel should not be held to a special, higher, biblical standard by which no other nation is judged.

At the same time, the range of political entities representing the Palestinian population should be held to the same standards: terrorism on either side cannot be justified; the end, Palestinian statehood, does not justify the means, whether the means are the killing of Israelis, or the publication of supersessionist biblical materials. Words harm.

Jews and Christians will disagree with each other, and among themselves, about how they understand the Middle East. Some support a two-state solution, Israel and Palestine. Some regard an independent Palestinian state as a direct danger to Israel. And others seek a single state, Palestine, to contain the entire land and its peoples. But the dominant desire among Jews, Christians, and Muslims, is for peace. There are deep resources in each tradition that oblige its adherents to work for peace, and working for peace has to consist of more than condemning only one side, or pushing only one agenda.

The more we know about each other, our similarities and our differences, the better able we will be to bring about this peace for which we all so much yearn. The goal is itself biblical: that the land will be the focus of justice to the nations. Isaiah 2.3 states,

Many peoples shall come and say,
"Come, let us go up to the mountain of the LORD,
to the house of the God of Jacob;
that he may teach us his ways, and that we may walk in his paths."
For out of Zion shall go forth instruction, and the word of the LORD from Jerusalem. [30]

NOTES

1. Eugene Korn, "response" (http://americamagazine.org/blog/entry.cfm?blog_id=2&entry_id=3850), points out that the Israeli Christian population has grown from 40,000 in 1948 to

155,000 in the twenty-first century, that in "15 years under PA control, [Christian] percentage in Bethlehem has dropped from 60% to 14% . . . while Gaza once had a significant Christian community, only 3,000 remain; 2,000 have left in the two years since Hamas wrested control." See also now Ethan Felson, "JCPA Background Paper: The Palestinian Christian Population" (http://org2.democracyinaction.org/o/5145/images/ JCPA%20Background%20Paper%20on%20Palestinian%20Christians%207%202.pdf). The facts adduced lead to the conclusion that "the demographic data are often distorted, sometimes significantly, in order to slander Israel. A population that is presented as drastically decreasing is, in reality, holding steady or slightly increasing" (p. 3).

2. http://www.thejerusalemfund.org/www.thejerusalemfund.org/carryover/documents/charter.html. Disclaimer: I cannot read Arabic and therefore cannot assure the accuracy of the translation.

3. Details in http://www.jewishvirtuallibrary.org/jsource/UN/israel_un.html.

4. Peter Beinart, "The Failure of the American Jewish Establishment," "The New York Review of Books" (May 12, 2010) [http://www.nybooks.com/articles/archives/2010/jun/10/failure-american-jewish-establishment].

5. http://www.jihadwatch.org/2010/12/melkite-patriarch-gregory-iii-jihad-attacks-on-middle-eastern-christians-have-all-been-a-zionist-plot.html (and elsewhere).

6. For three recent examples: J Street denounced the Presbyterian Church USA 2010 report; the Jewish Board of Deputies denounced the British Methodist 2010 Middle East Report; the Central Conference of American Rabbis denounced the Kairos-Palestine document.

7. http://www.nkusa.org/aboutus/index.cfm.

8. http://jstreet.org/.

9. James Besser, "Hyperbole about J Street," "James Besser's Political Insider," "The Jewish Week" 1/26/2–11 (http://www.thejewishweek.com/blogs/political_insider/hyperbole_about_j_street).

10. http://engage.jewishpublicaffairs.org/p/dia/action/public/?action_KEY=4504.

11. Gary Anderson, "Does the Promise Still Hold? Israel and the Land," *Christian Century* (January 13, 2009).

12. Hal Lindsey, "Israel, Nation of Miracles," WorldNet Daily Exclusive Commentary (posted April 1, 2004 [http://www.wnd.com/news/article.asp?ARTICLE_ID=37842]).

13. Texts frequently cited in support of this eschatological view include Joel 3.2 ("I will gather all the nations and bring them down to the valley of Jehoshaphat, and I will enter into judgment with them there, on account of my people and my heritage Israel, because they have scattered them among the nations. They have divided my land"); "they have divided my land" is then taken as predicting the Israeli withdrawal from Gaza, a view supported by Zephaniah 2.4 ("For Gaza shall be deserted; and Ashkelon shall become a desolation; Ashdod's people shall be driven out at noon, and Ekron shall be uprooted") and Zechariah 14.2 ("For I will gather all the nations against Jerusalem to battle, and the city shall be taken and the houses looted and the women raped; half the city shall go into exile, but the rest of the people shall not be cut off from the city").

14. Stephen Spector, *Evangelicals and Israel: The Story of American Christian Zionism* (Oxford: Oxford University Press, 2008). There is debate within Evangelical circles of regarding what constitute true Evangelical, or broadly "Christian" views; the debate is comparable to that found within Jewish communities regarding what appropriate "Jewish" views toward Israel should be.

15. http://www.echurchwebsites.org.uk/confrep-14–justice-for-palestine-israel-170510.pdf (p. 180).

16. See http://www.vatican.va/news_services/press/sinodo/documents/bollettino_24_speciale-medio-oriente-2010/02_inglese/b11_02.html.

17. http://melkite.org/Patriarch/PA38–Letters.htm (my emphasis).

18. http://www.echurchwebsites.org.uk/confrep-14–justice-for-palestine-israel-170510.pdf (section 3.4; 4.3.3.; the later section sites the State of Israel's own website, Declaration of Establishment of State of Israel http://www.mfa.gov.il/MFA/Peace+Process/Guide+to+the+Peace+Process/ Declaration+of+Establishment+of+State+of+Israel.htm [Accessed 8th November 2009]). This argument has shaky historical grounding. Recognition of the

destruction of Europe's Jews (the term "Holocaust" finds common use only in the late 1950s; *ha-Shoah* was coined in 1955) as needing to be redressed was not much of an issue in 1948. U.N. documents on partition do not mention the situation of Europe's Jews. In 1947, there were already half a million Jews in "Palestine"—and tensions between Jews and Arabs, as well as Jews and the British—made the situation untenable. The foundation of Israel results from this concern, as well as post-war Europe's general interest in decolonization. For the British, controlling Palestine had become too expensive in terms of troops, economic outlay, and public relations (internally and within the Arab world). Britain petitioned the United Nations to relinquish the mandate. The issue was less Western guilt: why would the West admit guilt? They saw themselves as righteous, having defeated Hitler—than a concern to remove the displaced Jews lest they resettle in France, Poland, Britain, and other countries not interested in absorbing refugees.

19. For examples, the 24th General Synod of the Disciples of Christ/Christian Church (July 2003) affirmed a resolution titled "An Alternative Voice to Christian Zionism." The British Methodists prepared such a report in 2011. The Episcopal Diocese of Jerusalem, "The Jerusalem Declaration on Christian Zionism," proclaimed Christian Zionism to be a "false teaching that corrupts the biblical message of love, justice and reconciliation"; the December 19, 2006, document is posted on the website for Global Ministries of the United Church of Christ/Christian Church Disciples of Christ (http://www.globalministries.org/mee/advocacy/the-jerusalem-declaration-on-chr.html). For other examples, see Paul Richard Wilkinson, *For Zion's Sake: Christian Zionism and the Role of John Nelson Darby*, Studies in Evangelical History and Thought (Milton Keyes: Paternoster, 2007). Wilkinson speaks of the move fully to blame Israel for the current crisis and to exculpate the Palestinians and the Arab League as "Christian Palestinianism" as opposed to "Christian Zionism."

20. The Chicago-based "International Fellowship of Christians and Jews" paid more than $29 million in 2001 to help Jews from the United States, Argentina, Ethiopia, and the former Soviet Union emigrate to Israel. The organization takes its motto from Ezekiel 39.28, "Then they will know that I am the Lord their God, for though I sent them into exile among the nations, I will gather them to their own land, not leaving any behind."

21. The larger area, of which Yehud and Samaria are both parts, the Persians called "Beyond the River" as in Ezra 7:21, the edict of King Artaxerxes of Persia (465–424).

22. E.g., Under "Ezra": "Ezra, the first of the post-captivity books (Ezra, Nehemiah, Esther, Haggai, Zechariah, and Malachi), records the return to Palestine under Zerubbabel" (http://www.biblestudytools.com/commentaries/scofield-reference-notes/ezra/ezra-introduction.html [1917 edition (online)]; under "Galatians" on how the congregation "had become the prey of the legalizers, the Judaizing missionaries from Palestine" [http://www.biblestudytools.com/commentaries/scofield-reference-notes/galatians/galatians-introduction.html].

23. See the superb discussion by Robert Wilken, *The Land Called Holy* (New Haven: Yale, 1994), esp. p. 48.

24. See Richard Lux, *The Jewish People, the Holy Land, and the State of Israel: A Catholic View* (New York/Mahwah, NJ: Paulist Press, 2010).

25. https://www.pc-biz.org/Explorer.aspx?id=3179&promoID=126

26. See http://www.vatican.va/news_services/press/sinodo/documents/bollettino_24_speciale-medio-oriente-2010/02_inglese/b11_02.html.

27. http://ncronline.org/blogs/all-things-catholic/thinking-straight-about-israel-jews-and-archbishop.

28. Interview by Julia Fisher with Bishop Riah Abu El-Assal, January 26, 2002, St George's Cathedral, Jerusalem, reported in Melanie Phillips: "The Demoralisation of Britain: Moral Relativism, the Church of England and the Jews" (http://www.yale.edu/yiisa/melaniephillipspaper111308.pdf).

29. See Paul Charles Merkley, *Christian Attitudes Towards the State of Israel* (Montreal: McGilll-Queens University Press, 2001).

30. My deep gratitude to Ted Smith, Jay Geller, and Martin I. Bresler for comments on drafts of this essay.

Chapter Six

Christian-Muslim-Jew

The Necessary Trialogue

James Carroll

The great Roman Catholic theologian Karl Rahner said, "The West is no longer shut up in itself. It can no longer regard itself simply as the center of culture, with a religion which could appear as the obvious and indeed sole way of honoring God. . . . Today everybody is the next-door neighbor and spiritual neighbor of everybody else in the world."[1] Rahner wrote those words in the middle of the last century. How much more true are they at the beginning of this one?

This new condition means that we, as a world of close neighbors, bumping up against one another, are all in the position of rubbing elbows with people who are not like us. By virtue of their presence, we have to understand, in a new way, who we are. This is particularly true in America. A nation like ours, having welcomed an unending stream of immigrants with their plethora of faiths and traditions, is especially suited for this re-examination of fundamental assumptions, especially called to it. In America, religiously, culturally, ethnically, and humanly diverse peoples have routinely encountered each other in the mundane neighborhoods of work and school and living. The testing of assumptions that inevitably follows such encounters is one of the reasons why America is suspect in the eyes of rigidly traditional people. Why don't they like us? Because here, through elbow rubbing, we are prepared to re-examine our most basic assumptions. It is part of what America is.

After September 11th, the Islamic presence in America which, frankly for most Americans had been somewhat invisible, drew particular attention. The still dominant assumption of the mainly Christian, or as we say "Judeo-Christian," character of this nation was quite efficiently punctured.

Americans discovered that there are more Muslims living among them than there are Presbyterians or Episcopalians. There are probably as many Muslims living in America—these numbers are inexact estimates—as there are Jews. Suddenly, with, on one side, Islam perceived as a religion that sponsors violence and, on the other side, a new feeling in America that God is blessing America's war on terrorism, religious differences have become flashpoints in our nation's life.

Meanwhile, across the globe fundamentalist truth claims rooted in various religions have been fueling conflicts with a ferocious new energy. In the Arab world, and in Europe, there has been a virulent outbreak of the old anti-Semitism, with some Muslims and many Arabs apparently believing that the September 11th atrocities were the work of Jews. And, with some in the West inclined to accept Osama bin Laden's deadly equation of the existence of Israel with the impoverishment of Arabs, Israelis had new reason to feel new levels of insecurity, especially as innocent gatherings at cafes and at bus stops became ever more targets of brutal violence. Ariel Sharon, meanwhile, quickly defined Israel as the front line of the new war on terrorism, with a Bush-like belligerence which some of us, frankly, have criticized. Yet few of Israel's critics see Sharon's "overwhelming force"—which is a Pentagon phrase—responses to Palestinian terror, in the context of America's licensing example of overwhelming force. No one should criticize Ariel Sharon without applying the same levels of criticism to George W. Bush. Yet, often that does not happen.

Likewise, few drew distinctions in these past two years between Israeli government policies and the segments of Israeli society itself that continued to question those policies, even while feeling those new levels of insecurity, even while still maintaining a firm commitment to the ideal of peace. Once again, a stereotyped and univocal fantasy of "the Jews" has emerged to be seen as a problem in the world. This resurgence of what must be labeled anti-Semitism is also well known.

Hannah Arendt warned of the doom that follows from the idea of eternal anti-Semitism, as if Jews are permanently fated to play the victim's role. As the war on terrorism has unfolded some, in a similar way, have reduced the idea of Islam to an eternal *jihad* as if the "clash of civilizations," (a phrase associated with Samuel Huntington but which he takes from Bernard Lewis,) between Islam and the rest of the world is somehow inevitable. Just as bigoted stereotypes about Jews and their religion were once more released into the common discourse, wildly distorted characterizations of Muslim belief and practice have been accepted as fact. The religions of both groups—and there is a long tradition of this in the Christian West—have been understood as motivating behavior that has grave import for the world, whether approved or condemned.

The irony in all this is that all at once the widely held twentieth-century idea that religion would grow increasingly irrelevant suddenly seemed unbelievably naive. The centrality of religion to life on earth, for better and for worse, has made itself very clear in this young twenty-first century. Yet, never had the dark side of religion been made more manifest. That is true because various forms of what must be labeled "religious fascism" have come into being. The Muslim suicide murderers, especially, wreaking such havoc in Israel—are religious fascists. But in hindsight we can also see that so were the Catholic and Protestant fanatics of the die-hard fringes in Northern Ireland, the place where my own story gets very personal. The Hindu who assassinated Ghandi, a man of his own people, was a religious fascist. And so was the Jewish student who murdered the great Yitzhak Rabin. What happens when intense religion and radical politics become intertwined? What territorial compromise is possible among people who claim that their hold on the land originates with God? What truce can interrupt Islamic violence if it is held to be somehow sacred, even if suicidal? Regarded across time, which religion is free of such demonic impulses? With numerous mainstream religions challenged from within by their own fundamentalists, and with expressly fundamentalist denominations growing across much of the world, the task of renewing the rational element in religion against fundamentalism; the task, that is, of affirming historically minded and ecumenically disposed religion has come to have broad importance. The capacity of each religion to engage in self-criticism and correction has come to be seen not only as an issue for religion but for the neighbors of the religious, neighbors whose very lives, now, are at risk by uncriticized and uncorrected attitudes.

I quoted the Catholic theologian Karl Rahner. His protégé, another hero of mine, the Catholic theologian Hans Küng, once wrote, "There will be no peace among nations without peace among the religions but there will be no peace among the religions without dialogue between the religions, but there can be no dialogue between the religions without each religion engaging in a fundamental re-examination of its basic assumptions."[2] That's what dialogue does.

So, events have forced a new agenda on the world's religions. How do we correct the foundations of our beliefs when they show themselves to be inhuman? And how can basic change in religious affirmation be made without undermining the authority of the tradition? We love religion because of the tradition. How can you change basic beliefs without undermining the tradition? This is an especially grave question because, in a time like ours of frighteningly rapid change, religion functions for many of us as the only connection with what went before, with what we call tradition. It can seem desperately important to wall off the realm of faith from everything else. Let this be one place where I do not have to face the pressures of change. Such an urge is natural because we can only handle so much uncertainty and so much change. Why can not religion be a place where we do not have to face uncertainty? Is not that an impulse we can all associate with? Yet it is now impossible.

History breaks down such walls, and the pressure to raise basic questions about belief and practice effects not just Islam, Christianity, and Judaism. Not so long ago, the world moved to the brink of a nuclear apocalypse because of the threat of war between Pakistan and India. In that case it was Hindus, too, who were prepared, in effect, to declare Armageddon in the name of tradition. So, wherever you look on this globe, there is the challenge to the devout to think critically about what they believe. In nothing, in America in the last three years, has this been as clear as the challenge of the conflict between the West and Islam.

This lecture's particular concern is with the question of Islam's relationship to the post-Holocaust dialogue that has been going on between Christians and Jews. I, myself, am privileged shortly to be going to a Christian, Jewish, Muslim trialogue in Jerusalem, at the Shalom Hartman Institute. This three-way encounter has been going on for five or six years right through the Intifada. Palestinians, West Bank Christians and Muslims come into West Jerusalem to pursue this most grave question. We three traditions, all descended from Abraham, have much in common and much to discuss. But even so, is it not true, really, that we people "of the West" are inclined to see the relationship with Islam as inevitably problematic, perplexing and even dangerous? Do not we see it, mainly, as a matter of "us against them?" We know from polling that more and more Americans in the last year, for example, have hardened in their attitudes toward Muslims. We know that, in the world of Islam, the War on Terrorism—and this certainly includes the war in Iraq—looks more and more like a Holy War coming from the old enemy. A Crusade, indeed. A Crusade against a *jihad*.

That is the danger the world is facing. I want to draw your attention— forgive me if it's obvious—to the way in which religion is essential to what is going on for both sides. Despite the broad assumption of secular people that modernity is the source of conflict, conflict with Islam is still overwhelmingly religious. The present conflict recalls, for example, the religious violence in Ireland. It comes as a big surprise in the secular world (and even among some church-goers and temple-goers) that religion can motivate behavior on more than one day in a week. It can motivate whole lives. Muslims know this.

Here is a list of current world conflicts with Islam (a list I noted in the work of theologian Jack Miles). Listed in this way, we can grasp the religious character of the depth of conflict the world is faced with. Currently, we see Roman Catholics against Muslims in the Philippines; Roman Catholics against Muslims on Timor; Russian Orthodox against Muslims in Chechnya; Maronite and Malachite Catholics against Muslims in Lebanon; Jews against

Muslims in Israel, the West Bank and Gaza; Christians of various kinds against Muslims in Sudan; Ethiopian Orthodox against Muslims in Eritrea; Anglicans and Roman Catholics against Muslims in Uganda; Greek Orthodox against Muslims in Cyprus; Serbian Orthodox against Muslims in Bosnia and Kosovo; Roman Catholics against Muslims in Algeria; Anglican and Roman Catholics against Muslims in Nigeria; Hindus against Muslims in Kashmir; Coptic Catholics against Muslims in Egypt, and, of course, the broad phenomenon in Europe and the Arab world, the rise of the particularly Muslim version of anti-Semitism, Muslims against Jews.

A reflection on this truly disturbing litany can go in several directions. Most obviously to the so-called clash of civilizations: is this inevitable? Eternal *jihad*? But a question must arise about the "Muslims" referred to in this litany: Do they, in fact, constitute one "civilization?" Is the so-called world of Islam, in fact, one world? That is the way mostly people in "the West" think of it.

The House of Islam is centrally religious, and it is the question of religion that is before us now, as it has not been in the West in many, many years. This is the context in which a Christian's reflection on the relationship among Jews, Christians and Muslims since the Holocaust and since 9/11 has sharp relevance. September 11 has become the all-purpose justification for the larger war on which the United States has now embarked. Will the United States simply treat Islam as an undifferentiated "world" phenomenon, as if Arabs and Indonesians are the same thing, and thus solidify the growing Islamic suspicion that the "West" is its enemy?

In truth, whether this dangerous new belligerence of the United States evolves into a holy war or not depends, in some measure, on our sophistication about religion. Sophistication about Islam, certainly. But sophistication, also, about religion as such. That, from this Christian's point of view, is discouraging to say the least, because our attitudes about religion are over-simple. Indeed, speaking of Americans generally, our attitudes about religion are childlike, even childish. That is a result of the feeling referred to before, that religion is a place that is walled off from the tensions of the world that require hard thought. Consider what the present crisis has revealed about our attitudes toward religion. Politicians and commentators, in this country especially, have gone to great lengths over the last couple of years to affirm the religion of Muslims, rejecting the terrorist claims that the heinous crimes of September 11th could be committed as an act of Islamic devotion. There is a good reason why we've tried to speak well of Islam. But something is lost in the well-intentioned assertion that Islam is a "pure" religion, entirely unrelated to the evil acts committed in its name. With so many violent conflicts being waged around the globe, as I just recited, exactly by people calling on the name of Allah, an old question must present itself and not just about Islam—is religion the solution or is it the problem? Britain's Prime Minister,

Tony Blair, said early on that the September 11th attacks were no more a reflection of true Islam than the Crusades were of true Christianity. Do you remember that?

Blair's purpose was a good thing. He wanted to head off anti-Muslim prejudice, but the comparison is instructive. We Latin Christians, we Roman Catholics would love to be able to say that the rampaging fanatics who slaughtered Jews in the Rhineland in 1096 and who, in 1099, murderously assaulted Jerusalem—we would love to say that they were acting in ways that had nothing to do with true Christian belief or practice. But, in fact—and this is what makes the Crusades so chilling—that Holy War was integrally tied to theology, the violence of God who wills the death of his only beloved son; and integrally tied to liturgy, the sign of the Cross which the Crusaders wore on their breasts; and integrally tied to authority, the Crusader Popes. Today, in the post-Enlightenment West, we have religion tied up in ribbons in a pretty box, as if it is one of those purely positive aspects of life. Religion is good, that is all. And we are quick to dismiss negative acts or attitudes that are spawned by religion as "not really religious."

My work has focused on the long, sad history of Church hatred of Jews, including mob violence, but also theologically sanctioned forced conversions, preacher-inspired blood libels, Vatican-enforced ghettos, the official racial sanction of "blood impurity," and the papacy's own use of anti-Semitism in its campaign against modernism in the nineteenth century. Here is the new rub of the argument that I am making. When the Vatican today asserts, as it did in the 1998 document, "We remember," and in the 2000 document, "Memory and Reconciliation," that the Catholic Church as the "Bride of Christ," is entirely sinless; and that crimes committed in the name of the Church—Crusades, Inquisition, and so on—were the acts of what the Vatican calls "sinful children" of the Church but never "the Church as such," it is furthering this deadly refusal to examine the way in which religion as such can prompt inhuman behavior. If religion prompts bad behavior, then, so they say, it is not "real" religion, not religion "as such." This lets religion off the hook. And today, that is dangerous.

We simply cannot let Islam off the hook in this way. And I say that as someone who does not let my own tradition off the hook. This means we cannot deplore the sins of "sinful members," as the Vatican does, without asking the hard question, which the Vatican does not, about where those sins come from? Were the endless acts of Christian anti-Semitism aberrations? Or were they tied directly to the anti-Jewish texts in the New Testament, which are about to be celebrated on film?[3] Were they tied directly to the foundational way the Church defined itself against Judaism? Were they tied directly to the totalitarian exercise of power by Emperor Popes? Were they tied to the traditional Catholic suspicion of dissent? Were they tied to the Vatican's rejection of Modernism? If anti-Semitism were an aberration, then an "apology" for the acts of "sinful members" would be enough. That is what my strongest Catholic critics accuse me of not appreciating, because I say the apology does not end it.

If anti-Semitism grew out of core beliefs and core practices, then apology is not enough. Core beliefs and core practices have to change—and that is what I say. Does that make me a Catholic basher? No more than it makes me a religion basher to say that religion, like every thing of the human condition, is ambiguous—partly good and partly bad. Religion has consoled the grieving; has overcome absurdity with meaning; has enabled major improvements in human life; and supports some of the world's greatest works for good. But religion also easily confuses the object of its worship of God with itself. Religion often prompts human beings to make absolute claims that lead inevitably to absolute disaster. Religion can lead to ranking by race, and by class, and by gender. The univocal claims of monotheists can lead to contempt for human beings who reject them. And the open-endedness of Pantheism can undermine the distinctions that are essential for thought. The religious impulse to die for the faith slides all too easily into the impulse to kill for it.

Thus, there is no crime of which Muslims, acting as Muslims, have been accused that Christians, to cite only one other religion, do not stand accused by history. In nothing is this more clear for us, for us Catholics especially, than in our relationship with Jews. This history teaches us that to be religious is first to be repentant. And so with Islam. Just as some Christians like to draw an absolute line between the pure virtue of religion and the bad deeds of sinners who act in its name, some defenders of Islam, like Tony Blair that day, have trouble seeing that violence can also come out of basic Islamic assumptions. Blair and others do that for a good reason, but, to repeat, the evidence suggests that religion as such is ambiguous—the source of consolation and the source of violence—and this is true of Islam.

Islamic attitudes toward God, revelation, tradition, law, prayer, fasting, after-life, and human responsibility deserve full respect. They deserve to be known and honored by non-Muslims which, to our shame, they are not. Knowledge of the complexities of Islamic history, the glories of *Convivencia* in Iberia, the pluralism of Bosnia-Herzegovina, and the diversity of Islamic practice all around the globe. Do we in the "West" know, for example, that there are more Muslims in India than any other nation? India is the world's largest democracy, yet we ask if Islam is compatible with democracy? Knowledge like this is particularly important as an antidote to the crude stereotyping to which Muslims have long and recently been subjected.

The first principle—and we Christians and Jews have learned this from each other—the first principle of inter-religious dialogue is that each religion must be defined, or rather must define itself, on its own terms. When Jews and Christians sit down, Christians do not tell Jews what they believe. That's over. Jews don't tell Christians what they believe. That's over. And so now with Islam. We have a lot of learning to do. In the West this has rarely happened. For example, "Mohammedanism" is the way this religion was referred to not so long ago, you may remember that. It is a word that Muslims have always deplored because it suggests an impulse to see the Prophet as a figure analogous to Christ, when the incarnational center of this religion is not the Prophet but the text, the Koran. The word Mohammedanism does violence to Islamic belief. It is a British word, a colonial word. Similarly, it is misleading to understand Islam using points of reference that originate from outside of it. Thus, for example, "fundamentalism"—as in "Islamic fundamentalism." But "fundamentalism" is a word that was coined in the twentieth century about a certain brand of evangelical Protestantism in America. It is not a word that does any kind of justice to the serious belief of a religious Muslim, and Muslims properly resent that word. It has no reference to the world in which they live. And, finally, before we people of the West ask too glibly of Islam, as a Bernard Lewis book title does, "What Went Wrong?"— we in the West might better ask what we haven't asked fully enough. (I learned this from the scholar Said Nasser.) We might better ask the question, thinking of the Holocaust—What went wrong in Europe? That's the question Muslims want to hear addressed. It was out of the Christian culture, not a Muslim one, which genocide came.

Having said all of that it is still important to acknowledge that the religion of Islam does stand against much of what is taken for granted in the West— and this is especially true in the broad Islamic suspicion of what we call the Enlightenment. Whether one thinks of the currency of anti-Semitic rhetoric, especially among Arab Muslims, or the experience not so long ago of the writer Salman Rushdie, whose problem transcended the Arab world, or even the terrifying growth in some parts of the Islamic margin of an acceptance, even a celebration, of suicide-murder; or whether one thinks of that litany of conflicts around the world that I recited earlier, in all of this one sees a disturbing sign of a broad gulf separating the Islamic view and the view of the post-Enlightenment world. It is not clear whether that gulf can be overcome.

Let us acknowledge the difficulty here. These questions are only now beginning to be confronted, only now beginning to be worked out—less through "clash," I hope, than through dialogue. And as the Mel Gibson film *The Passion of the Christ* suggests, Muslims are not the only ones who have rigidly fundamental tendencies when it comes to their texts. The danger of that "clash of civilization" will be far less if all of us understood that we are alike as human beings. Russian Orthodox, Malachite Christians, Jews, Anglicans, Roman Catholics, Coptic Catholics, Muslims, Hindus, people of no faith—we are alike as human beings. In nothing more is this true than the fact that our noblest impulses come inevitably intertwined with opposite inclinations that betray them, and that is true of all of us.

We religious people must submit to the judgment of history. If that is our broad attitude about ourselves, then it is no offense if we expect such self-critical and reforming impulses of each other. This is especially so at a time when foundational impulses of all kinds, including religious ones, are underwriting self-righteousness and triumphalistic contempt for the Other. These impulses threaten the world now with mass violence, which means the urgent need is for religions and for nations to re-examine those assumptions in the light of what they lead to, and, where necessary, to correct them.

I am talking mainly about "religion," but everything I am saying could also be applied to America, whose response now in some important ways is too triumphalisltic, too self-righteous, too certain of itself, and too violent. We assume a close alliance with God. We assume God's blessing. All of this is why the trialogue, among Muslims, Jews and Christians, matters so much and that is why the task within that trialogue of religious self-criticism, has become so urgent.

After September 11th, obviously, Islam *must* engage in such reckoning, and we are properly desperate for signs that Muslim leaders and scholars are beginning to do this. But Muslims will be far more able to engage in this difficult process if they perceive those who have long acted like their enemies are doing so as well. Christian self-criticism in relation to anti-Semitism can be a model here for the self-criticism we Christians must engage in relationship to Islam. Christians have, in fact, since the Holocaust begun to confront the truth of our complicity in the anti-Jewish contempt that made it possible. But Christianity has done no such thing in confronting its relationship to the anti-Muslim bigotry and violence that has been part of European relationships with Islam since the Crusades. The Crusades were a nearly 300 year long holy war against Islam, which is why President Bush's inadvertent use of the word "crusade" swept through the Islamic world like an alarm bell going off.

The need for self-criticism applies to every religion, and it is up to practitioners of each religion to say exactly how. Jewish settlers on the West Bank who invoke a divine sanction to claim disputed land have this obligation. Christians who uncritically celebrate the death of Jesus Christ on film, without regard to the story's violence, or to its character as source of the oldest slander—"Christ killer"—have this obligation. Hindus who justify a nuclear threat in the language of Apocalypse have this obligation, and so do Muslims when suicidal murderers act in the name of Allah. Those of us who are religious take on the task of such self-criticism in the presence of the Other, not just for political hope or even only for peace, but because there is simply no other way to fulfill the commandment that binds us all—to honor God by loving our neighbors as ourselves.

NOTES

1. James Carroll, "Enhancing Democracy: The Key to Religious Reform." Speech of November 2 at the Annual Call to Action Conference, Milwaukee, Wisconsin. Subsequently published by the "National Catholic Reporter," November 15, 2002.

2. 1989 UNESCO Conference on World Peace and Dialogue Among Religions; Alan L. Berger, *Trialogue and Terror: Judaism, Christianity, and Islam After 9/11* (Eugene: Cascade Press, 2012), p.2.

3. Mr. Carroll is referring to the Mel Gibson film *The Passion of the Christ* released on Ash Wednesday, 2004.

Chapter Seven

What Have You Done?

Wrestling with the Sixth Commandment

John K. Roth

You shall not murder. (Exodus 20:13)

For Jews and Christians, indeed for any human being, no ethical conviction is more fundamental than *murder is wrong*. "You shall not murder," we read in the Ten Commandments as they are recorded in the Hebrew Bible's Book of Exodus. Some versions of the Decalogue's sixth commandment substitute *kill* for *murder*. In either case those key words require definition if the commandment is to make sense, but how much difference does it make if the Sixth Commandment contains one of those words rather than the other? The answer is *a great deal*. That response and the question that prompts it make an apt place to start what I call wrestling with the Sixth Commandment, an engagement with the imperative that is the most necessary, although not sufficient, condition for human civilization. [1]

The wrestling in this lecture has multiple parts, which can be identified in part by four additional questions: (1) How has the Sixth Commandment functioned and fared in history? (2) What does this commandment reveal about humankind? (3) What does the Sixth Commandment suggest about God? (4) What place does this commandment have in humanity's future? As we shall see, the struggles involved with those issues are, quite literally, matters of life and death.

DEFINITIONS

As a prelude to addressing the four questions above, two further steps need to be taken. The first involves definitions that inform this lecture's wrestling. According to the most reliable biblical scholarship, *murder*, not *kill*, is the best English term to use in translating the Hebrew text. That decision is significant, for the meanings of *murder* and *kill*, although closely related, are not identical.

All murder is killing, but not all killing is murder. To kill means to inflict or cause death, which also happens in murder, but distinctions exist because killing acts can be accidental and unintentional. Killing acts of that kind are not murder, which typically requires an intention, often including premeditation and careful planning, to inflict or cause death. In addition, murderous intentions are usually inflamed by anger, malice, envy, greed, fear, hate, revenge, or some other violence-inciting emotion. Not all killing actions fit that description, but typically murderous ones do.

Historically, the Sixth Commandment, along with others in the Decalogue, has been understood to be addressed to human beings—to Jews, to Christians, and indeed to all persons and communities—whose distinctiveness includes a capacity for murder that is not found in any other part of the natural world. Various interpretations of its meaning can be found, but they all share and depend upon the understanding that the imperative applies to human beings who are commanded not to do certain things that are within their power. Obvious though this point may be, awareness of it helps to underscore other crucial differences between *kill* and *murder*.

The Sixth Commandment is unequivocal and absolute. Allowing no exceptions, it does not say, "Murder is wrong in situation X, but it may be permissible in situation Y." Murder, the commandment entails, is wrong—period. Killing, however, is not so easily interpreted that way, unless one stipulates that *killing* means *murder*. In fact, unless killing is qualified in that way, or in some other way that restricts the meaning of that term to forms of killing that are intentional but unjustifiable or inexcusable, a commandment that said "You shall not kill" would be so ambiguous, even nonsensical, that it would be impossible for human beings to obey it no matter how good they might be or how hard they might try.

To see why that situation holds, notice that human life depends on killing. That statement, of course, is as problematic as it is evident, as much in need of qualification as it is bold. Therefore, to avoid misunderstanding, I need to clarify what I do and do not mean by it. I do not mean, for example, that human life depends on war; it does not, although sometimes war is unavoidable and even necessary to defend human life. Nor do I mean that human civilization depends on capital punishment; it does not, although there may be times and places where justifiable reasons for executions can be found.

What I do mean is that human life and civilization cannot exist, let alone thrive, unless people eat, quench their thirst, obtain shelter, raise and educate their young, and, in short, take the actions that are necessary to sustain human life. Unfortunately, those actions cannot be taken without killing. As the philosopher Philip Hallie cogently put the point, "We are in the food web. We are killers, if only of plants."[2]

In addition, if human life, in the biblical words of Genesis, is to be "fruitful and multiply," it unavoidably becomes even more lethal than Hallie said. Human beings are thinkers and doers; they are political, social, and also religious creatures who plan, strive, and build. Scarcely any of humankind's initiatives can be pursued without dislocations and destructions of one kind or another. Even the most environmentally conscious projects that men and women carry out have lethal consequences for living creatures somewhere.

An absolute and unequivocal prohibition against killing is not what the Sixth Commandment can mean if it is coherent. With due qualification, human life depends on killing, but a corollary of that truth is that human existence and especially its *quality* also depend on careful discrimination between killing that is justifiable or excusable and killing that is not. Absent such discrimination, including laws and sanctions to implement the difference socially and politically, it is hard to imagine that human civilization could long endure. Instead, to use Thomas Hobbes's bleak description from 1651, human existence would likely be in "that condition which is called war, and such a war as is of every man against every man. . . . In such condition there is . . . continual fear and danger of violent death; and the life of man solitary, poor, nasty, brutish, and short."[3]

Not even the most thorough, rigorous, and truthful interpretation of the Sixth Commandment, however, may be able to provide a complete analysis of killing that is justifiable or excusable and killing that is not. After acknowledging that some kinds of killing are necessary for basic sustenance of human life, the category of killing may still remain larger than the category of murder. At least in many cases, if not ordinarily, murder is not the category into which one places killing in self-defense, for example, or killing to prevent the murder of another person or to combat warring aggression. Even when unjust war unleashes killing that is met with armed resistance, a gray zone of moral classification may exist, and it will be debatable whether all the killing done by the warring aggressor, wrong though it surely is, should be called murder. In short, there remain cases of killing, justifiable or unjustifiable, that are not necessarily cases of murder or at least not clearly so. That realization, however, does not cut slack for killing; at least it should not, because most killing can and should be found wrong and condemned without inevitably and always being classified as murder.

PERSPECTIVES

Much killing, but not all, is murder, but now two more questions must be addressed for the Sixth Commandment to make sense: When is killing murder? What constitutes murder? My response to those questions emerges from the perspectives that inform my thinking about the Sixth Commandment. My perspectives are those of a Protestant Christian philosopher/theologian whose work has concentrated for more than thirty years on the Holocaust, Nazi Germany's attempt to destroy the Jewish people, and on other genocides as well. This outlook reminds me, again and again, of an unmistakable instance of murder, namely, the murder that the Hebrew Bible identifies as the first one. Genesis 4 tells that story, which depicts Cain's slaying of his brother Abel.

When God favored Abel's offering but "had no regard" for Cain's, the latter's anger got the best of him. "Let us go out to the field," said Cain to the apparently unsuspecting Abel. "And when they were in the field," the biblical text continues, "Cain rose up against his brother Abel, and killed him." The story reports that God responded: "What have you done? Listen; your brother's blood is crying out to me from the ground!" Cain's killing made him "a fugitive and a wanderer on the earth," one who "went away from the presence of the Lord," but God spared Cain's life, marking him "so that no one who came upon him would kill him."

At rock bottom, murder takes place when one person kills another intentionally, deliberately, and unjustifiably. (Much hinges on the latter term in particular, a point to which we will return in due course.) Cain's killing of Abel was murder—*homicide*—or nothing could be. Moreover, like the Sixth Commandment itself, the Genesis narrative leaves no doubt that murder is wrong. That same account, however, raises as many questions as it answers. For instance, was Cain's killing of Abel clearly premeditated? Genesis does not say so explicitly, although far from being excluded, the text definitely invites such an inference. Furthermore, when Cain "rose up against his brother," was that action murderous from the outset? Again, the text allows for the possibility that it might not have been that way, although Cain's "rising up" resulted in killing that was unlikely to have been accidental. Otherwise, Cain probably would not have tried to fend off God's question—"Where is your brother Abel?"—by denial and evasion: "I do not know; am I my brother's keeper?"

The ambiguities do not end there. When Cain questioned whether he should be held accountable as his brother's keeper, was he implying that creation did not yet have a moral structure that condemned murder as the Sixth Commandment would do explicitly later on? Cain's defense might have been that he unfairly received an *ex post facto* judgment from God. Who says, and where and when was it said, Cain might have protested, that I am to be Abel's keeper? However, if Cain made a legalistic move of this kind, Genesis shows that God had none of it. Prior to Cain's murdering Abel, the biblical account in Genesis brims with language about what is good, about the knowledge of good and evil, about obedience and disobedience. The Genesis tradition, moreover, makes clear not only that God "created humankind in his image, in the image of God he created them; male and female he created them" but also that "God blessed them." Could it make any good sense for God to create human beings in God's image, bless them, and then permit them with impunity to slaughter one another intentionally? At the end of the day, ambiguity notwithstanding, no credible reading could interpret Genesis as doing less than defining murder quintessentially or as doing anything other than finding murder wrong—period.

The clarity notwithstanding, a troubling darkness lurks in the question and response above. It will need revisiting, but the basic point is maintained within Jewish tradition, which, among other things, holds that when God gave Moses the Ten Commandments at Sinai, they were etched on two stone tablets, five commandments on each. The first five identified human duties to God; the second five underscored obligations that persons have to one another. Tradition holds further that there are parallels between the two sets of five commandments. Thus, the Sixth Commandment "You shall not murder" is especially linked to the First Commandment "I am the Lord your God, who brought you out of the land of Egypt, out of the house of slavery; you shall have no other gods before me." Murder—the intentional, deliberate, and unjustifiable killing of one human being by another—is wrong for reasons that go deep down because they violate the First Commandment.

God created human life in God's image. In God's sight, and surely in ours, that act was good. It was also awesome, even sacred, for in the ultimate sense, no human being has the power to create human life—not even the wonders of twenty-first century science contradict that fact—and murder destroys human life in ways that are beyond our repair and recovery. God may or may not resurrect the dead, but human beings utterly lack the power to do so. The result is that no human act rivals murder in defying, disrespecting, and denying God. The Christian philosopher Stephen Davis succinctly sums up the primary point: "Murder, then, is a crime both against the victim and his family and friends, and also (and most importantly) against God." [4]

Here it is worth noting that, according to the biblical scholar David Flusser, the Christian New Testament "does not use the term 'Ten Commandments' even once," but the injunction against murder is emphasized in multiple instances, and especially by Jesus in ways that are thoroughly consistent with the Jewish tradition that he observed. [5] In Matthew 19:16–22, Mark 10:17–22, and Luke 18:18–23, for example, Jesus stresses the importance of obeying God's commandments and explicitly condemns murder. Paul does the same in Romans 13:9, adding that the Sixth Commandment, along with those prohibiting adultery and theft, "are summed up in this word, 'Love your neighbor as yourself'" (Romans 13:10).

Meanwhile, for one reason or another—and here lurks another troubling problem related to the Sixth Commandment—Cain, who did not have the advantage of reading Genesis or Exodus, let alone the New Testament, may not have known as clearly as the readers of those texts that killing Abel was wrong. Genesis says little about the moral upbringing that Cain and Abel received from Adam and Eve, their biblical parents. Nor does it indicate much about what the brothers knew about God and God's expectations, except that they understood enough "in the course of time" to bring offerings to God. Abel, apparently, knew better than Cain what would please God. Whether Cain's misjudgment resulted from ignorance or from a disrespectful holding back of what he should have given to God, the result was the introduction of murder, which ever since has bloodied and scarred creation almost beyond belief. To illustrate the latter point consider two further episodes. Linked to Cain's murder of Abel even though they are millennia removed from that act, these examples also help to shape my perspectives on the Sixth Commandment.

TWO EPISODES

Richard Rhodes's *Masters of Death: The SS Einsatzgruppen and the Invention of the Holocaust* details how Nazi Germany's mobile killing units murdered more than 1.3 million Jews in eastern Europe during World War II. "Maps in Jewish museums from Riga to Odessa," writes Rhodes, "confirm that almost every village and town in the entire sweep of the Eastern territories has a killing site nearby."[6] Gratuitous and sadistic violence accompanied the slaughter. Rhodes describes one instance as follows: "A woman in a small town near Minsk saw a young German soldier walking down the street with a year-old baby impaled on his bayonet. 'The baby was still crying weakly,' she would remember. 'And the young German was singing. He was so engrossed in what he was doing that he did not notice me.'"[7]

Although such brutal murder should rightly leave one speechless, there are many things that ought to be said about it. One of them is that if such action is not an example of unjustifiable killing, nothing could be. Of course, the young German and his Nazi superiors, SS leader Heinrich Himmler and Adolf Hitler himself first and foremost among them, would have argued differently. In their Nazi eyes, the mass killing of Jews was not only justifiable but also imperative. To them, Jews were such an unrelenting, pestilential threat to the "superior" German *Volk* that Jewish life—including, significantly, the Jewish tradition that emphasized the Sixth Commandment—must be eradicated root and branch. Himmler was not, however, an advocate of gratuitous and sadistic violence. He would have disapproved of young Germans who found joy in impaling infants on their bayonets. He wanted "decent" killers instead.

Hitler, Himmler, and the young German soldier in Rhodes's account were neither insane nor completely irrational. They had a worldview that made sense to them, and they acted on it.[8] Nevertheless, rational and ethical scrutiny far better and deeper than theirs underscores how much the Nazis' reasoning, planning, and acting were misguided and immoral. For no matter how sincerely Hitler and his followers held their beliefs or how valid they took them to be, those convictions and the mass murder that flowed from them were based on error and terror, on deceit and delusion, on theft and tyranny, on falsehood and aggression, on hate and disrespect for human life other than their own. That catalog does not exhaust the criteria that brand killing unjustifiable, but no killing arising from those conditions, dispositions, or motivations can reasonably be justified.

Unjustified and unjustifiable, so much of the killing done by Nazi Germany and its collaborators was not only murder but also *mass murder*. In 1944, Raphael Lemkin, a Jewish lawyer who fled from Poland during the Holocaust, named such crimes when he coined the term *genocide*, which derives from the Greek word *genos* (race) and the Latin suffix *cide* (killing). It refers to instances of mass murder, such as Nazi Germany's assault on the Jews, that do not target individuals alone but aim at the murder of entire groups. Owing considerably to Lemkin's dogged persistence, the United Nations adopted the 1948 Convention on the Prevention and Punishment of the Crime of Genocide, which defined that crime in terms of "acts committed with intent to destroy, in whole or in part, a national, ethnical, racial, or religious group, as such."[9]

Cain committed homicide and fratricide but not genocide. The United Nations' definition indicates that genocide can take place without direct murder, but typically genocide is no less an occasion for murder than is the case with homicide and fratricide. Granting some genocidal exceptions, all three are instances of murder; all three involve the intended, deliberate but unjustifiable taking of individual lives. In genocide, however, the murderous aim is immensely escalated, and a person's life is at risk not for anything in particular that he or she has done but simply because one exists at all as a member of a targeted group. The fact that the group is targeted is crucial, because all human individuals are fundamentally defined by factors of group identity of one kind or another. Indeed there can be no individual human life without such identities. Unfortunately, not even genocide is the end of the matter where mass murder is concerned, and thus we come to the second episode that influences my wrestling with the Sixth Commandment. It involves calculations of time and distance.

In 1994, the political scientist R. J. Rummel, a demographer of what he calls *democide*, published an important book called *Death by Government*. Writing before he could have taken account of the late twentieth-century genocidal atrocities in Bosnia, Rwanda, and Kosovo or the twenty-first century genocide in the Darfur region of Sudan, Rummel estimated that "the human cost of war and democide"—he defined *democide* as "the murder of any person or people by a government, including genocide, politicide, and mass murder"—is more than "203 million people in [the twentieth] century."[10] (What the precise figure would be today, God only knows.)

"If one were to sit at a table," Rummel went on to say, "and have this many people come in one door, walk at three miles per hour across the room with three feet between them (assume generously that each person is also one foot thick, navel to spine), and exit an opposite door, it would take over *five years and nine months* for them all to pass, twenty-four hours a day, 365 days a year. If the dead were laid out head to toe, assuming each to be an average of 5 feet tall, they would reach from Honolulu, Hawaii, across the vast Pacific and then the huge continental United States to Washington, D.C. on the East coast, *and then back again almost twenty times*."[11]

While Rummel may have thought that such calculations would make the abstraction of huge numbers more concrete, it is not clear that he even convinced himself, for he placed an endnote number at his calculation's conclusion. Note 14 reads as follows: "Back and forth, over 4,838 miles one way, near twenty times? This is so incredible that I would not believe the calculation and had to redo it several times."[12]

THE SLAUGHTER BENCH OF HISTORY

Turning now to the first of the four questions that I identified at the outset, consider that the philosopher G. W. F. Hegel called history a slaughter bench.[13] Although he may not have acknowledged the point explicitly, he did so largely because the Sixth Commandment has neither functioned nor fared nearly as well as God and humankind should desire. Things could always be worse, even to the point of *omnicide*, the total extinction of life that may now be within the willful killing and murderous prowess of human beings, but humanity's murderous ways lend all too much credence to the point made by the Holocaust survivor Elie Wiesel when he said, "At Auschwitz, not only man died, but also the idea of man. . . . It was its own heart the world incinerated at Auschwitz."[14]

Meanwhile, the Sixth Commandment has had normative status, and it probably has had some braking effect on humankind's propensity for violence. Arguably, however, an honest historical appraisal leads to the conclusion that the most distinctive quality about the Sixth Commandment is the extent to which it has been violated—disregarded, dismissed, and disrespected. Coupled with those characteristics, one must add that the Sixth Commandment has never been backed sufficiently by credible sanctions, divine or human, that would ensure full respect for and obedience to it. [15]

"What have you done?" God asked Cain after he murdered Abel. The slaughter-bench history of homicide, genocide, and democide, plus the potential of omnicide, call into question the functional status of the Sixth Commandment. A commandment that is not obeyed may still be a commandment, but its functional status depends on obedience and credible sanctions against disobedience. An injunction that is not heeded lacks credibility. When Nazi Germany unleashed the Holocaust, the force of the injunction "You shall not murder" was impugned to the degree that millions of Jews were slaughtered. It took the violence of a massive world war, which left tens of millions more corpses in its wake, before the Third Reich was crushed and the Holocaust's genocidal killing centers were shut down. At least in biblical terms and in the Jewish and Christian traditions, God is the source and the ultimate vindicator of the Sixth Commandment. If God is not acknowledged and obeyed, God's existence is not necessarily eliminated, but God's authority is curtailed. And if God's authority lacks credibility, then the nature of God's existence is affected too. How has the Sixth Commandment functioned and fared in history? Two of the words that must be used in response to that question are *poorly* and *badly*.

DISAGREEMENT

What does the Sixth Commandment reveal about humankind? Beyond the fact that human beings have often been what Richard Rhodes called "masters of death" who flagrantly and repeatedly disobey the prohibition against murder, this commandment also shows how contentious, confident, and confused the commandment against murder can make us. Those three qualities make an ill-fitting package.

In late May 2005, I drove across the United States from Washington, D.C., to my home in California. I had spent the 2004–2005 academic year at the United States Holocaust Memorial Museum, where I wrote a book about ethics during and after the Holocaust. On my way west, somewhere outside of Little Rock, Arkansas, a billboard caught my attention. Not the only one of its kind in the United States, it said: "You call it abortion. God calls it murder."

What about abortion? Few issues are more vexed than whether God calls abortion murder and how human beings know God's mind on that matter. More than once in this area, violence has eclipsed dialogue. What about euthanasia, another issue that pitted Americans, families even, against one

another in the 2005 media-hyped, "right to die" case involving Terri Schiavo? Absent the Sixth Commandment and the contentious ways in which the
Decalogue, including wrangles over the relationship between civic displays
of Exodus 20:1–17 and American constitutional requirements about the separation of church and state, it is hard to imagine that the Schiavo case would
have riveted and ripped the republic as it did. [16]

The Sixth Commandment creates confidence, although not necessarily
confidence that is warranted and wise, when people think they know exactly
what it means and precisely to what it applies. But such claims, including
their assumptions about "God's will," rarely produce more agreement than
disagreement. Whether intended or unintended, one consequence of confidence about the meaning of the Sixth Commandment is often disagreement,
frequently contentious disagreement. Typically, confusion—recognized and
acknowledged or not—accompanies disagreement of that kind. It remains to
be seen whether even the most careful inquiry can produce the clarity and
insight that are needed, but such wrestling should be one of the Sixth Commandment's most critical by-products.

Unmistakably, the Sixth Commandment declares that homicide is wrong.
It requires us to find genocide and democide wrong as well. How it applies in
other acts that take life away—along with war and capital punishment, abortion and euthanasia are two of the most crucial examples in our time—may
not be as clear, but at the very least respect for the Sixth Commandment
should make us deliberate thoughtfully and humbly as we wrestle with the
silence, and therefore the need for interpretation, that is embedded in its
unmistakable clarity that murder is forbidden.

WHAT HAS GOD DONE?

In wrestling with the Sixth Commandment, God's question to Cain—"What
have you done?"—can be put to God as well. God's prohibition of murder is
clear, but arguably not clear enough because the commandment's meaning is
neither completely self-evident nor as thoroughly detailed as it might be.
Even if the taking of any life is in some sense wrong, and such a case can be
made, God's specific positions—to the extent that they exist—on war, capital
punishment, abortion, and euthanasia appear not to be entirely free of ambiguity, leaving men and women to contend for and about the interpretations
that make the best sense. The complications, however, are not restricted to
matters of interpretation. They also involve God's relation to murder, which
is made the more troublesome because of the Sixth Commandment.

Could it be that the Sixth Commandment is violated by God, the very One
who established it? That question does not imply, God forbid, that God is a
murderer, but it does raise the possibility that God can be found wanting for

failing to intervene against murderers and, to that extent, for being a bystander if not an accomplice when murder takes place.

When that possibility is raised, theology usually offers justifications or excuses for God in an exercise called *theodicy*. Where murder is concerned, theodicy typically gives God a pass by arguing that human beings and they alone are responsible for their actions because God gave them freedom to choose. Freedom's defense for God, however, is more problematic than it seems.[17] As homicide, genocide, and democide make clear, God's gift of freedom has taken an immensely murderous toll. History shows that human beings can and will use their freedom to murder wantonly and to a large extent with impunity because the murdering is never stopped soon enough. Auschwitz makes us ask, "Where was humanity?" Auschwitz can also make us ask, "Where is God?" and it does so because of the Sixth Commandment.

"You shall not murder"—this commandment reveals much about God. The revelation is awesome but not only because God's commanding moral voice resounds within it. The revelation is also awesome because God's refusal or inability to prevent human beings from murdering one another ramps up humankind's responsibility for itself. The Sixth Commandment reveals God to be One who takes human accountability far more seriously than men and women are likely to do.

THE SIXTH COMMANDMENT AND THE FUTURE

The Sixth Commandment will continue to be what I called it at the outset: the imperative that is the most necessary, although not sufficient, condition for human civilization. No less clear is the fact that this commandment will continue to be violated, often immensely and with a large measure of impunity. Furthermore, the God who prohibits murder is also the One who will do relatively little, if anything, to stop human beings from committing homicide, genocide, democide, and perhaps even omnicide.

The Jewish philosopher Emmanuel Lévinas, who lost much of his family in the Holocaust, insisted that "You shall not murder" means nothing less than "you shall defend the life of the other."[18] The Sixth Commandment and the task that Lévinas rightly identifies as following from it show that nothing human, natural, or divine guarantees respect for either of those imperatives, but nothing is more important than making them our key responsibility, for they remain as fundamental as they are in jeopardy, as vitally important as they are threatened by humankind's murderous destructiveness and indifference.

NOTES

1. Among the sources that have been most helpful in my thinking about the Decalogue, I want to mention especially William P. Brown, ed., *The Ten Commandments: The Reciprocity of Faithfulness* (Louisville, KY: Westminster John Knox Press, 2004).

2. Philip Paul Hallie, "Cruelty: The Empirical Evil," in Paul Woodruff and Harry A. Wilmer, eds., *Facing Evil: Light at the Core of Darkness* (LaSalle, IL: Open Court, 1988), p. 128.

3. Thomas Hobbes, *Leviathan* (Indianapolis, IN: Bobbs-Merrill, 1958), pp. 106–7. To a considerable degree, human existence is perpetually in the state of war that Hobbes identified. The reason has much to do with humankind's repeated and escalating violations of the Sixth Commandment.

4. Stephen T. Davis, "Genocide, Despair, and Religious Hope: An Essay on Human Nature," in John K. Roth, ed., *Genocide and Human Rights: A Philosophical Guide* (New York: Palgrave Macmillan, 2005), p. 38.

5. David Flusser, "The Decalogue in the New Testament," in Ben-Zion Segal and Gershon Levi, eds., *The Ten Commandments in History and Tradition* (Jerusalem: Magnes Press, Hebrew University of Jerusalem: 1990), p. 221.

6. Richard Rhodes, *Masters of Death: The SS-Einsatzgruppen and the Invention of the Holocaust* (New York: Alfred A. Knopf, 2002), p. 121.

7. Ibid., p. 140.

8. On this point, see Claudia Koonz, *The Nazi Conscience* (Cambridge, MA: Harvard University Press, 2003).

9. For more detail on these matters, see Carol Rittner, John K. Roth, and James M. Smith, eds., *Will Genocide Ever End?* (St. Paul, MN: Paragon House, 2002).

10. R. J. Rummel, *Death by Government* (New Brunswick, NJ: Transaction Publishers, 1997), pp. 13, 31. Observations about Rummel's data by the Holocaust historian Yehuda Bauer are worth noting: "Rummel has been criticized for exaggerating the losses. Even if the criticisms were valid, a figure lower by 10 or 20 or even 30 percent would make absolutely no difference to the general conclusions that Rummel draws." See Yehuda Bauer, *Rethinking the Holocaust* (New Haven, CT: Yale University Press, 2001), pp. 12–13, 277 n.17.

11. Rummel, *Death by Government*, pp. 13, 31.

12. Ibid., p. 28.

13. See G. W. F. Hegel, *Introduction to the Philosophy of History*, trans. Leo Rauch (Indianapolis: Hackett Publishing Company, 1988), p. 24.

14. Elie Wiesel, *Legends of Our Time* (New York: Avon Books, 1972), p. 230.

15. If there is life beyond death, God's judgment may provide sanctions that condemn murder beyond all doubt and without remainder. Unfortunately, that outcome comes too late to be effective in history, for neither the murdered nor their murderers have returned to tell what God may have done with them. Nor has God made that situation crystal clear. Meanwhile, within history, murder is sometimes punished but not with sufficiently credible deterring impact. History's mounds of murdered dead grow larger and larger.

16. It is not even clear that the disputes about the Schiavo case have been entirely laid to rest by the autopsy report that was released on June 15, 2005, which found that her collapse in 1990 had not been caused by physical abuse or poison but had left her with irreversible brain damage and in a condition that could properly be described as a persistent vegetative state. See, for example, Timothy Williams, "Schiavo's Brain Was Severely Deteriorated, Autopsy Says," *New York Times*, 15 June 2005.

17. For elaborations of my views on these matters, see, for example, my contributions to Stephen T. Davis, ed., *Encountering Evil: Live Options in Theodicy*, rev. ed. (Louisville, KY: Westminster John Knox Press, 2001).

18. Emmanuel Lévinas, "In the Name of the Other," trans. Maureen V. Gedney, in Jill Robbins, ed., *Is It Righteous to Be? Interviews with Emmanuel Lévinas* (Stanford, CA: Stanford University Press, 2001), p. 192.

Chapter Eight

Redeeming Sacred Texts from their Sacrilegious Uses

Mary C. Boys

It is difficult for religiously committed persons to acknowledge that their sacred texts are prone to sacrilegious uses. Learning that narratives that inspire and sustain can be—and indeed have been—used as weapons often evokes resistance and denial; to encounter the shadow side of one's religious tradition brings both sorrow and shame. Thus, how we "trouble tradition" in wrestling with "problem passages" requires educational wisdom and pastoral sensitivity.

The Bible, of course, is full of problematic passages that appear to sanction violence, demean women, condone slavery, and discriminate against particular groups. Frederick Buechner, well-known writer and Presbyterian minister, playfully describes the Bible as a

> disorderly collection of books which are often tedious, barbaric, obscure and teem with contradictions and inconsistencies. It is a swarming compost of a book, an Irish stew of poetry and propaganda, law and legalism, myth and murk, history and hysteria . . . hopelessly associated with tub-thumping evangelism and dreary piety, superannuated superstition and blue-nosed moralizing; with ecclesiastical authoritarianism and crippling literalism. [1]

The sacred texts in the Christian tradition most prone to sacrilegious use are those that deal with the suffering (passion) and death of Jesus. These texts, the "passion narratives," give rise to a narrative that is fundamental to Christian identity; collectively, they give rise to a story as elemental to Christianity as the Exodus is to Judaism. Yet have been used in ways that I can only call sacrilegious in their disparagement and vilification of Jews and Judaism. The charge, initially leveled in the New Testament, developed with considerable rhetorical effect in early church writings, and a common staple of church teaching for nearly two millennia, constitutes the theological core of anti-Judaism. In short, the passion narratives seem to be a case study in problem texts precisely because they are both deadly and life-giving. All depends on the telling.

Accordingly, I have organized my remarks in a fivefold rubric of "tellings:"

- A Trembling Telling
- A Troubling Telling
- A Tragic Telling
- A Transformed Telling
- A Transforming, Trembling Telling

I hope the adjectives will become clear over the course of my lecture, but first a word about "telling."

Tell is a simple word—more widely accessible than "interpretation" and "hermeneutics," terms we who make our living in the "academy" tend to use. But its simplicity may be deceptive: To tell a story involves more than might initially meet the eye (or ear). Even if we are merely reading aloud what is already in writing, we reveal what we think is significant in emphasizing certain words or phrases. And when the church "tells" the story of the passion and death of Jesus, it does so in elaborate and complex ways: in the Gospel proclaimed in liturgical solemnity, in its prayers, in the symbols of cross and crucifix that mark our churches (and delineate Protestantism and Catholicism), in hymnody and art—and in the retelling that is the sermon.

Now to the five tellings.

A TREMBLING TELLING

Stories of Jesus' death are lodged in the core of Christian identity. They offer an encounter with the way Jesus experienced the human condition, including betrayals by those closest to him, his own fear of death, uncertainty about God's will, and the endurance of terrible suffering and an ignominious death. These stories cause us, in the words of that magnificent spiritual, to "tremble, tremble, tremble."[2]

> Were you there when they crucified my Lord?
> Were you there when they crucified my Lord?
> Oh, sometimes it causes me to tremble, tremble, tremble.
> Were you there when they crucified my Lord?
> Were you there when they nailed him to the tree?
> Were you there when they nailed him to the tree?
> Oh, sometimes it causes me to tremble, tremble, tremble.

Were you there when they nailed him to the tree?
Were you there when they laid him in the tomb?
Were you there when they laid him in the tomb?
Oh, sometimes it causes me to tremble, tremble, tremble.
Were you there when they laid him in the tomb?
Were you there when God raised him from the tomb?
Were you there when God raised him from the tomb?
Oh, sometimes it causes me to tremble, tremble, tremble.
Were you there when God raised him from the tomb?

This spiritual offers us a glimpse into the power of the passion stories. An enslaved people could identify with the suffering Jesus; in some way, he had taken on their pain as well. The passion stories are especially revelatory for marginalized peoples: Jesus, through whom we Christians see God revealed, is one with the marginal peoples of this world—all those whom brutal rulers, whether Pontius Pilate or Hitler or Pol Pot considered expendable, of non-human status.

The death-resurrection of Jesus lies at the heart of the church's liturgical life and spirituality, as well as in its creeds and doctrines. It has evoked centuries of reflection, given rise to powerful rituals, inspired beautiful art and music, stimulated tomes of theology, motivated persons to sacrifice themselves for a cause greater than they, and sustained persons through times of horrifying suffering. The stories of Jesus' death symbolize all that is sacred in Christianity.[3]

The story has also been told in ways that have glorified suffering, condoned passivity in the face of violence, and constricted the meaning of salvation by associating it only with the death of Jesus, as if his life and teaching had little meaning. These are troubling tellings, but there is another even more troubling telling: We know from history that misinterpretations of the passion narratives have rationalized hostility to and violence against Jews. As Gerard Sloyan, a respected New Testament scholar (and Catholic priest) lays out the charge: "The chief actual sufferers from Jesus' death by crucifixion have been, paradoxically, not Christians but Jesus' fellow Jews."[4]

A TROUBLING TELLING

The writers of the Gospels differ from one another in the way they tell the story of Jesus' passion (arrest, beating, trial[s]) and death. But common to all their accounts is this: Jews are primarily responsible for the death of Jesus. Two texts in particular have been especially troubling. The Gospel of Matthew (27:25) has a scene in which Pontius Pilate, the Roman procurator, acclaims his innocence before an unruly crowd. He washes his hands in their presence, saying, "I am innocent of this man's blood; see to it yourselves. Then the people as a whole answered: 'His blood be on us and our children!'" The Gospel of John (19:14–16) puts this accusation in sharpest relief in the scene in which "the Jews" demand of the Roman governor, Pontius Pilate, "Crucify him, crucify him."

This is troubling because Imperial Rome had far more to do with the death of Jesus than the Gospels reflect; I will return to this historical claim later. Even more troubling is the way in which early Christian teachers built upon this charge as the rivalry with Judaism widened and deepened.

Early Christian apologists had to justify Christianity, a minority religion without legal status in the Roman Empire, vis-à-vis Judaism, which was well established and respected, and undergoing its own process of transformation as it adapted to the loss of the Temple and Jerusalem. They believed a new era had arrived, and that Judaism would, therefore, give way to Christianity. Judaism no longer had a Temple since the Romans destroyed it in 70 C.E., and after 135 C.E. Jerusalem had become a Roman city, *Aelia Capitolina*. So history seemed to confirm what their theology claimed—Judaism had been unfaithful to the covenant, and now its time was over. [5]

Already by the mid-second century, the accusation had moved out of Judea: Justin Martyr, in his *Dialogue with Trypho*, accused Trypho: "He was pierced by you." In late second century, the bishop of Sardis (in modern Turkey), Melito (d. ca. 190), preached an eloquent sermon articulating what became the leitmotif of anti-Judaism: in killing Jesus, the Jews had murdered God. Origen (ca. 185–254) intensified the accusation: The Jews had committed "the most impious crime of all when they conspired against the Savior" of humankind in the "city where they performed to God the customary rites" that symbolized profound mysteries. "Therefore," he concluded, "that city where Jesus suffered these indignities had to be utterly destroyed. The Jewish nation had to be overthrown, and God's invitation to blessedness transferred to others, I mean the Christians, to whom came the teaching about the simple and pure worship of God" (*Against Celsus* 4.2.3.).

Major Christian figures of the fourth and fifth centuries, Augustine of Hippo (354–430) and John Chrysostom (347–407), intensified the separation. Augustine argued that the Jews, though responsible for the death of the Son of God, were ignorant of his true identity because they misread their own scriptures. They preserved faithfully the books of Scripture, but Jews read them "as the face of a blind man appears in a mirror—by others it is seen, but by himself it is not seen." (*City of God* 18.46) Because the Jews had rejected Jesus, they were cursed to wander in exile as reprobates. Yet in Augustine's thinking, they should not be killed so that the world will see the consequences of rejecting the Christ.

Chrysostom authored some of the most vitriolic denunciations of Jews: "Where Christ-killers gather, the cross is ridiculed, God blasphemed, The Father unacknowledged, the Son insulted, the grace of the Spirit rejected." (*Homily One Against the Judaizers* 1.6). (We understand something of the rhetorical style of this period when we see how Chrystostom recycled some of the same vitriol in attacking Arian Christians, whom he regarded as heretics.)

How can we not be troubled by a telling of the passion and death of Jesus that portrays Jews as blind to the ways of God, unfaithful, cursed, a deicide people? Yet as troubling as this telling is, it eventuated in tragedy.

A TRAGIC TELLING

In this section, I can only adumbrate developments in Christian life that are a source of enormous shame: ways in which accusations of Jewish responsibility for the death of Jesus become theological hate speech legitimizing, even at times inspiring, violence against Jews. (Parenthetically, there is a long legacy of church teaching that "sinners were the authors and the ministers of all the sufferings that the divine Redeemer endured" [*Roman Catechism* I, 5, 11], but it is not possible to pursue this legacy here.)

Once Emperor Theodosius declared Christianity the official religion of the Roman Empire ca. 379 C.E., the church had greater capacity to exercise its theology in the political and cultural sphere. Jews became subject in many areas to decrees that restricted their rights and effectively reduced them to second-class citizens. Yet Augustine's dictum that Jews not be killed held force; Christian society tolerated the presence of Jews in *their* society.

In the twelfth and thirteenth centuries, there was a tragic turn to violence against Jews. The Crusaders (so called because of the crosses that marked their tunics) set out to destroy the "infidel" Muslims, but found other infidels—Jews—en route. The church became more preoccupied with rooting out heretics, and as Christians began to learn more about rabbinic Judaism (in part through the infamous disputations), they realized that contemporary Judaism was shaped by the Talmud; Jews were no longer merely blind to the Christ whom their Scriptures prophesied, but practitioners of a heretical religion. [6] Moreover, in theological circles, most notably in the work of Thomas Aquinas, the Jews who killed Christ were not so much ignorant as they were guilty of "voluntary ignorance," that is an express desire to be ignorant; voluntary ignorance increases the degree of sinfulness. [7]

All this led to the conviction among many that contemporary Jews no longer deserved the protection of the church. Popular legends about Jews as ritual murderers became widespread in this period. During the thirteenth century, Christians charged Jews with desecrating the Host so as to reenact their original deicide. They accused them of blood libel—using the blood of Christians, preferably children, for their Passover rituals. Preachers spread tales based on such fabrications and vilified Jews in passionate sermons. The violence against Jews—both verbal and physical—suggests that anti-Judaism had come to resemble what the modern world calls anti-Semitism. It had, however, one major difference: Christianity provided no sanction for genocide.

What role did these tragic tellings of the passion story play in the Shoah? This is not a question I have sufficiently researched, but it is clear that the Nazis drew significantly on the Christ-killer myth in the curriculum of German schools. Most notable is the 1938 work of Ernst Hiemer, *Der Gifpilz* (*The Poison Mushroom*), a collection of seventeen short stories for young readers and a key text making the ideology of the Third Reich widely accessible. Among its chapters is "What Christ Said about the Jews." A peasant mother, returning from working in the fields, stops with her three children near a roadside shrine of Christ:

> Children, look here! The Man who hangs on the Cross was one of the greatest enemies of the Jews of all time. He knew the Jews in all their corruption and meanness. Once he drove the Jews out with a whip, because they were carrying on their money dealings in the Church. He called the Jews killers of men from the beginning. By that he meant that the Jews in all times have been murderers. He said further to the Jews: Your father is the Devil! Do you know, children, what that means? It means the Jews descend from the Devil. And because they descend from the Devil, they live like devils. So they commit one crime after another. Because this man knew the Jews, because He proclaimed the truth to the world, He had to die. Hence, the Jews murdered him. They drove nails through his hands and feet and let him slowly bleed. In such a horrible way the Jews took their revenge. And in a similar way they have killed many others who had the courage to tell the truth about the Jews. Always remember these things, children. When you see the Cross, think of the terrible murder by the Jews on Golgotha. Remember that the Jews are children of the Devil and human murderers. [8]

Such explicit linkage of purported Jewish responsibility for the death of Jesus with vilification of contemporary Jews is evident also in the shocking incident in 1942 in which a Slovakian rabbi called upon the local archbishop to plead for Catholic help in resisting the Nazi policy of deporting his town's Jews:

> Since the rebbe did not yet know of the gas chambers, he stressed the dangers of hunger and disease, especially for women, old people, and children. The archbishop replied: "It is not just a matter of deportation. You will not die there of hunger and disease. They will slaughter all of you there, old and young alike, women and children, at once—it is the punishment that you deserve for the death of our Lord and Redeemer, Jesus Christ—you have only one solution. Come over to our religion and I will work to annul this decree." [9]

I do not believe that this utterly immoral "telling" of the story of the death of Jesus by this archbishop was typical—but even one such example is scandalous and appalling.

A TRANSFORMED TELLING

In the wake of the Shoah, a group of Christians and Jews formed the International Council of Christians and Jews in 1946. A year later they gathered in Seelisberg, Switzerland; the Christian participants issued a document, "Ten Points of Seelisberg: An Address to the Churches." Five of their ten points involved interpretation of the death of Jesus:

> 6. Avoid using the word *Jews* in the exclusive sense of the enemies of Jesus and the words *The Enemies of Jesus* to designate the whole Jewish people.
> 7. Avoid presenting the Passion in such a way as to bring the odium of the killing of Jesus upon all Jews or upon Jews alone. It was only a section of the Jews in Jerusalem who demanded the death of Jesus, and the Christian message has always been that it was the sins of mankind which were exemplified by those Jews and the sins in which all men share that brought Christ to the Cross.
> 8. Avoid referring to the scriptural curses, or the cry of a raging mob: *His Blood be Upon Us and Our Children,* without remembering that this cry should not count against the infinitely more weighty words of our Lord: *Father Forgive Them, for They Know not What They Do.*
> 9. Avoid promoting the superstitious notion that the Jewish people are reprobate, accursed, reserved for a destiny of suffering.
> 10. Avoid speaking of the Jews as if the first members of the Church had not been Jews. [10]

These points anticipated later statements from various churches, most famous of which is the Second Vatican Council's 1965 *Nostra Aetate* #4 that "what happened in His passion cannot be charged against all the Jews, without distinction, then alive, nor against the Jews of today." Although the full formulation in *N.A.* regarding the death of Jesus is problematic insofar as it claims "True, the Jewish authorities and those who followed their lead pressed for the death of Christ," subsequent documents have drawn on recent biblical scholarship to provide more nuanced wording.

The story of the development of this statement is both fascinating and dramatic, but not one we can trace here. *Nostra Aetate* is indeed a flawed document, not nearly as forceful as many had hoped, but, most importantly, it inaugurated a serious reassessment of Christian teaching in many churches. The charge of "Christ-killer" lingers, but it no longer has the same force in most of Christianity, and in many cases has been explicitly and repeatedly repudiated.

Two intertwined factors play a major role in this repudiation: the churches' reassessment of their relationship with Judaism in the wake of the Shoah, and developments in biblical scholarship. While I have used "the churches" in the plural, at this juncture I am going to restrict my observations to developments in the Catholic Church, since it has a well-developed set of interpretational principles that provides substantial tools for a transformed telling of the passion, death and resurrection of Jesus.

To start with the scholarship: It is well known that Catholicism struggled initially with historical criticism—that is, methods that situate biblical texts in their literary cultural and historical contexts. "Struggle" is in fact too kind; historical criticism was condemned in official church teaching around the turn of the twentieth century in the so-called Modernist crisis. Yet beginning in the 1940s a more open attitude became evident. Today, an official Vatican document, *The Interpretation of the Bible in the Church* (1993), calls historical criticism "indispensable."

Indeed, historical criticism is indispensable in understanding the crucifixion of Jesus. For the sake of clarity, let me outline the principal findings:

1. Second Temple Judaism was heterogeneous, and the proper matrix in which we must situate the teachings of Jesus. As a consequence, to generalize about "the Jews," and especially to make claims that Jesus taught "x" while the Jews taught "y" falsifies the picture (e.g., Jesus taught love, but Jews the law).

2. From the 60s of the first century B.C.E., Second Temple Judaism existed under the vise of Imperial Rome. There is now a wealth of scholarship attesting to the way in which Rome enforced its rule by violence. Crucifixion was an especially effective deterrent to any who might challenge the Empire. It was "highly organized, massive state terrorism, intended to intimidate the vast peasant and slave populations of the empire into passivity."[11] Thousands of Jews met their death this way.

3. There is a consensus among biblical scholars that Pontius Pilate, governor of Judea from 26–36 C.E., appointed by the Roman Empire (and later removed for excessive cruelty) likely alone had the authority to impose the sentence of crucifixion, though it is highly probable that some Jewish authorities, likely members of the temple priesthood, may have been involved. Philo wrote that under Pilate there were "executions without trial constantly repeated" (*On the Embassy to Gaius*, 302). The likely charge against Jesus was sedition: a threat to the order of the state.

4. The Gospels, composed some thirty to forty years (or more) after the death of Jesus, were shaped by the devastation unleashed by Rome's destruction of the Temple and Jerusalem in the wake of the Jewish

War. The evangelists seem to have interpreted this devastation as divine punishment.

5. The period of Gospel composition likely witnessed rivalry and disagreement between the Jewish followers of Jesus and other Jews. It is probable that these tensions fueled a sense of betrayal because of the memory that some Jewish authorities were complicit in the death of Jesus. Moreover, Roman imperial power made it dangerous for the followers of the Way of Jesus (not yet separate from Judaism) to highlight the role of the state in the crucifixion of Jesus.

6. The Gospel accounts were not intended in the first instance to be historically reliable documents. Rather, they provided a particular community's "telling" of the story of Jesus. Gerard Sloyan says about the evangelists: "As modern reporters, they were a flat failure. As ancient dramatists, they were more than a little successful; in assigning human responsibility for Jesus' death, in light of subsequent history they were tragically successful." [12]

Taking these six factors into account, we may rightly conclude that the accounts in the Gospels, shaped by the experience of the evangelists and their communities in the latter third of the first century C.E., downplay Roman imperial power, especially as exercised by Pontius Pilate, the Roman procurator of Judea, and assign greater culpability to Judean Jews (Matthew) or to "the Jews" (John).

Such scholarship plays an elemental role in how the Catholic Church at official levels now teaches about the death of Jesus, for example, the 1993 *Interpretation of the Bible in the Church*. Clearly to be rejected also is every attempt at actualization set in a direction contrary to evangelical justice and charity, such as, for example, the use of the Bible to justify racial segregation, anti-Semitism or sexism whether on the part of men or of women. Particular attention is necessary, according to the spirit of the Second Vatican Council (*Nostra Aetate*, 4), to avoid absolutely any actualization of certain texts of the New Testament which could provoke or reinforce unfavorable attitudes to the Jewish people. The tragic events of the past must, on the contrary, impel all to keep unceasingly in mind that, according to the New Testament, the Jews remain "beloved" of God, "since the gifts and calling of God are irrevocable" (Rom. 11:28–29).

Since *Nostra Aetate* various Catholic agencies at the international, national, and local levels have issued various documents that refine and extend the interpretative moves made in that foundational text regarding the death of Jesus. The most important have even been collected in a small book, *The Bible, the Jews, and the Death of Jesus,* published by the United States Conference of Catholic Bishops. This is an important collection, indicative of the possibilities of transforming the tradition.

But the Messiah has not yet come (whether for the first or second time). There is far too little education about interpreting Scripture. The average person has few, if any, tools for reading biblical texts in context. The great wave of enthusiasm for Scripture study that followed Vatican II seems diminished. Too often the sermon retells the Gospel narrative for the day without attention to context, thereby losing one of the key teachable moments. Moreover, the passion narratives are proclaimed on the Sunday inaugurating Holy Week (variously called Palm or Passion Sunday) and on Good Friday, all too often without sufficient commentary.

Catholicism is a commentary tradition—but the commentary needs to be made more accessible. Would that every congregation had available in the pews a Catholic equivalent of *Etz Chayim* (the Torah and Haphtarah commentary of the Rabbinical Assembly and the United Synagogue of Conservative Judaism). If Catholicism is to honor the sorts of interpretative moves or "tellings" found in recent official documents, it must make a major educational commitment to helping persons learn to interpret texts, most especially problematic passages.

TRANSFORMING, TREMBLING TELLING

By way of a brief conclusion, I believe it absolutely crucial that we Christians learn to tell our story in ways that do justice to its complex history. By history here I mean not simply the "back story" of the crucifixion—particularly the iron grip of Imperial Rome—but the long history of how our ancestors in faith used it against Jews. This is a matter of justice in the relationship of our two peoples, and it is also requisite if we are to tell our story accurately. Indeed, this history must give us pause—the sacrilegious uses to which we have put the story of the death of Jesus cause us to tremble, tremble.

Yet even more is involved if we are to redeem these stories. They are inextricably connected to a Way of Life in the following of Jesus that saves us from excessive self-absorption, fear and enslavement to the destructiveness of sin. The life, death and resurrection of Jesus call us to a Way that is transforming, in large measure because it patterns our daily lives. To be a disciple is to take up our cross.

By striving to love our enemies, we lessen the world's violence and the violence within our own being. By engaging in acts of foot-washing and table service, we are redeemed from the constriction of selfishness and become part of a realm larger than ourselves—an activity that partakes of the coming reign of God. By forgiving others (and ourselves), we experience deliverance from an anger that can so easily corrode us by sapping our psychic energy. By responding to those in need, we mediate God's healing.

In short, the death of Jesus calls us to participate in the world's salvation by giving freely of our lives to others. The magnitude of this call causes us to tremble, tremble.

NOTES

1. Frederick Buechner, *Wishful Thinking: A Theological ABC* (New York: Harper & Row, 1973) 8–9.

2. In his commentary on this spiritual, James Cone writes: "Because black slaves knew the significance of the pain and shame of Jesus' death on the cross, they found themselves by his side. [. . .] Through the blood of slavery, they transcended the limitations of space and time. Jesus' time became their time, and they encountered a new historical existence. Through the experience of being slaves, they encountered the theological significance of Jesus' death: through the crucifixion, Jesus makes an unqualified identification with the poor and the helpless and takes their pain upon himself." *The Spirituals and the Blues: An Interpretation* (New York: Seabury, 1972), 53–54.

3. In my own Catholic tradition, we speak of the passion-death and resurrection as the "paschal mystery," (from the Greek, *pascha*, derived from Hebrew p*esach*)—that is, Jesus' "passing over" from death to life. In a sense, the Eucharist is the Haggadah from which we retell this story and enact it ritually.

4. Gerard S. Sloyan, *The Crucifixion of Jesus: History, Myth, Faith* (Minneapolis: Fortress, 1995), 2.

5. See Robert L. Wilken, *Judaism and the Early Christian Mind* (New Haven and London, 1971: Yale University Press, 1971, 1 38; 222–230.

6. The church "had awakened to the reality that Judaism did not cease to develop on the day of Jesus' crucifixion, on that day when the New Testament presumably replaced the old. If this New Testament charted the only legitimate direction in which the religion of biblical Israel could develop, and if the Jews had survived solely to testify to that Old Testament which had given birth to Christianity, then a postbiblical or talmudic Judaism was an impossibility. [. . .] The value of the Jews in a Christian world depended on their blindness, their ignorance of Christian truth, their testifying to that very truth unknowingly, despite themselves." Jeremy Cohen, *Christ Killers: The Jews and the Passion from the Bible to the Big Screen* (Oxford: Oxford University Press, 2007), 88–89.

7. It must, however, be understood that their ignorance did not excuse them from crime, because it was, as it were, affected ignorance. For they saw manifest signs of His Godhead; yet they perverted them out of hatred and envy of Christ; neither would they believe His words, whereby He avowed that He was the Son of God. Hence He Himself says of them (John 15:22): "If I had not come, and spoken to them, they would not have sin; but now they have no excuse for their sin." And afterwards He adds (John 15:24): "If I had not done among them the works that no other man hath done, they would not have sin." And so the expression employed by Job (21:14) can be accepted on their behalf: "(Who) said to God: depart from us, we desire not the knowledge of Thy ways." (*Summa theologica* 3.47.5, http://www.newadvent.org/summa/4047.htm)

8. Cited in Gregory Paul Wegner, *Anti-Semitism and Schooling Under the Third Reich* (New York and London: RoutledgeFalmer, 2002), 162. Wegner says, "No other society has ever devoted such a focused effort at integrating anti-Semitic thinking into curriculum intended for young children. [. . .] The language of religion expressed by various Nazi curriculum writers became another effective way in which Jews could be categorized as the negative other. The image became all the more potent through the exploitation of Golgotha. The charge of deicide against the Jews, one which survives to this day in anti-Semitic circles, carried a powerful emotional appeal for Nazi propagandists both inside and outside schools" (181).

9. Irving Greenberg, "Cloud of Smoke, Pillar of Fire: Judaism, Christianity, and Modernity after the Holocaust," in Eva Fleishner, ed., *Auschwitz: Beginning of a New Era? Reflections on the Holocaust* (New York: KTAV, 1977), 11–12.

10. In *More Stepping Stones to Jewish–Christian Relations: An Unabridged Collection of Christian Documents 1975–1983,* Helga Croner, ed. (New York and Mahwah, N.J.: Paulist Press, *1985),* 32–33. Also available http://www.bc.edu/research/cjl/meta-elements/texts/cjrelations/resources/documents/interreligious/Seelisberg.htm

11. Stephen J. Patterson, *Beyond the Passion: Rethinking the Death and Life of Jesus* (Fortress, 2004), 8.

12. Sloyan, *The Crucifixion of Jesus*, 42.

Chapter Nine

The Catholic Church and the Holocaust

Toward an Honest Assessment

John T. Pawlikowski

In dealing with the question of the Catholic Church and the Holocaust we need to keep in mind that institutional Catholicism docs not represent the totality of the church. The church, in the words of the Second Vatican Council, is also the "people of God." The record of the church at large, especially at the level of lay membership, was sometimes considerably better in terms of a response to the Holocaust than the institutional church leadership. The ZEGOTA movement in Poland is a case in point. This essay will confine itself to the response of Catholic leadership. But the reader needs to be aware that this does not necessarily tell the full story.

For a century or so the institutional Catholic Church battled the forces of liberalism and what was termed frccmasonry in Europe. As Ronald Modras has documented, Poland was one of the principal focal points of this effort.[1] This "hundred years war" was rooted in the belief on the part of popes and Vatican officials that fundamental notions of human rights and religious freedom would undermine Catholic moral hegemony in countries where Catholics constituted a majority, such as Italy, Austria and Poland. And even in countries such as Germany and France where Catholics did not dominate the political scene, Catholic leadership frequently fought strongly against such notions which were labeled "satanic" in origin. While such opposition on the part of the papacy, the Vatican and local church leaders did not automatically generate support for genocide and ultimately the Holocaust, it certainly weakened sustained protest against genocidal or near-genocidal actions on the part of governments and eventually against the Holocaust. Moral opposition to genocide and the Holocaust is ultimately based on notions of individual human equality. By trashing notions of human equality in the nineteenth and early parts of the twentieth century, Catholicism contributed, if only indirectly, to prevailing notions of religious and racial superiority that would provide an indispensable seedbed for genocides and the Holocaust. The failure of Vatican Council I to respond to growing anti-Semitism as a major social force in Europe is a case in point.

This hundred year war against liberal notions of human dignity and human rights only came to an end at the Second Vatican Council. After a fierce battle within the Council, the bishops endorsed for the first time the importance of notions of human rights and religious liberty in the Declaration on Religious Freedom (1965). Pope John XXIII made a major contribution to the about-face through his social encyclical *Pacem in Terris* (1963) released shortly before his death. If these documents had been available at the time of the Holocaust, they may well have made some difference in the quality of the Catholic response to Hitler's central attack on the Jews as well as his attack on the Poles, the Roma, the disabled and gay people.

After many years of delay the Vatican released a comprehensive statement on the Holocaust titled *We Remember*[2] on March 16, 1998. Its principal architect was Cardinal Edward Idris Cassidy, then president of the Holy See's Commission for Religious Relations with the Jews. But Cardinal Cassidy had to submit the text to the Vatican's doctrinal office headed by Cardinal Joseph Ratzinger (who later became Pope Benedict XVI) and to the Vatican Secretariat of State Cardinal Angelo Sodano. The latter in particular mandated changes in the document which would be responsible for future controversy. Perhaps the most important positive aspect of the document is that it came with a strongly positive introduction written by Pope John Paul II.

In some quarters, mostly Catholic, the document was greeted with considerable enthusiasm. A number of Jewish leaders also saw very positive elements within it. It clearly acknowledged the Holocaust as an historical fact—Holocaust denial was not an acceptable Catholic option. This has been reiterated by Pope Benedict XVI, Cardinal Walter Kasper and other Catholic leaders in response to the controversy over the lifting of the ban of excommunication for Bishop Richard Williamson and three other bishops in the heretical Society of St. Pius X. Even though this situation was handled in a very poor manner both by the Pope and other Vatican officials resulting in very vocal criticism from some bishops, theologians and Catholic organizations, in the end it resulted in a strong affirmation that Holocaust denial cannot be condoned in any way within Catholicism. The crisis in fact showed the depth of the bonds that had been forged between many Catholics and the Jewish community in light of Vatican II's Declaration on the Church and the Jewish People.

But *We Remember*, despite its genuine contribution to an understanding of the Holocaust, exhibits some serious drawbacks as several respected publications such as *Commonweal* and *The Tablet* made clear at the time of its release. Most of these criticisms were discussed at length in a major symposium on the document with Cardinal Cassidy as an active participant held at the Catholic Theological Union in Chicago under the auspices of the school's Cardinal Joseph Bernardin Center and the Tanenbaum Center for Interreligious Understanding in New York in March 1999.[3]

We Remember clearly implicates Catholics at all levels of the Church—even at the very highest levels, as Cardinal Edward Cassidy has reiterated, in the sin of anti-Semitism during the Holocaust. Its main drawbacks in this regard are its failure to link such anti-Semitism to the ordinary teachings of the church, especially as proclaimed in preaching, and to its depiction of the Catholic-Jewish relationship in church art over the centuries. The document tends to portray anti-Semitic Catholics as fringe members of the church, as people who refused to follow authentic church teachings. This is in fact a falsification of the actual historical record. Many national statements, such as those issued by the German and Polish bishops in 1995 and the French bishops in 1997 are far more forthright in this regard.

The German bishops emphasized that during the first part of the twentieth century an anti-Jewish attitude was evident in German society, including within the church. This anti-Jewish attitude bore consequences during the Nazi era:

> This was one of the reasons why, during the years of the Third Reich, Christians did not offer due resistance to racial anti-Semitism. Many times there was failure and guilt among Catholics. Not a few of them got involved in the ideology of National Socialism and remained unmoved in the face of the crimes committed against Jewish-owned property and the life of the Jews. Others paved the way for crimes or even became criminal themselves.[4]

The Polish episcopacy addressed the issue of Catholic culpability on two occasions. In a pastoral letter read in all churches on January 20, 1991, they spoke "of those who remained indifferent to that inconceivable tragedy. In particular, we mourn the fact that there were also those among Catholics who in some way had contributed to the death of Jews. They will forever remain a source of remorse in the social dimension."[5] And on the fiftieth anniversary of the liberation of Auschwitz-Birkenau they issued a letter titled "The Victims of Nazi Ideology" in which they wrote the following: "Unfortunately, there were also those who were capable of actions unworthy of being called Christian. There were those who not only blackmailed, but also gave away Jews in hiding into German hands. Nothing can justify such an attitude . . ."[6]

In many ways the strongest declaration came from the French Catholic bishops in September 1997. They clearly saw their admission of responsibility as a necessary step of cleansing and healing in preparation for the new millennium. "It is a well-proven fact," say the French bishops, that for centuries, up until Vatican Council II, an anti-Jewish tradition stamped its mark in different ways on Christian doctrine and teaching, in theology, apologetics, preaching, and in liturgy. It was on such ground that the venomous plant of hatred for the Jews was able to flourish. Hence, the heavy inheritance we still bear in our century, with all its consequences which are so difficult to wipe out. Hence are still open wounds. [7]

The document clearly admits the failure of Church authorities to challenge this anti-Semitic shadow on Christian theology and practice:

For the most part, those in authority in the Church, caught up in a loyalism and docility which went far beyond the obedience traditionally accorded civil authorities, remained stuck in conformity, prudence, and abstention. This was dictated in part by their fear of reprisals against the Church activities and youth movements. They failed to realize that the Church, called at that moment to play the role of defender within a social body that was falling apart, did in fact have considerable power and influence, and that in the face of the silence of other institutions, its voice could have echoed loudly by taking a definitive stand against the irreparable. [8]

In light of these statements *We Remember* could have been stronger and more explicit in terms of Catholic culpability during the Holocaust. *We Remember* could have, and should have, made it clearer that in speaking about the "wayward sons and daughters" of the church who fell into the sin of anti-Semitism that they did so because of what they had learned from teachers, theologians (the Church Fathers in particular), and preachers as well as from art work in churches where Jews were depicted as blind and decrepit. Yet we know from many studies on anti-Semitism by scholars, including Catholic scholars such as Edward Flannery[9] and Frederick Schwietzer[10] that for centuries anti-Semitism had permeated Catholic education and preaching and the popular culture they generated. The famous facade of the medieval cathedral in Strasbourg, France, with its depiction of the vibrant church as a young woman and the bedraggled and blindfolded synagogue presented in the guise of a bent-over old woman, is an apt illustration of how deeply anti-Semitism was embedded in the church's attitudes. *We Remember* is remiss in not connecting the sinful actions of its members relative to Jews much more directly to the anti-Semitic perspectives presented them within the tradition of Catholic worship and education. Pope John Paul II's recognition of anti-Semitism in Christian history in his plea for forgiveness for offences against the Jews made during his wider liturgy of pardon on the first Sunday of Lent 2000, a plea he repeated in the note he placed in Jerusalem's Western Wall during his historic visit to that city, represented a significant advance on *We Remember*.

The second problematic area of *We Remember* is its contention that there exist no substantive links between Christian anti-Judaism (a hostility toward the Jewish religion) and Nazi anti-Semitism. There is some basis for a distinction between Christian anti-Judaism and Nazi anti-Semitism. The church preached that Jews should be rendered miserable and marginal in human society and, at least in the case of St. Augustine as Paula Fredriksen has argued in her recent volume on Augustine and the Jews,[11] should be kept alive despite the mark of Cain that they bear. Nazism proposed the total annihilation of the Jews. Both are morally repugnant. But they are different. Nonetheless *We Remember* has overdrawn the distinction. Nazi ideology certainly was more than an enhanced version of Christian anti-Semitism. It drew on sources other than classical Christian anti-Semitism such as new theories of bio-racism. Yet when all is said and done, *We Remember*'s argument that there was no inherent connection between Nazi ideology relative to the Jews and classical Christian anti-Semitism is basically false, especially at the level of popular opinion during the Nazi era. Among Europe's Christian population, Christian anti-Judaism and anti-Semitism had everything to do with widespread acquiescence and even collaboration with the Nazi policy of Jewish destruction. I like to speak of classical Christian anti-Judaism and anti-Semitism as providing a seedbed for Nazism. Nazi ideologues drew upon classical anti-Jewish church legislation while developing the laws they would use to dispossess Europe's Jews and exploited Catholic-based cultural entities such as the Oberammergau passion play to promote Nazi ideology among the masses.

As we come to the papacy of Pope Benedict XVI and his outlook both on anti-Semitism in general and its formative role in terms of Nazism we encounter a mixed picture. Benedict XVI entered the papacy with some track record with respect to Catholic-Jewish relations, particularly on the theological front. At the end of the nineties and in early 2000 as Cardinal Ratzinger he did offer some succinct perspectives that seemed to make him receptive to new theological thinking on the Jewish–Christian relationship. These perspectives came in two articles, one book, and in the laudatory introduction he writes for the 2001 Pontifical Biblical Commission's two-hundred-plus-page monograph on *The Jewish People and Their Sacred Scripture in the Christian Bible.*[12] The articles were "The Heritage of Abraham: The Gift of Christmas," which was published in the December 29, 2000, edition of *L'Osservatore Romano* and a spring 1998 essay in *Communio* entitled "Inter-religious Dialogue and Jewish-Christian Relations." The latter piece was eventually incorporated into a full-length book (though in a somewhat different translation) *Many Religions; One Covenant: Israel, the Church and the World.*[13]

In the two major articles Ratzinger seemed to propose an understanding of the Jewish–Christian relationship as one in which the two communities move along distinctive, but not separated, paths toward an eschatological culmination. Hence there is only one covenant, not two, but pre-eschatologically there exist two different paths. Ratzinger clearly affirms that the Jewish community advances to final salvation through continuing obedience to its revealed covenantal tradition. In the end Christ will confirm that Jewish covenant. Thus Christ remains central to ultimate Jewish salvation; though it is not fully clear whether Ratzinger believes Jews must explicitly acknowledge Christ to attain full salvation in the end.

The 2001 Pontifical Biblical Commission's document, despite some significant limitations in the way it portrays post-biblical Judaism, makes an important contribution to the development of a new constructive theological understanding of the Jewish–Christian relationship. One important assertion in this document which Cardinal Ratzinger explicitly endorsed in his Introduction to it maintains that Jewish messianic interpretations are not in vain. In other words, there exists an authentic, parallel interpretation of the texts of the Hebrew Scriptures with regard to messianic hopes that stands side-by-side with that offered by Christianity through the New Testament. Unfortunately there has been no further development of this perspective since Cardinal Ratzinger has assumed the papacy. As I like to put it, Benedict has thus far never cited Ratzinger on this topic. In fact, there seems to be some regression in his thinking of late when compared with his endorsement of the 2001 Pontifical Biblical Commission's document. In addressing the yearly meeting of the Pontifical Biblical Commission in April 2009 he argued that the authentic interpretation of Sacred Scripture is possible only within the Church community and its traditions. This would seem on the surface to rule out the claim in the 2001 document that Jewish interpretations of the Bible with regard to messianism can be understood as valid. This is but one example of the significant ambiguity on theological issues in the Jewish–Christian dialogue that has marked Pope Benedict's pontificate since its inception. This reality was recently highlighted in a collection of letters from thirty-five Christian, Jewish and Muslim scholars written to the Pope in connection with his visit to Jordan, Israel, and Palestine in May 2009.[14]

This ambiguity appears to have taken a positive turn in Pope Benedict's address at the synagogue in Rome in January 2010. In his remarks he spoke of the Jewish covenant in the present tense and positively cited both traditional Jewish religious sources and the 2001 Pontifical Biblical Commission's document.

Based on these remarks it would appear the Pope understands the Jewish covenant as in force still today. Two questions remain, however, about the ultimate significance of the synagogue statement. Will we see this same attitude toward the Jewish covenant reaffirmed when Pope Benedict is speaking internally to the Catholic community? In other words, will such an outlook become a permanent feature of his thinking or will it remain confined to the address at the synagogue? Secondly, how will those at the Vatican and the United States Conference of Catholic Bishops who have been promoting the perspective of the late Cardinal Avery Dulles and who have been responsible for statements that refer to the Jewish covenant in the past tense now adjust their thinking in light of the Pope's address? In the controversy regarding the theology of the Jewish–Christian relationship over the past year they have frequently dismissed the many positive statements of Pope John Paul II on the Jewish–Christian relationship as not part of so-called "settled doctrine" (a theologically and canonically dubious term). Will they treat the January address at the Rome synagogue in the same manner and, if so, will they be called to task on it? Only time will tell the full impact of the synagogue address. Will it remain an isolated statement in terms of contemporary Catholic self-identity or refocus Catholic thinking back toward the continuing positive link between the two living covenants that was inherent in *Nostra Aetate* and reaffirmed on numerous occasions by Pope John Paul II?

On questions related to anti-Semitism and the Holocaust the same ambiguity that exists on the theological level is also evident. Benedict XVI gave a number of brief addresses in the context of the Jewish–Christian relationship in the early days of his papacy. The first was in connection with a June 9, 2005, visit to the Vatican by representatives of the International Jewish Committee for Interreligious Consultations (IJCIC). This is a global body established by the major organizations within the world Jewish community for official dialogue with the Vatican and the World Council of Churches. The second statement was delivered by the Pope during his visit to the synagogue in Cologne as part of his participation in World Youth Day 2005. The third was a letter to Cardinal Walter Kasper, President of the Holy See's Commission for Religious Relations with the Jews, on October 26, 2005, the day prior to the Vatican's official commemoration of the fortieth anniversary of Vatican II's *Nostra Aetate*, the conciliar text on the Church's relationship with non-Christian religions whose chapter four put the Catholic–Jewish relationship on a totally new footing. In all these statements Pope Benedict expressed his firm determination to follow in the footsteps of Pope John Paul II whose pontificate is credited with providing chapter four of *Nostra Aetate* a solid grounding in Catholicism. "It is my intention to continue on this path"—these words italicized in the official text released by the Vatican from the June 2005 meeting with the international Jewish leadership constitute the most important statement in these initial addresses. [15]

In these initial statements as a whole, but especially in the more substantive Cologne statement, Pope Benedict rejects anti-Semitism in any form. On this point he has been firm and consistent throughout his papacy. While he has refrained from applying the term "sinful" to anti-Semitism, something that John Paul II did on several occasions, there is little doubt that Benedict XVI shares with his predecessor a fundamental intolerance for anti-Semitism in any guise. He was quite forceful on this point in his address in Cologne: "Today, sadly, we are witnessing the rise of new signs of anti-Semitism and various forms of a general hostility towards foreigners. How can we fail to see in this a reason for concern and vigilance? The Catholic Church is committed—and I reaffirm this again today—to tolerance, respect, friendship and peace between all people, cultures and religions." He repeated this condemnation of anti-Semitism in remarks to Jewish leaders on his visit to France where he insisted that anti-Semitism "can never be theologically justified." [16]

Pope Benedict's remarks regarding the Holocaust, particularly in his Cologne address and his statement at the Birkenau extermination camp in late May 2006 where he was present during his visit to Poland remain somewhat more questionable. For one, his Cologne address makes no mention of the statements of the German, French, Polish and other hierarchies mentioned previously. Even more surprisingly, he omits any reference to the Vatican's official statement *We Remember*. In both speeches and subsequently in his address to Jewish leaders from the United States soon after the debacle surrounding the lifting of the ban of communication on four bishops from the Society of St. Pius X, including the notorious Holocaust denier Bishop Richard Williamson, [17] the Pope acknowledged the brutal horrors of the Holocaust, including the specific attack on the Jews. This Pope is no Holocaust denier. This we can assert with full certainty. At Cologne he made his own the words of Pope John Paul II in January 2005 on the occasion of the sixtieth anniversary of the liberation of the Auschwitz-Birkenau extermination camp: "I bow my head before all those who experienced this manifestation of the *mysterium iniquitatis*," "The terrible events of the period," the Pope continued "must never cease to rouse conscience, to resolve conflicts, to inspire the building of peace." [18] There is little doubt that Pope Benedict regards the Holocaust as one of the darkest moments in European history. In remarks at a general audience on November 30, 2005, he termed the Holocaust of the Jews as "an infamous project of death." [19]

It is with regard to the parentage of the Holocaust that Pope Benedict's remarks have raised some eyebrows. In a front page article in the December 19, 2000, issue of *L'Osservatore Romano* he argued that "it cannot be denied that a certain insufficient resistance to this atrocity on the part of Christians can be explained by the inherited anti-Judaism in the hearts of not a few Christians." But this remains a rather isolated text in the overall Ratzinger/Benedict corpus. Both at Cologne and in Birkenau and then again in statements during the Bishop Williamson controversy, as well as in his May 2009 address at Yad Vashem, he presents the Holocaust as primarily, even exclusively, a neo-pagan phenomenon which has no roots in Christianity but instead constituted a fundamental challenge to all religious belief, including Christianity. No reputable scholar on the Holocaust would deny its neo-pagan roots nor its fundamental opposition to all religious perspectives. But equally reputable scholars, and I would count myself among them, would also insist on surfacing the Holocaust's links with classical anti-Semitism.

The Holocaust succeeded in a culture that supposedly was deeply impacted by Christian values for centuries. I have always opposed drawing a simple straight line between classical Christian anti-Semitism and the Holocaust as though Nazism was merely the final and most gruesome manifestation of this cancer within Christianity. Clearly Nazi ideology was influenced by modem philosophy and modem racial biology. But we cannot obfuscate the fact that, as I noted earlier, traditional Christian anti-Semitism provided an indispensable seedbed for the spread of this vicious ideology. In his various addresses on the Holocaust Pope Benedict seems to be supporting a rather fringe interpretation which understands it as solely an attack on religion in all its forms rather than as a phenomenon that draws heavily on a continuing anti-Semitic base in the heart of Christianity at that time. His remarks can easily leave the impression, intended or not, that the Holocaust was simply the result of secular, modernizing forces in Europe at the time of the Nazis not dissimilar from the secularizing forces that affect Europe today in particular and which as Cardinal Ratzinger and now as Pope he has strongly criticized. Various Catholic publications have expressed concern about Pope Benedict's reluctance to acknowledge Catholic culpability relative to the Holocaust. [20]

During his visit to the synagogue in Rome Pope Benedict for the first time made reference to the 1998 Vatican document on the Shoah *We Remember* and acknowledged Catholic culpability in terms of anti-Semitism and the Holocaust. He quoted directly from the moving words of Pope John Paul II spoken at the liturgical ceremony in Rome on the first Sunday of Lent 2000 and repeated in a note John Paul II placed in the Western Wall in Jerusalem during his visit there. While this recognition of Catholic complicity on the part of Pope Benedict is a positive step forward it would have been good if he had added some words of his own on the matter given his German Catholic ancestry. And his rather weak defense of Pius XII during the Nazi era in response to Jewish expressions of conccrn at thc synagogue ceremony somewhat undercut the force of his making his own the significant words of John Paul II.

When we ask why Pope Benedict has been so reluctant to confront the issue of Christian responsibility during the Holocaust several answers may emerge. One possibility is that he fails to understand the depth of Christian complicity. He certainly is aware that there were some Christians who supported Nazism. But he seems to regard them as few in number and as rather isolated individuals in terms of the overall response of the Christian community. Fr. Patrick Desbois, who chairs the French Episcopal Commission on Catholic-Jewish Relations and whose recent work in uncovering mass Jewish graves from the Holocaust period described so poignantly in his book *The Holocaust by Bullets*,[21] reported to us at a meeting at the United States Holocaust Memorial Museum received by the late Cardinal Lustiger of Paris from Pope Benedict XVI in response to a letter the Cardinal had written to the Pope supporting the work of Fr. Desbois. In the papal letter Benedict expresses shock to learn of the information of Catholic collaboration in the mass killings of Jews in the Ukraine. It would seem that Benedict XVI has never made himself aware of the full depth of Catholic complicity in the Holocaust.

An even stronger influence on Benedict's seeming reluctance to grapple with Catholic complicity may in fact be his general ecclesiological outlook. Benedict has shown a strong tendency to regard the church primarily as an eternal, transcendental reality fundamentally unaffected by events in human history. Scholars have shown how the present Pope has referenced Vatican II's statement on the Church and the Modern World (*Gaudium et Spes*) very infrequently in contrast to Pope John Paul II for whom it was a central document in his understanding of the nature of the church even though John Paul II also had some difficulty linking Catholic complicity during the Holocaust with "the church as such."

In his Cologne address Pope Benedict did urge Catholic and Jewish scholars to take up together the difficult historical issues in the church's relationship with the Jewish People. This sounds similar to the so-called historians' project of several years ago launched by Cardinal Edward Idris Cassidy, the then President of the Holy See's Commission for Religious Relations with Jews and the International Jewish Committee for International Consultations. This project's goal was a thorough examination by a joint Catholic-Jewish scholarly team of the documentation from the Vatican archives originally released during the pontificate of Pope Paul VI. Unfortunately this effort ended in some acrimony and faced strong resistance from forces within the Vatican dedicated to the beatification/canonization of Pope Pius XII. The effort eventually fell by the wayside when Cardinal Cassidy departed the Vatican curia despite the Cardinal's urging his successor Cardinal Walter Kasper to continue the effort. If Pope Benedict were to follow through on this proposal at some point and re-establish a similar joint commission to continue this effort and even move beyond the materials from the Paul VI pontificate it would be an important step forward. It would show some awareness on his part of a link between the actions of church members, including church leaders, and the legacy of Christian anti-Semitism.

The most contentious single issue remaining on the Catholic–Jewish agenda relative to the Holocaust is the assessment of the papacy of Pius XII. The discussion became somewhat further polarized with the release of the Vatican's document on the Holocaust in 1998. A positive section on Pius XII was forced upon the document as a condition of its release by the then papal Secretary of State Cardinal Angelo Sodano. Cardinal Edward Cassidy has publicly confirmed this reality on several occasions. Most of the material came from Fr. Peter Gumpel, S.J., the promoter of Pius XII's cause for beatification/canonization. Cardinal Cassidy has indicated that in the original text there was little mention of Pius XII given the continuing controversy surrounding his stance during the Nazi era on both the popular and scholarly levels.

For a decade or more I have been arguing that the term "silent" should be removed as an adjective describing his papacy.[22] It unnecessarily polarizes the discussion. While in a limited sense, i.e., speaking out publicly, it is basically true; most people expand the term to mean he did nothing to save Jews. There is now substantial evidence that he took some actions, albeit through diplomatic channels, and did not interfere in any way with his representatives, especially papal nuncios, who did undertake concrete actions to rescue Jews. The remaining questions, and they are indeed crucial questions, include "did he act soon enough" and "did he do all he could, even in the difficult circumstances in which he found himself behind enemy lines?" The second question could also be put another way, "was saving the Jews a high priority on the papal agenda?" My personal answers to these questions remain negative at this stage of the scholarship on Pius XII. But they are open to revision should significant documentary evidence emerge from the various archival material still awaiting exploration.

We also need further research on the theological and social context in which Pius XII was working during the Nazi era and how that context may have influenced his outlook on the Jewish question. There have been two lines of scholarship on Pius XII that have never been brought together. As Papal Nuncio in Germany, and then as Papal Secretary of State under Pope Pius XI, Pius XII supported the notion of a distinctive Catholic social order for most of his life. He shared in Catholicism's century-long critique of the liberal social model. While he certainly opposed Nazism in principle—as his important contribution as Secretary of State to Pius XI's encyclical denouncing Nazism bears witness—his priority for most of his period in leadership was the defense of the Catholic Church against Bolshevism and Liberalism. In concert with many other Catholic leaders at the time, Pius XII came to the conclusion that Fascism and Nazism posed a somewhat less dangerous threat to Catholicism's continuing impact on the public order. In that context, defense of Jewish or Polish victims (Pius XII was also criticized on this point) became an important but secondary concern in the face of this difficulty. From the theological perspective Pius XII regarded the Catholic Church as indispensable for ultimate human salvation. Hence he saw his role as its head as one that demanded full commitment to its continued functioning in the midst of very challenging circumstances.

As we move into the early 1940s we begin to see some shift in Pius XII's general outlook on the social order. In the well-known Christmas addresses delivered via radio to a war ravaged Europe, he began to speak about the need for an entirely new social order beyond the earlier debate regarding the liberal, fascist and communist options. The people, some of them Catholics, who eventually founded the European Coal and Steel Community which laid the foundation for the current European Union, were in part inspired by this new papal perspective. And scholars on the post–World War II social encyclicals make a direct connection between the vision of these Christmas messages and the subsequent statements from Popes John XXIII, Paul VI and John Paul II.

The interesting, and still relatively unexplored, area is how this shift in Pius XII's outlook on the social order may have affected his approach to Jewish victimization. We do notice from the documentary material now available to us some of the Pope's behind-the-scenes efforts to save Jews. Is there a connection? Perhaps, but solid documentary evidence is still lacking. Among the interesting material is a letter written by Rabbi Herbert A. Friedman. He was a chaplain in the U.S. military who was sent with another chaplain to meet with Cardinal Augustus Hlond regarding the Kielce massacre. Friedman reports that they left that meeting rather disillusioned as the Cardinal told them that Jews were to blame for their fate. Subsequently they met with Pius XII at Castel Gondolfo on the same matter. Friedman describes this visit in far more favorable terms saying the Pope told them that Cardinal Hlond was wrong in what he told them a few months earlier. He also indicated that he was now having some reservations about the Concordat with Hitler. While they were at the papal summer residence Pius XII also showed them a garden where some two hundred Jewish orphans were playing, children to whom the Pope had personally given sanctuary. Three weeks later Pius XII issued the requested pastoral letter and, as Friedman puts it, "the fires in Poland slowly died down."[23]

Another immediate postwar situation casts a more negative light on the record of Pius XII. The Pope got into a controversy with the noted Catholic philosopher Jacques Maritain who was then serving as the French ambassador to the Vatican. Maritain was urging the Pope to speak out forcefully about German Catholic responsibility during the Nazi era. He was supported in this, at least partly, by the German Bishops' Conference who in a 1945 statement argued that all those who participated in the atrocities of the Nazi era must be brought to justice. Pius XII resisted Maritain's advice and in fact took steps to undercut the German Bishops' statement. As a result, Maritain tendered his resignation as French ambassador in protest and deposited some very unflattering comments about Pius XII's leadership in the French archives. Catholic historian Michael Phayer who has studied this situation describes Pius XII as the first "Cold War Warrior."[24]

There are several other aspects of the question of Pius XII and the Jews that need further exploration. One is the issue as to whether he gave tacit support to Jewish rescue efforts even though he may have communicated such support indirectly. There is some evidence emerging that a number of key Catholic resistance groups in France and Italy understood their efforts as in line with the wishes of the Pope himself. The French resistance movement, if we are to believe the memoirs of the late Catholic scholar Henri de Lubac,[25] took inspiration for their efforts to rescue Jews from the "generic" statements of Pius XII on racism and the well-known work of the Assisi Underground, according to one of its leaders. Padre Rufino Niccacci speaks of receiving Pius XII's order for Jewish rescue efforts "loud and clear" even though he was quite critical of the Pope for not speaking out publicly.[26] And I find it difficult to imagine that London Cardinal Hinsley's appearance at a mass rally in New York in 1943 in which he explicitly named the Jews as primary victims of the Nazis did not receive Vatican clearance. Likewise, the 1942 U.S. Bishops' Statement in which they denounced the Nazi effort to exterminate Jews in Poland likely came with the encouragement of the then Apostolic Delegate in Washington, Archbishop Cicognani, who likely provided them with vital information received from the Vatican which in turn obtained it through Dr. Gerhart Riegner of the World Jewish Congress in Geneva.

We may certainly question whether Pius XII's apparent policy to rely on subordinates to challenge the Nazis publicly on the Jewish question was sufficient. But some credit must be accorded him for these positive activities. Many, if not most, required at least his tacit support. And he could have put a halt to most of them if he had wished.

A second remaining issue has to do with reactions to his activities by Jewish and Western political leaders during the period of Nazism. Some have argued that criticism from the Jewish side of Pius XII began only after the appearance of the play *The Deputy* by Rolf Hochhuth. But such a claim is overly simplistic. While it is true that Jewish criticism of the Pope during the period of the war itself was rather muted, this should not be interpreted according to Gerhart Riegner as a sign of satisfaction on the part of the international Jewish leadership with Pius XII's commitment to Jewish rescue. Quite the contrary, in the words of Riegner,[27] The lack of great public pressure on Pius XII from the Jewish side was due primarily to the recognition of the Vatican's rather isolated location within a Fascist state.

Also noteworthy was the vocal criticism of members of the Polish Government in Exile based in London which pressured the Vatican to speak out more publicly on the extermination of Jews.[28] This criticism went hand-in-hand with internal criticism in Poland, mostly on the issue of Polish victimization under the Nazis, which became so intense at times that the Vatican commissioned the Jesuits to prepare a defense of Pius XII. This aspect of the situation, brought to light in the writings of scholars such as Richard Lucas[29] and John Morley,[30] deserves fuller consideration than it has received thus far in analyses of Pius XII's overall record.

Another remaining research task is to continue to see if any evidence exists of overt anti-Semitism in the more personal writings of Pius XII and in the records of people who interacted with him on a regular, in some cases daily, basis. The archival materials released some years ago during the pontificate of Paul VI certainly seem free of overt anti-Semitism. But we at least have to wonder if there is anything more. Surely Pius XII shared the anti-Judaic theology prevailing at the time. But did this theology ever spill over into more direct anti-Semitism? I sincerely hope the record will finally show up negative in this regard. But it is simply too early in the research to halt this effort.

Finally, a word or two is in order relative to the continuing debate over the so-called Hidden Encyclical of Pope Pius XI and Pius XII's rejection of it. This remains an important area for further research as it may yield some additional information regarding the dynamics within the Vatican at the time of the papal transition from Pius XI to Pius XII. But to allege that there was a "conspiracy" to block its publication that involved Pius XII as maintained in such works as *The Hidden Encyclical of Pius XI*[31] is to go far beyond the current documentary evidence. Michael Marrus is quite correct in his argument on this point.[32] That this proposed encyclical was not published after Pius XI's death is a fact. That the section on the Jews, despite its bottom line of a call for assistance to the Jewish community in the face of Nazism, is horrible and would have been a theological liability, is also a fact. Whether issuing it in view of its pronounced liabilities would have assisted the cause of European Jewry at the time is something that will likely remain unresolved. Most probably Pius XII rejected publication because of his overarching policy of relying exclusively on back channels regarding the Jewish question. If there was any "suppression" involved, it may have lain far more with the Jesuit General Superior at the time, Fr. Ledóchowski, given that the authors of the encyclical were two members of his congregation. But to make rejection of this text a central issue in a negative assessment of Pius XII's record is to put forth a very shaky argument in terms of the information available to scholars at this time.

Certainly the issue of Pius XII will remain an important question in the discussion of the Catholic Church and the Holocaust. This is as it should be because the issue goes far beyond the record of Pius XII himself. Whatever that record will be when all relevant scholarly work has been completed will remain with him. There is nothing the contemporary Church can do to change that, nor should it try. But the Church is in a position to alter its self-understanding today in light of what we have learned from a study of his response to the Holocaust. And the major lesson must surely be that there is no authentic understanding of the church that does not involve seeing the protection of the human rights and dignity of all people as integral to such an understanding. Emphasis on the "diplomatic model" of the church that prevailed during the Holocaust era has been exposed as morally flawed, No longer can the Catholic Church, or any other religious institution, allow a mind-set to prevail in which those outside its membership are viewed as "unfortunate expendables," a term coined by Holocaust scholar Nora Levin to describe the situation of the Jews under the Nazis, in its own struggle for survival in trying political circumstances.

It is my hope that the Catholic leadership will commit itself to the pursuit of continuing research on the record of Pius XII and the church at large during the Holocaust. The recent closed scholarly conference held at Yad Vashem involving Catholic and Jewish scholars is surely a step in the right direction. But such conferences must involve reputable scholars from both communities and not be limited to persons who either praise or condemn him without qualification and whose scholarly work in some cases is open to serious critique. The Vatican can hope to defuse some of the conflict over the Pius XII issue only if it commits itself to sound and open scholarly discussion of the issues involved rather than lend its support to people who simplistically argue that "he did all he could."

A study of Pius XII's and the Vatican's conduct during the Nazi era provides Catholics today with extremely valuable reference points as the church confronts new social situations in many parts of the world, especially those in which genocide remains an ongoing possibility. They can learn how violent religious language such as that found in the anti-Semitic rhetoric of classical Christian faith expression can "soften" a society for genocide. But it can also come to understand the power of major linguistic change such as that which has occurred in Catholicism relative to the Jews after the Second Vatican Council. Religion remains a powerful force in most current societies. If religious language in a given society continues to demean people who do not share in the dominant faith system and even denies them full rights of citizenship it certainly opens the door for possible physical assault on such groups when social tensions arise. On the contrary, positive language about the "religious other" can serve as a barrier to such assaults.

Religion also has a role to play in insuring that groups in society are not "neutralized" in terms of their fundamental humanity. The Holocaust scholar Henry Friedlander showed some years ago how the neutral language in reporting daily death counts in the Nazi extermination camps showed parallels with the language used by the U.S. military in reporting Vietnamese casualties during the Vietnam war.[33] Religion must always fight against such "neutralization," even of an enemy. For if neutralization of particular groups in society is allowed a foothold, it exposes these groups to the possibility of more violent attacks which again, in times of social crises, can turn into genocidal or near-genocidal actions against them.

Study and reflection on the Holocaust must remain at the top of Catholicism's contemporary agenda. This is an absolute requirement if the church is to speak with integrity and influence to contemporary moral challenges. But it is equally necessary for the kind of refined self-definition of the church that will enable it to stand at the forefront of a defense of human dignity that escaped it during the dark night of the Holocaust.

NOTES

1. Ronald Modras, *The Catholic Church and Anti-Semitism: Poland, 1933–1939* (Chur, Switzerland: Harwood Academic, 1994).

2. The text of *We Remember* can be found in United States Catholic Conference, *Catholics Remember the Holocaust* (Washington, DC: United States Catholic Conference, 1998), 47–56.

3. Cf, Judith H. Banki and John T. Pawlikowski, eds., *Ethics in the Shadow of the Holocaust: Christian and Jewish Perspectives* (Franklin, WI and Chicago: Sheed & Ward, 2001), 3–231.

4. *Catholics Remember the Holocaust*, 10.

5. Ibid., 14

6. Ibid.

7. Ibid., 34.

8. Ibid., 32

9. Edward Flannery, *The Anguish of the Jews: Twenty-Three Centuries of Anti-Semitism*, rev. ed., foreword by Philip A. Cunningham (New York/Mahwah, NJ: Paulist, 2004).

10. Marvin Perry and Frederick M. Schweitzer, *Anti-Semitism: Myth and Hate from Antiquity to the Present* (New York and Houndmills, UK: Palgrave Macmillan, 2002).

11. Paula Fredriksen, *Augustine and the Jews: A Christian Defense of Jews and Judaism* (New York/London: Doubleday, 2008).

12. Pontifical Biblical Commission, *The Jewish People and Their Sacred Scriptures in the Christian Bible* (Vatican City: Libreria Edifice Vaticana, 2002). For a discussion of the document, cf. the special issue of *The Bible Today*, May/June 2003.

13. Cardinal Joseph Ratzinger, "Interreligious Dialogue and Jewish-Christian Relations," *Communio*, 25:1 (1998): 29–41; *Many Religions—One Covenant* (San Francisco: Ignatius Press, 2000); "The Heritage of Abraham: The Gift of Christmas," *L'Osservatore Romano* (29 December 2001): 1.

14. Carol Rittner and Stephen D. Smith, eds., *No Going Back. Letters to Pope Benedict XVI on the Holocaust, Jewish-Christian Relations & Israel* (London: Quill Press in association with The Holocaust Centre, 2009).

15. Pope Benedict XVI, "First Major Meeting with World Jewish Leaders," *Origins,* 35:6 (23 June 2005): 88–89; "Visit to Cologne Synagogue," *Origins* 35:12 (1 September 2005): 205–207. Pope Benedict XVI's 26 October 2005, "Message to Cardinal Kasper" is available on the website of the Center for Jewish–Christian Learning at Boston College, www.bc.edu/research/cjl

16. Pope Benedict XVI, "Visit to the Cologne Synagogue," 206 and "French Visit: Meeting with Jewish Leaders," *Origins* 38:16 (25 September 2008): 248.

17. Pope Benedict XVI, "Meeting with American Jewish Leaders," *Origins* 38:38 (5 March 2009): 597–599.

18. Pope Benedict XVI, "Visit to the Cologne Synagogue," 206.

19. The text can be found on the website of the Center for Christian-Jewish Learning at Boston College, www.bc.edu/research/cjl/

20. Meinrad Scherer-Edmunds, "Never Again! The Pope's Visit to the Cologne Synagogue Was Both a Milestone and a Missed Opportunity," *U.S. Catholic* 70:11 (November 2005), 50. Also cf. *Commonweal* editorial, "Misremembered," 10 April 1998 and *Commonweal* editorial, CXXX111 12 (16 June 2006): 5, and my response in *Commonweal* 13 (16 July 2006): 2

21. Father Patrick Desbois, *The Holocaust by Bullets: A Priest's Journey to Uncover the Truth Behind the Murder of 1.5 Million Jews*. Foreword by Paul A. Shapiro (New York and Houndmills, UK: Palgrave Macmillan, 2008).

22. John T. Pawlikowski, "The Papacy of Pius XII: The Known and the Unknown," in Carol Rittner and John K. Roth, eds., *Pope Pius XII and the Holocaust* (London and New York: Leicester University Press, 2002), 56–69.

23. Cf. Letter of Rabbi Herbert A. Friedman to Dr. Eugene J. Fisher, National Conference of Catholic Bishops, 27 May 1997.

24. Michael Phayer, *The Catholic Church and the Holocaust, 1930–1965* (Bloomington and Indianapolis: Indiana University Press, 2000).

25. Henri de Lubac, *Christian Resistance to Anti-Semitism: Memories from 1940–1944* (San Francisco: Ignatius Press, 1990).

26. A. Ramatti, *The Assissi Underground: Priests Who Rescued Jews* (New York: Stein an Day, 1978), 50/

27. Gerhart M. Riegner, *Never Despair—Sixty Years in the Service of the Jewish People and the Cause of Human Rights* (Chicago: Ivan Dee in association with the United States Holocaust Memorial Museum), 2006.

28. Cf. Dariusz Libionka, "Against a Brick Wall. Interventions of Kazimierz Papee, the Polish Ambassador at the Holy See, with Regard to German Crimes in Poland. November 1942–January 1943," *Holocaust Studies and Materials: Journal of Polish Center for Holocaust Research,* 2008, 270–293

29. Richard Lukas, *Forgotten Holocaust: The Poles under German Occupation 1939–1944* (Lexington, KY: University Press of Kentucky, 1986), 16.

30. John Morley, *Vatican Diplomacy and the Jews during the Holocaust: 1939–1943* (New York: KATV, 1980), 209.

31. Georges Passelecq and Bernard Suchecky, *The Hidden Encyclical of Pius XI* (New York: Harcourt Brace & Company, 1997).

32. Michael Marrus, "The Vatican and Racism and Antsemitism, 1938–1939: A New Look at a Might-Have-Been," *Holocaust and Genocide Studies,* 11:3 (Winter 1997): 378–395.

33. Henry Friedlander, "The Manipulation of Language," in *The Holocaust: Ideology, Bureaucracy, and Genocide,* ed. Henry Friedlander and Sybil Milton (Millwood, NY: Kraus International Publications, 1980) 103–113.

Chapter Ten

Human Dignity and
Jewish–Christian Relations

Donald J. Dietrich

If we watch the TV news or read the news in papers or on computers, we are usually immersed in a sea of violence in which frequently the only feel-good story revolves around a dog or is on the back pages. Yet, Steven Pinker in his book, *The Better Angels of Our Nature: Why Violence Has Declined*[1] makes the case that our civilization has become more benign as the eighteenth century has progressed into the twenty-first. Seemingly, there has emerged a "climate of change," since the Enlightenment and the birthing of human rights, and this climate has led to reduced violence, even if we take into account the Holocaust as well as other instances of war and sanctioned murder.

As I approached the ambivalent issue of human dignity and violence for this lecture, I again came to realize how complex this topic really was and is, especially in light of the Holocaust, that cataclysmic evil that unfolded during the Third Reich (1933–1945). I could repeat as background the sordid history of Christian contempt encased in anti-Semitism, very much a theological and an institutional issue, but, I am sure you have heard it all from the early Christian charges of deicide to the so-called explication of the Jewish conspiracy in the *Protocols of the Elders of Zion.*[2] Even a casual glance at Amazon.com or Google under the heading "Holocaust" indicates the fantastic amount of research that has tried to expose this dark side of humanity. The "how" and the "why" of this evil eruption are still being plumbed in academic conferences and in the environs of the Holocaust Museum in Washington. Certainly, religion seems to have nurtured sanctioned murder. Christianity, it is now affirmed, was a necessary condition for the Holocaust. And yet, we can also see traces of religion actually building a more beneficent cultural climate that can support reflections on human dignity.

I began by investigating the climate that has been constructed in Jewish–Christian relations. There are, of course, all kinds of low points in these relations. But I start with a few of the highpoints and an array of reflections in the spirit of Raphael Lemkin's observation that "the function of memory is not only to register past events, but to stimulate human conscience."[3] Lemkin was a Jewish lawyer who fled Poland during the Holocaust and eventually ended up in the United States. He coined the term "genocide" and helped move the United States to adopt the 1948 Convention on the Prevention and Punishment of the Crime of Genocide. Significantly, he stresses memory and history as we deal with moral topics. There has been a sustained history of Jewish–Christian relations grounded in dialogue as well as some definitely negative insertions into the conversation.

In the United States, there have been Jewish–Christian partnerships and conversations, including self-critical ones, since the 1890s at least. In the 1930s, for example, Mildred Eakin at Drew University was studying the problematic teachings about Jews in Christian texts and was working to advance Jewish–Christian dialogue. Victoria Barnett at the Holocaust Museum has observed that two tracks of Jewish–Christian dialogue exist in the United States. One emerges out of Holocaust Studies, but another weaker strain has been nurtured without the Holocaust at its foundation.[4] The Holocaust, however, has been a seminal influence. As James Carroll aptly puts the point: "That it took the Holocaust to open an honorable and reciprocal dialogue between Christians and Jews is an outrage."[5] Parts of the post-1945 problem impacting on the dialogue revolve around relativizing Christianity in a world of pluralistic faith traditions as well as the problematic handling of the role of Pius XII and his canonization process, which is still controversial in Jewish–Christian relations. With Pius XII, tentative answers may well be the best that can be hoped for among theologians and historians. But the dialogue can be seen as the foundation for the climate leading to reflections on human dignity.

Institutionally, the issue of Jewish–Christian relations has emerged over the last few decades. In 1947, an international group of Jews and Christians gathered at Seelisberg, Switzerland. This international meeting of 65 Jews and Christians not only marked the formal founding of the International Council of Christians and Jews (ICCJ), which had taken place informally the year before, but also produced a crucial document known as the "Ten Points of Seelisberg: An Address to the Churches." This document reflected a dual challenge that the Holocaust raised for Jewish–Christian relations; (1) to clarify the historical record of what happened; and (2) to explore honestly what this history could mean for the interfaith relationship. The National Conference of Christians and Jews was initiated in the United States in 1928, but the ICCJ's post-Holocaust founding became the real catalyst for Jewish–Christian dialogue and launched aggressive efforts to combat anti-Semitism.[6]

In the post-Holocaust milieu, an interesting dialogue also evolved between Abraham Joshua Heschel, a Jewish scholar, and Reinhold Niebuhr, his Protestant counterpart. There are two sides to the Jewish–Christian dialogue as set forth by Niebuhr and Heschel: what Christianity and Judaism have in common and what they can accomplish together. One similarity shared by Christianity and Judaism is their common attitude toward history. Judaism and Christianity both have accepted discrete faith events in history as the genesis of the disclosure of the eternal mystery to humanity. Although Jews and Christians accept their faith by different events, they both affirm the importance of historical revelation. They both also address the identical human condition and ultimately agree that God is the source of man's redemption and the fulfillment of human history. Rabbi Heschel has also affirmed that Judaism has an interest in the destiny of Christianity, which also has a stake in Judaism.[7]

Additionally, however, more is needed for the dialogue than just the use of our cognitive abilities. Jewish–Christian dialogue, according to Heschel, will not progress if Jews and Christians focus merely on ritual, doctrine, institution, symbol, and theology. The real source for mutual understanding between Christians and Jews as well as the most fruitful level for interreligious dialogue is what Rabbi Heschel calls "depth theology." His theology of "wonder" and "radical amazement" teaches that Jews and Christians ought to live with "reverence and awe for the mystery that surrounds them" until they are "overwhelmed by glory."[8] Unfortunately, interfaith conversation is always threatened by what he calls the claim to cognitive finality, i.e., to absolute truth. The hope for meaningful dialogue between Jews and Christians is constantly threatened by factions of both religions, which insist that interaction is not possible because the other faith tradition is wrong, invalid, misguided, or a lie. An empathetic or emotional quality has to be present and this implies an authentic embrace of the Other.

There are always questions concerning the nature of interreligious dialogue. Do Christians and Jews run the risk of ignoring some of their faith practices and beliefs just for the sake of creating a conversation in the first place? As Niebuhr and Heschel would argue, none of this will happen if we approach interfaith dialogue from a position of respect, understanding, and acceptance. We have to be affectively attuned. This is why Niebuhr was such a strong critic of proselytization and Christian missionizing to convert Jews.[9] Both of these men helped set a tone for the serious engagement of Jews and Christians. Such engagement blossomed in the Catholic world with Vatican II (1962–65), a council of renewal and celebration.

In October 1965, the Second Vatican Council promulgated *Nostra Aetate*, its "Declaration on the Relation of the Church to Non-Christian Religions." A crucial document in Jewish–Christians relations, *Nostra Aetate* did not explicitly reflect on the Holocaust, but it did reject key elements of the Church's "teaching of contempt" against Jews and Judaism. *Nostra Aetate* decried "Hatred, persecution, displays of anti-Semitism, directed against Jews at any time and by anyone." Additionally, it rejected the pernicious deicide charge by proclaiming that the crucifixion of Jesus "cannot be charged against all Jews, without distinction, then alive, nor against the Jews of today." Furthermore, emphasizing the Jewish origins of Christianity *Nostra Aetate* affirmed that "God holds the Jews most dear."[10]

In hindsight, *Nostra Aetate*, which arrived two decades after Nazi Germany's defeat, may seem too little, too late, but it was groundbreaking for Christians and Jews at the time by opening doors for further steps in its revisionist direction. In retrospect, it can tentatively also be said that if *Nostra Aetate*'s teachings had been part of the institution's ethos and taken to heart, the Holocaust might have been blunted or, at least, not been accompanied with such widespread passive and active Christian support. *Nostra Aetate,* however, did not really do enough to call into question the assumption that Christianity considered itself superior to Judaism. This presumption ensured that Christianity became a necessary condition for the Holocaust. *Nostra Aetate*'s message was reinforced by Benedict XVI's book, *Jesus of Nazareth*, in which the Pope asserted that the Jewish people cannot be held guilty for the death of Jesus Christ. Abraham Foxman of the Anti-Defamation League noted that the book's release was an important and historic moment for Catholic–Jewish relations, one that would translate the teaching of *Nostra Aetate* into the pews. He suggested that Christians were beginning to deal with their supersessionist inclinations.[11]

Nostra Aetate is only one document issued by Vatican II and so really has to be embedded into the contemporary culture being outlined for renewal by the Catholic Church. Other documents embellish *Nostra Aetate* by stressing the universality and unity of the human race as well as the dignity of the human person. To see how this dialogue could play out, a look at the issue of covenant is useful. The dialogue between Catholics and Jews that has expanded for over four decades since *Nostra Aetate* has created a vision of reconciliation and deepened the spiritual bonds that Christians and Jews seem to share as a covenantal people. At the same time, the dialogue also has expressed in the foreground some fundamental theological differences and the painful legacy of the past experience of Jewish–Christian relations. From a Catholic perspective, Jews and Christians both belong to the one people of God, but the commonality has been lived in mystery through brokenness and fracture. Christians will have to enter into dialogue with a Judaism that is deeply injured, while also acknowledging that God's covenant with the Jews has never been revoked. The goal of both traditions is to give visible witness to the mystery of the covenant that is shared. Cardinal Walter Kasper has stated that Christians do not have as yet a comprehensive theology of Judaism, thus leaving many issues unresolved. [12] The people of God, comprised of Jews and Christians, still seems divided by fundamental theological issues and is tragically fractured, although healing has begun.

The ambivalence encased in this healing phenomenon can be observed in the March 1998 document, *We Remember: A Reflection on the Shoah*, a document widely anticipated to be the Catholic Church's long-awaited confrontation with the Vatican's problematic posture during World War II. *We Remember* referred to the Shoah as an unspeakable tragedy, emphasizing the fact that this disaster occurred in Europe with its long-standing Christian civilization. This fact raises the question of the relation between the Nazi persecution and the attitudes through the centuries of Christians toward Jews, even though no satisfactory response was provided. The document rightly stated that the history of Jewish–Christian relations has been tormented and quite malignant. It repudiated, however, anti-Semitism as well as racism and condemned absolutely all forms of genocide. [13]

Especially in Jewish circles, but also among many Christians, including Catholics, the reception for *We Remember* was mixed. Two perspectives in the document led to negative reactions; (1) *We Remember* argued that the Shoah was the work of a thoroughly modern neopagan regime. Nazi anti-Semitism, the document asserted, had its roots outside of the Christian community, and in pursuing its aims, it attacked the Church and persecuted her members. While acknowledging that some Christians were definitely oppressed and martyred for opposing Nazism, many readers of the document maintained that it centered on these points in Christianity's favor, and that recent research has increasingly objected to these benign observations. Specifically, *We Remember* unconvincingly separated Nazi anti-Semitism from Christian anti-Judaism. Differences do exist, but the document overly emphasized the distinctions, while connecting the exclusionary ideological principles too little. (2) *We Remember* acknowledged that Christian conduct during the Holocaust "was not that which might be expected from Christ's followers" and went on correctly to say that "for Christians, this heavy burden of conscience of their brothers and sisters during the Second World War must be a call to penitence." Certainly, individual Christians were guilty. Many Jews and Christians insisted that such language, however, did not properly allocate responsibility for Christian failure. *We Remember* had little, if anything, to say about the deficient behavior of the Roman Catholic institutional church during the Holocaust. The document created the doubtful impression that the Catholic rank and file, and not so much their leaders, were responsible for Christian failings. [14] The institution and its theology were portrayed in a favorable aspect, which in light of social psychology and learning theory is almost an impossible position to maintain, since the institution is historically responsible for theological traditions, including the historical development of anti-Judaism/anti-Semitism. Vatican II had correctly described a sinful church, composed of imperfect humans. *We Remember* tried to maintain the Church institutionally as a perfect society, a position rooted in medieval philosophy and presumably outdated after 1965. *We Remember*, therefore, was engaged in theological revisionism to protect the institution and not to respond to Holocaust victims.

While *We Remember* noted that Jewish–Christian relations had long been tormented and quite negative, the question "why?" did not get much attention. An adequate response to this issue would require definitively grappling with assumptions on the Christian side about the truth and so-called superiority of Christianity in relation to Judaism. This issue has been and still is tendentious.

In September 2000, several Jewish scholars responded to Christian efforts by drafting *Dabru Emet* (Speak truth) for publication in the New York Times. This document emphasized that, although irreconcilable differences were still present between Jews and Christians, both traditions also shared unique perspectives, including belief in the same God and normative texts from the Hebrew Bible. The document also took into account the positive changes that had emerged in the Christian community with respect to the Jewish people. Correctly asserting that Christianity's anti-Jewish teachings and policies had nurtured the Holocaust and so reflected Christian ideology from top to bottom, *Dabru Emet* encouraged "the continuation of recent efforts in Christian theology to repudiate unequivocally contempt for Judaism and the Jewish people." It declared that Nazism "was not solely a Christian phenomenon" and expressed profound gratitude for righteous Christians who had helped Jews during those dark times. The shifts that Christianity still had to take, it noted, could be labeled profound.[15] Some potholes would be encountered as the institutional Catholic Church tended in a more conservative direction that was more interested in defending the pre–Vatican II position than in exploring new paths. The tension between the two Catholic camps would be exacerbated as the new century began. The conversation between the two faith traditions has been spirited and controversial, which is not surprising given the distinct stakes at risk.

The Catholic Church unfortunately issued a document, *Dominus Jesus* (Lord Jesus), in the late summer of 2000. A declaration "On the Unity and Salvific Universality of Jesus Christ and the Church," *Dominus Jesus*, urged repeatedly that the Church's doctrines and dogmas in the declaration must be "firmly believed." The document contained at least two claims that considerably impacted the complexity of Jewish–Christian relations. One assumption was that "the salvation of all" comes uniquely, singularly, exclusively, universally, and absolutely through Jesus Christ. The other asserted that the

Church is intended by God to be "the instrument for the salvation of *all* humanity," a condition entailing that the "followers of other religions," even if they have received a trace of divine grace, remain "in a gravely deficient situation" compared to those who are fully within the Church. Such an approach was not conducive to maintaining dialogue.[16]

Dominus Jesus naively claimed that its absolutist teachings about Jesus Christ and the Church really expressed no disrespect for "the religions of the world." Subsequent Vatican commentary trying to blunt the outrage felt by many, insisted that the declaration was designed actually to guide Catholic theologians and the Catholic faithful. But a document is generally published for universal consumption, even if not for agreement. The Church's message evoked dissonance. *Dominus Jesus* insisted that the Vatican's version of Christianity should and does supersede every other religious tradition. In an increasingly pluralistic world, and definitely in a post-Holocaust context, that stance has to be seen as problematic. Adding fuel to the fire were some statements made by Cardinal Avery Dulles of New York.[17]

Dulles asserted that Vatican II had never resolved the question of Jewish covenantal inclusion from a traditional Christian perspective. He constructed his attack in a major address given at a 2005 conference in Washington, D.C., celebrating the fortieth anniversary of *Nostra Aetate*. In his address he maintained that there was a need to reintroduce the teaching of St. Paul's Letter to the Hebrews, in which several passages seem to present the Jewish covenant as abrogated following Christ's life. By the standards of Vatican II the Hebrews letter would need a great deal of hermeneutical exegesis in order to be sustainable in the developing Catholic approach to Judaism.[18]

Certainly, *Nostra Aetate* and successive documents did not resolve all the questions attached to a Christian theological perspective on the Church's relationship with Judaism. There is still the seeming contradiction between Paul's letter to the Romans 9–11, which insists that God's covenant with the Jews will not be revoked. Romans is the basic building block for the church's view of Judaism and basically ignores mentioning the problematic texts in Hebrews. Vatican II focused conciliar and papal authority by its selection of Romans 9–11 with its insistence on Jewish covenantal inclusion after Christ as the prevailing text for understanding Judaism's role today in a theological environment. This view has been sustained in subsequent Vatican statements and in the many pronouncements of John Paul II on Jewish–Christian relations. Dulles, therefore, stands on extremely shaky grounds from the standpoint of official Catholic teaching. Dulles himself has assured some persons privately that he was actually presenting a strictly "personal" position in his speeches and articles.[19] But why publish in scholarly venues, if you are only articulating private opinions? There are other places for such statements.

The real problem is that no one in the Vatican with its ecclesial hierarchies has publicly challenged Dulles' view. There seemingly has to be a public affirmation of *Nostra Aetate*, not just disputatious articles around divergent points, which cannot advance the dialogue begun by Vatican II. Do the declarations on Jewish–Christian relationship, it has to be asked, have relevance only when Christians are speaking to Jews or are they brought into the picture more universally when Christians are theologically conversing with themselves? In other words, should not Jewish–Christian relations be affecting institutional theology, since this was the charge of Vatican II? [20]

What do other church leaders and theologians say? There have emerged rays of hope with respect to bringing the theology of Jewish–Christian relationship into the mainstream of church thinking. The writings of such theologians as Johann Baptist Metz, who has asserted that the overall theological implications of the documents on Jewish–Christian relationship issued by the Christian churches during the last decades have significant implications in renewing the Christian tradition. Metz has insisted that the theological implications of the conversation go far beyond the parameters of the restricted Jewish–Christian dialogue. Especially after the Holocaust, Metz argues, they involve a revision of Christianity itself. [21] Metz himself is an "event" driven theologian and roots his scholarship in history, which some would suggest could lead to a relativization. He has stated that if the event, i.e., the Holocaust, is repellent, then there has to be a critique of the theology behind the culture that has shaped historical realities.

Metz's argument has also been replicated in the Leuenberg Church Fellowship, an association of Reformation churches in Europe. Its 2001 document, *Church and Israel,* has stressed that the relationship between the Church and Israel is not marginal, but actually represents a central dimension of Christian ecclesiology. The relationship with Israel can be seen as an indispensable foundational element for the Christian faith. From this perspective the Church has to reflect on its relationship with Judaism, because it has been linked to the Jewish community from its inception. Jewish and Christian theologies seemingly have to be linked. [22]

Additionally, such projects as the Oxford University–Princeton University Study Group have also struggled with the significant questions relative to the identities of both Jews and Christians as scholars increasingly have been showing that Jesus had no intention of beginning a totally new religious community and that Jews and Christians were interlocked for several centuries. Such scholarship should pose fundamental challenges for Christian and Jewish self-identities. A question has emerged. Will there be a retreat from scholarly efforts on the grounds that "faith" cannot be determined by historical scholarship or will all tools be available to the theologian? [23]

In the Catholic hierarchy, confusion reigns with respect to the Jewish–Christian relationship. Cardinal Joseph Bernardin became attached to the very complex picture of the "parting of the ways" offered by Dr. Robin Scroggs of the Chicago Theological Seminary. Research has suggested that the separation may well be pushed into the fourth century. [24] Cardinal Walter Kasper has asserted in his writings that there is no need to proselytize Jews because they have authentic revelation as a covenantal people. He has also referred to the notion of Christ's universal salvific work, but has not explicated how these notions can be integrated. Most Catholic theologians have generally called a halt to missionizing Jews. Cardinal Dulles, however, has written a strong critique of this position. [25] Even the new Good Friday prayer seems to reflect a bit of pre–Vatican II thinking of conversion. Evangelization still has remained a central issue given the conversation around covenant and Christ's injunction to teach all nations. It is perhaps also important for the Church to re-examine its self-identity as it has emerged in Jewish–Christian dialogue in order to engage with other religious traditions. The story is obviously continuing and issues have not been satisfactorily resolved for all concerned, but at least civil discussions have continued, and authentic problems are being addressed.

Christians will likely never come to the precise point where their Christological affirmations will lead to a theology of religious pluralism that will resonate with the perspectives of Judaism or any other world religion. They may, however, narrow the issue in the spirit of *Nostra Aetate,* which contends that every faith tradition contains a bit of God's revelation. Additionally, the development of new thinking about Christianity exemplified in the Jewish document *Dabru Emet* will not resolve all theological concerns about church teachings. But in the globalized world, in which interreligious understanding is not merely confined to the realm of theological ideas, but directly impacts the lives of persons living together as a civic community, theologians and others can ill afford to shrink from this challenge.

Beyond factions in the ecclesial establishment, what has been emerging in the concrete world? An op-ed story, "Honoring All Who Saved Jews" by Eva Wiesel appeared in the *New York Times.* It concerned Yad Vashem, the memorial for righteous gentiles. In Eva's case she was promoting the story of how she was saved from the Nazis by an Arab Muslim in the town of Mahdia in Tunisia. Human dignity on the ground seems to know no bounds. There is also Alan Wolfe's book, *Political Evil: What It Is and How to Combat It.* Wolfe asserts that we have religion that can help us understand that evil exists and politics as well as psychology that can help explain why it persists. Combining the two can offer a means to avoid the twin traps of bland indifference and overweening self-confidence, which have bedeviled those concerned with the nexus of politics and religion so much in a world marked by terror, genocide, and ethnic cleansing. In essence, those interested in this conundrum can understand the dynamics of evil as a first step in expunging it. [26]

What have Vatican II and such theologians as Metz contributed to an articulation of human dignity? Decades have passed since Vatican II set the tone for the new Catholic sensitivity toward history, contingency, and human dignity. But there seems to be a dissonance in what is being articulated by members of the hierarchy carefully guarding the program of the institutional church and theologians as well as lay Catholics, who are concerned with the complexities introduced with the real world's focus on marching soldiers. How can we portray this world of praxis and what does it mean in exploring the meaning of human dignity?

In the search for the concrete meaning of moral values, issues concerning the formation of conscience and the paths leading to moral development have become crucial concerns. Conscience as an ongoing human, i.e., historical, process of assessment and judgment is not simply the authoritative voice of God spoken in the Scriptures through words directed toward men and women. Reason, emotion, and memory are all evaluated by affective capacities as well as by abstract analysis and critical reflection. Despite the skepticism of postmodernists, some Christian philosophers and theologians think that there is considerable evidence, based on experience, of a common human morality that can be uncovered through an ongoing dialogue concerning God and the human condition and that such a development can occur in conversations in every faith tradition. From the most optimistic perspective, this dialogue can use personal/historical peculiarities to lead to a universal authentication of the common good. Conscience itself relies on the moral questioning that transpires in the communities, to which men and women belong. Moral anchorage is developed through the communities where persons are born and deliberately choose values through familial, religious, professional, and political relationships. People generally construct those values and principles that fit the specific communities that matter to them. Such a community is being created in Jewish–Christian relations, when viewed from its most adventurous and positive side. [27]

An evolving dissatisfaction with the traditional theological concept of "nature" has helped some theologians focus on the "human person" and "human dignity" rather than simply on abstract "humanity." Such post–Vatican II theologians as Metz are more historically attuned and have continued dissolving the traditional natural law paradigm by suggesting that more relevant moral standards should be rooted in the dignity of the human person who lives in concrete history. Vatican II's "Decree on Religious Freedom" opened with this very crucial statement: "A sense of the dignity of the human person has been impressing itself more and more deeply on the consciousness of man." [28]

In revisiting the meaning of the historical human condition and responding to real contingencies, those at Vatican II insisted that the right to religious freedom, for example, emanated from the very dignity of the human person. Their discussions shifted from the "scholastic" nature to the biblical, historical person, wherein human dignity now became the first principle of moral reasoning. God's revelation, they insisted, embraced the entire human person and race. Humanity was to be viewed from a holistic perspective as the imaging forth of God's love and as the co-creator with God of this world. Individuality as a philosophical concept was to distinguish each human from every other, while personhood, more of a theological and affective notion, was to bind humans to one another. [29]

Especially since 1945, existential and personalistic patterns of moral reflection along with the re-appropriation of the reality that theology and reason are embedded in history have led some theologians to view change, pluralism, and even diversity as positive contributions to human development. Because humans are in the Judeo-Christian tradition sharing the Genesis notion of the "image of God" and have one destiny, a shared moral program among persons in these communities can be derived and explicated as the primary creational task at every level of society. Such theologians as Metz and his disciple, Didier Pollefeyt, have focused their work on the Christian message of compassion for the marginalized victims of sociopolitical oppression, who as humans reflect the image of God. Metz's experiences in Nazi Germany, for example, as well as his reflections on the Holocaust make him a good contemporary representative of the reform theology that has been gestating in the Catholic tradition. [30]

For Metz, instrumental in developing this new political perspective, theology has meant speaking to God in history. Metz's orientation has been dictated by the need to respond to historical facts and to uncover what dynamically structures political societies. From this perspective, attending to God always means to speak about what Vatican II has called the "signs of the times." The sign, without which no Christian in our context should speak of God today, is Auschwitz and all that the Final Solution has meant up to the present. Political theology, historically centered on the person, has been generated in a culture, inspired by Vatican II, but one that also includes sanctioned, administrative murder. This context has promoted authentic discussion in devising a Jewish–Christian relation that can make some sense. The barbarities, for which Auschwitz stands, have to be considered a challenge to religion and the norms of human rights, explored in dialogue with all religious traditions. [31]

Political theology, conceived as a way of doing theology after Auschwitz, developed a hermeneutic, i.e., a way of interpretation, that was designed to address the sufferings of people in society and history. Political theologians have argued that the theodicy question, i.e., why does a good God permit evil, has to be the foundation for contemporary God talk. Auschwitz as an event represents a drastic rupture in historical consciousness and the traditional philosophical responses to evil both among Christian and Jewish theologians. Traditional theodicy has been exposed in recent works as perpetrating amoral justifications for evil and rationalistic caricatures of the life of faith. The Holocaust, two World Wars, and several instances of genocide, i.e., sanctioned murder, have been designated as historical landmarks that have reshaped Christian and Jewish reflections on evil and suffering, as well as God's response to brutality. Traditional theodicy, based on human freedom, may be seen as legitimizing suffering and undermining protest and resistance.[32] What is needed in theology is a space for resistance, in which freedom confronts and, hopefully, limits evil in our sociopolitical milieu.

Jews and Christians can recognize a way to handle the ambiguities of traditional theodicy by stressing the insight revolving around the human role in constructing society. Both religious traditions contain a stress on the fact that men and women have a responsibility to create a just and equitable society. When tempted to ask why God allows or even causes evil, one can respond that God has created in humans the instrument to alleviate evil. Such an approach can lead to a line of thought in both traditions that the work of creating the kingdom of God in this sinful world is ongoing.

Metz developed an intolerance for all theologies that did not recognize the socially critical character of faith. The Bible with its two scriptures was viewed by Metz, for example, as a narrative primarily concerned with resistance to socially caused suffering and as fundamentally eschatological in impulse. Faith and suffering were not to be seen as contradictory. The kind of faith that is plausible in the face of suffering, according to Metz, is the prophetic model of biblical faith that faced collective suffering. Metz has elaborated his model of political faith by using categories of memory, narrative, hope, and solidarity.[33]

For Metz, World War II and the Holocaust assumed a primary memory role that has shaped his theology. He has asserted that the Christian response to suffering ought to give the Holocaust victims authority with respect to the religious interpretation of this catastrophe and should remind theologians of the sociopolitical fractures that seem to characterize modern culture. Theologians, then, have several duties. First, there has to be a radical transition from systematic, i.e., philosophical, concepts to subject concepts. Second, a theology sensitive to the violation of human dignity must have the capacity to provide a broad and deeply analytical grasp of the present in light of the past. Third, theology must protect the narratives of the victims. Fourth, theologians have to criticize every act of distancing themselves from the suffering of others. The suffering person must be allowed to speak.[34]

In brief, theory alone cannot change the world because this would reduce political activity to merely instrumental manipulation. As can be seen from past experiences, "scientific theory" and its accompanying technology have historically tended to elicit authoritarian or totalitarian behavior in practice. Theory needs the corrective of concrete praxis. The history of our times has warned men and women about promoting any ideology as the system of principles that could be used to organize society.[35] Praxis is delineated as and necessitated to be dialectical and intentionally transformative. Liberating praxis has as its goal the commitment to and solidarity with other persons.

In light of what Metz has suggested, the book, *Genocide in Jewish Thought* by David Patterson, illuminates the role of theology in this post-Auschwitz era. His book begins with a telling quote from Primo Levi: "They will even take away our name: and if we want to keep it, we will have to find the strength in ourselves to do so."[36] Patterson contends that the roots of genocide have penetrated into modes of thought as well as into social mores, economic conditions, and political movements. The foundational feature of the mode of thought at the heart of genocide is a thought process that restricts men and women into the isolation of a rational, abstract ego and that blinds them to the faces of their fellow human beings. Patterson's basic themes are: (1) the mass murder of humanity originates with an abstract view of humanity, which sees concrete individuals of flesh and blood as faceless individuals of a species; (2) a corrective to mass murder can be found in a concrete mode of thought; (3) Jewish thought exhibits a felicitous model for such a grounding.[37] Genocidal actions are rooted in speculative abstractions, which is what Metz would also affirm.

Patterson has quite correctly analyzed traditional Christian thought. Abstract thinking opens the way to mass murder through depersonalization. Such abstract modes of thought are characterized by egocentric, creed-based approaches to life that deny the flesh-and-blood life for the sake of an other-worldly realm.[38] Philosophical abstractions prominent, for example, in traditional Christian theology and in the Enlightenment are also dangerous and include: individualistic freedom without the mediation of the community, autonomy, self-legislation, and egocentrism. Such aspects of thinking about humanity can be dangerous.[39] Freedom can liberate and provide the values at the base of democratic political systems and so can be seen as beneficial. But what about freedom present in autonomous creatures who plan the biological components of a faceless, racist society as the Nazis tried to do? Jewish thought would stress, asserts Patterson, that authenticity is constructed by concrete action toward one another as persons, not by abstract belief in itself.[40] Patterson's view concludes that religion is not necessarily at the core of genocide. Indeed, the religion that is at the core of genocide is the religion of egocentric idolatry (traditional, philosophical Christianity) and not the religion of the God of Abraham, Isaac, and Jacob.[41] Annulment of the ego is at the core of their commandments. Viktor Frankl caught the core of Patterson's thought in his *Man's Search for Meaning* when he says that the salvation of man is "through love and in love," which means that relationships trump everything.[42]

In conclusion, probing beneath the everyday surface[43] of civilization has become imperative because Auschwitz as a fact has insisted that we question the basic value assumptions at the very core of our culture—the nature of progress, the effect of science and technology on our culture, the significance of the nation state, the role of religion, and certainly the concept of individualistic morality, which for too long has absolved corrupt institutions. John XXIII has suggested that at the basis of any human coexistence that should be well ordered and fruitful must lie the principle that every human being is in essence a person. A person is defined by concrete relationships or as Frankl says by love. Relationships are noted for inclusivity and a lack of marginalization. Real relationships delicately balance individualism and sacred dignity. Genesis 1:26 can help us understand this relational issue. Here God says: "let us make man." Whom is God addressing? Some Jewish sages have thought that God was talking to the potential Adam, whom God's plan envisages, but who can only be fully actualized if God and His creation cooperate. This initial covenant made the free person a partner with God to fulfill creation's destiny or to destroy it.[44]

Reflecting on religion and public policy is necessary. Religion can certainly lead into or nurture barbaric activities. But it can also serve as a transformative agent in redirecting persons toward a beneficent goal by helping to create a more propitious climate. Despite controversy among its participants, the Jewish–Christian relationship has opened a way to enter into the dialogue that can focus on the common good and human rights as long as it is recalled that a conversation cannot be one-sided. The relationship can and, indeed, has helped create a cultural climate, in which human values can be explicated more fully. And, finally, it perhaps can open ways in which the dialogical approach can be expanded into other religious traditions. The task before us as co-creators is that the challenge of the dialogue must be met enthusiastically.

NOTES

1. Steven Pinker, *The Better Angels of Our Nature: Why Violence Has Declined* (New York: Penguin, 2011).

2. Donald J. Dietrich, *God and Humanity in Auschwitz: Jewish–Christian Relations and Sanctioned Murder* (New Brunswick, NJ: Transaction Publishers, 1995), pp. 15–60; Edward Flannery, *The Anguish of the Jews: Twenty-Three Centuries of Anti-Semitism* (New York: Paulist Press, 1985).

3. Israel Charney, ed. *The Encyclopedia of Genocide* (Santa Barbara, CA: ABC – Clio, 1999). 2:79.

4. John Roth, "The Holocaust's Impact on Jewish–Christian Relations in the United States: Looking Back and Forward from 2011," in a paper presented at the Organization of American Historians in Houston, Texas on March 19, 2011, pp. 36–37.

5. James Carroll, *Constantine's Sword: The Church and the Jews* (New York: Houghton Mifflin, 2011), p. 54.

6. Roth, pp. 11–12; Victoria Barnett, "Interreligious Dialogue since the Holocaust: Turning Points and the Next Steps," in Carol Rittner, ed., *Learn Teach Prevent: Holocaust Education in the 21st Century* (Greenburg, PA: Seton Hall University, 2010), pp. 19.

7. Reinhold Niebuhr, "The Relations of Jews and Christians in Western Civilization," in Robert McAfee Brown, ed., *The Essential Reinhold Niebuhr: Selected Essays and Addresses*

(Binghampton, NY: Vail-Ballou Press, 1986), pp. 182–190; Abraham Heschel, "No Religion is an Island," in Susannah Heschel, ed., *Moral Grandeur and Spiritual Audacity* (New York: Farrar, Straus, and Giroux, 1995), p. 242.

8. Abraham, Heschel, "What We Might Do Together" in Susannah Heschel, *Moral Grandeur*, pp. 295–297.

9. Abraham, Heschel, "No Religion," p. 247.

10. See the text *Nosta Aetate* in Geoffrey Wigoder, *Jewish–Christian Relations since the Second World War* (Manchester, UK: Manchester University Press, 1988), pp. 143–144.

11. Roth, pp. 14–15, 42.

12. Dietrich, *God and Humanity*, pp. 91, 162–169, 176–182ff.

13. *Catholics Remember the Holocaust* (Washington, DC: Secretariat for Ecumenical and Religious Affairs, National Council of Catholic Bishops, 1998), pp. 47–56; *Catholic Teaching on the Shoah: Implementing the Holy See's We Remember* (Washington, DC: Secretariat for Ecumenical and Religious Affairs, National Conference of Catholic Bishops, 2001).

14. Roth, pp. 17, 43.

15. See, http://www.sacredheart,edu/pages1924_dabru_emet_september_10_2000_.cfm.

16. Roth, p. 20; http://www.vatican.va/,,,/rc_con_cfaith_doc_20000806_dominus_jesus_en.

17. Roth, p. 20.

18. John Pawlikowski, "Moving the Christian-Jewish Dialogue to a New Level: Can It Happen?" a paper presented at the Stadt Heidelberg–ICCJ Agreement in Heidelberg, Germany, 2008, p. 3; http://catholiccincinnati.org/wp-content/uploads/2010/11 Moving the Christian-Jewish Dialogue.pdf.

19. Pawlikowski, p.3.

20. Ibid., 4.

21. Ibid., 6.

22. Ibid.

23. Ibid., 8.

24. Ibid., 9.

25. Ibid., 11–12

26. Eva Wiesel, "Honoring All Who Saved Jews," in *New York Times,* December 28, 2011, p. A21; Alan Wolfe, "Evil Intent," *Boston College Magazine*, 71:3 (2011), pp. 22–26.

27. Donald J. Dietrich, *Human Rights and the Catholic Tradition* (New Brunswick, NJ: Transaction Publishers, 2007), pp. 181–182.

28. Dietrich, *Human Rights*, p. 182.

29. Ibid.

30. Ibid., 182–183.

31. Ibid., 183.

32. Ibid., 183–184; Johann Baptist Metz, "Theologie als Theodizee," in Willi Oelmüllerk, ed., *Theodizee: Gott vor Gericht?* (Munich: Funk-Verlag, 1990), pp. 103–108; Sarah Pinnock, *Beyond Theodicy: Jewish and Continental Thinkers Respond to the Holocaust* (Albany, NY: State University of New York Press, 2002), pp. xi, 1, 7, 20–21.

33. Pinnock , p. 81.

34. Johann Baptist Metz, "Communicating a Dangerous Memory," in Fred Lawrence, ed., *Communicating a Dangerous Memory: Soundings in Political Theology* (New York: Scholars Press, 1987), p. 39; Ekkehard Schuster, *Hope Against Hope: Johann Baptist Metz and Elie Wiesel Speak Out on the Holocaust* (New York: Paulist Press, 1999).

35. Dietrich, *Human Rights* p. 193; Richard Bernstein, *The Restructuring of Social and Political Theory* (New York: Harcourt Brace, 1976), pp. 217

36. Primo Levi's quote in David Patterson, *Genocide in Jewish Thought* (Cambridge University Press, 2012), p. 1.

37. Patterson, p. 2

38. Ibid.

39. Ibid.

40. Ibid., 9.

41. Ibid., 13.

42. Viktor Frankl, *Man's Search for Meaning* (Boston: Beacon Press, 2006), p. 37.

43. Dietrich, *God and Humanity*, pp. 292ff.

44. André Neher. "The Silence of Auschwitz." In Michael Berenbaum and John K. Roth. Eds., *Holocaust: Religious and Philosophical Implications* (New York: Paragon House, 1989) pp. 12–13.

Selected Bibliography

In addition to the bibliography noted by contributors to this volume, I have included books published in the twenty-first century relevant to the topic. The majority of these works deal with Jewish–Christian dialogue, although some treat dialogical issues that shed light on the role religion can play in seeking to change the world.

Allen, John L. Jr. "Thinking straight about Israel, the Jews and the Archbishop." *National Catholic Reporter.* October 27, 2010.
Anderson, Gary. "Does the Promise Still Hold? Israel and the Land." *Christian Century,* January 13, 2009.
Banki, Judith H. and John T. Pawlikowski, eds. *Ethics in the Shadow of the Holocaust: Christian and Jewish Perspectives.* Franklin, WI: Sheed & Ward, 2001.
Bard, Michael. "United Nations: The U.N. Relationship with Israel." *The Jewish Virtual Library,* last modified December 2013, http://www.jewishvirtuallibrary.org/jsource/UN/israel_un.html.
Beinart, Peter. "The Failure of the American Jewish Establishment." *New York Times*, May 12, 2010, http://www.nybooks.com/articles/archives/2010/jun/10/failure-american-jewish-establishment.
Berger, Alan L., ed. *Trialogue and Terror: Judaism, Christianity, and Islam after 9/11.* Eugene: Cascade Publishing, 2012.
Berger, Alan L. and David Patterson. *Jewish-Christian Relations: Drawing Honey from the Rock.* St. Paul: Paragon House, 2008.
Bergoglio, Jorge Mario and Abraham Skorka. *On Heaven and Earth.* Translated by Alejandro Bermudez and Howard Goodman. New York: Image.2013.
Besser, James. "Hyperbole about J Street." *The Jewish Week*, January 26, 2011, http://www.thejewishweek.com/blogs/political_insider/hyperbole_about_j_street).
Bishop Riah Abu El-Assal, interview with Julia Fisher January 26, 2002, St George's Cathedral, Jerusalem.
Bleich, J. "Entering a non-Jewish House of Worship." *Tradition* 44, no. 2 (2011): 73–102.
Borowsky, Irvin J. *Defining New Christian/Jewish Dialogue.* New York: Crossroad, 2004.
Boys, Mary. *Has God Only One Blessing?* Mahawa, NJ: Paulist Press, 2000.
———. *Redeeming Our Sacred Story: The Death of Jesus and Relations between Jews and Christians.* Mahwah: New Jersey, 2014.

————. *Seeing Judaism Anew: Christianity's Sacred Obligation.* Lanham, MD: Rowman and Littlefield, 2005.

Brill, Alan. *Judaism and Other Religions: Models of Understanding.* New York: Palgrave Macmillan, 2010.

————. *Judaism and World Religions: Encountering Christianity, Judaism, Islam, and Eastern Traditions.* New York: Palgrave Macmillan, 2012.

Carroll, James. "Additional Perspectives on *Passion of the Christ.*" *Harvard Divinity Bulletin,* Summer (2004): 34

————. *Constantine's Sword: The Church and the Jews.* New York: Houghton Mifflin, 2001.

————. *Toward a New Catholic Church: The Promise of Reform* Boston: Houghton Mifflin, 2002.

Catholic Church. *Catholic Teaching on the Shoah: Implementing the Holy See's We Remember.* Washington, DC: Secretariat for Ecumenical and Religious Affairs, National Conference of Catholic Bishops, 2001.

Connelly, John. *From Enemy to Brother: The Revolution in Catholic Teaching on the Jews 1933–1965.* Cambridge: Harvard University Press, 2012.

Cook, Michael. "The Mel Gibson Ordeal: An Insider's Account." *The Chronicle: Hebrew Union College-Jewish Institute of Religion,* Issue 63, 2004, 14–15.

————. *Modern Jews Engage the New Testament: Enhancing Jewish Well-Being in a Christian Environment.* Woodstock, VT: Jewish Lights, 2008.

Cunningham, Philip. *The Catholic Church and the Jewish People: Recent Reflections from Rome.* New York: Fordham University Press, 2007.

Cunningham, Philip, Joseph Sievers, Mary C. Boys, Hans Hermann Henrix and Jesper Svartvik, eds. *Christ Jesus and the Jewish People Today: New Explorations of Theological Interrelationships.* Eerdmans Publishing Company, 2011.

Davis, Stephen T. "Genocide, Despair, and Religious Hope: An Essay on Human Nature." In *Genocide and Human Rights: A Philosophical Guide,* edited by John K. Roth. New York: Palgrave Macmillan, 2005.

Desbois, Patrick. *The Holocaust by Bullets: A Priest's Journey to Uncover the Truth behind the Murder of 1.5 Million Jews.* New York: Palgrave Macmillan, 2008.

Dietrich, Donald J. *Human Rights and the Catholic Tradition.* New Brunswick, NJ: Transaction Publishers, 2007.

DiSegni, Riccardo. "Steps Taken and Questions Remaining in Jewish-Christian Relations Today." In *The Catholic Church and the Jewish People from Vatican II to Today.* Pontifical Gregorian University, October 19, 2004. Available on line at https://www.bc.edu/dam/files/research_sites/cjl/texts/center/conferences/Bea_Centre_C-J_Relations_04–05/DiSegni.htm.

Donahue, William. Qtd in David Berger, "Jews, Christians, and 'The Passion.'" *Commentary,* 117, May, 2004, 30.

Flannery, Edward. *The Anguish of the Jews: Twenty-Three Centuries of Antisemitism,* Revised edition. New York: Paulist, 2004.

Frankl, Viktor. *Man's Search for Meaning.*Boston: Beacon Press, 2006.

Fredriksen, Paula. *Augustine and the Jews: A Christian Defense of Jews and Judaism.* New York/London: Doubleday, 2008.

Frymer-Krensky, Tikva Novak, David Novak, Peter Ochs, David Fox Sandmel, and Michael A. Signer, eds. *Christianity in Jewish Terms.* Boulder: Westview Pess, 2000.

Gibson, Mel. "Interview with Diane Sawyer." ABC, February, 2004.

Greenberg, Irving. "Anti-Semitism in 'The Passion.'" *Commonweal,* May 7, 2004, 12.

————. *For the Sake of Heaven and Earth: The New Encounter between Judaism and Christianity.* Philadelphia: Jewish Publication Society, 2004.

Grob, Leonard and John K. Roth, eds. *Encountering the Stranger: A Jewish Christian, and Muslim Trialogue.* Seattle: University of Washington Press, 2012.

Gushee, David P. *Righteous Gentiles of the Holocaust: Genocide and Moral Obligation.* St. Paul: Paragon House , 2003.

Janssen, Peter E. *Adventures in Dialogue: The Jerusalem Rainbow Group.* Jerusalem: Ein Karem, 2013.

Jewish Council for Public Affairs. http://engage.jewishpublicaffairs.org/p/dia/action/public/?action_KEY=4504

Jihad Watch. "Melkite Patriarch Gregory III: Jihad attacks on Middle Eastern Christians Have All Been a Zionist Plot," by Robert Spencer, Dec 17, 2010, http://www.jihadwatch.org/2010/12/melkite-patriarch-gregory-iii-jihad-attacks-on-middle-eastern-christians-have-all-been-a-zionist-plo.html (and elsewhere).

JStreet. *The Political Home for Pro-Israel, Pro-Peace Americans.* http://jstreet.org/.

Kessler, Edward H., Judith Banki, and John T. Pawlikowski, eds. *Jews and Christians in Conversation.* Cambridge: Orchard Academic, 2002.

Korn, Eugene. "The People Israel, Christianity and the Covenantal Responsibility to History." In *Covenant and Hope: Christian and Jewish Reflections,* edited by Robert Jensen and Eugene Korn, 145–172. Grand Rapids: Eerdmans Publishing Co., 2012.

———. Qtd. in Tim Reidy, "The Holy Land and the Church in the Middle East." *America, The National Catholic Review,* January 31, 2011, http://americamagazine.org/node/127227.

Korn, Eugene B. and John T. Pawlikowski, eds. *Two Faiths, One Covenant?: Jewish and Christian Identity in the Presence of the Other.* Lanham, MD: Rowman & Littlefield Publishers, 2005.

Kotzkin, Michael. "Facing the Unresolved Issue in Interfaith Dialogue." *Forward Forum,* October 28, 2005, 11.

Kujawa-Holbrook, Sheryl. *God beyond Borders: Interreligious Learning among Faith Communities.* Eugene: Pickwick, 2014.

Levinas, Emmanuel. "In the Name of the Other." In *Is It Righteous to Be? Interviews with Emmanuel Levinas.* Edited by Jill Robbins. Translated by Maureen V. Gedney, 192. Stanford: Stanford University Press, 2001.

Levine, Amy-Jill. *The Meaning of the Bible: What the Jewish Scriptures and the Christian Old Testament Can Teach Us.* New York: HarperOne, 2011.

Levine, Amy-Jill and Marc Z. Brettler. *The Jewish Annotated New Testament* New York: Oxford University Press, 2011.

Lindsey, Hal. "Israel, Nation of Miracles." *WorldNet Daily Exclusive Commentary,* April 1, 2004, http://www.wnd.com/news/article.asp?ARTICLE_ID=37842]).

Melkite Greek Catholic Church Web site. http://melkite.org.

Niebuhr, Gustave. *Beyond Tolerance. Searching for Interfaith Understanding in America.* New York: Viking, 2008.

Patterson, David. *Genocide in Jewish Thought.* New York: Cambridge University Press, 2012.

Patterson, Stephen J. *Beyond the Passion: Rethinking the Death and Life of Jesus.* Minneapolis: Fortress, 2004.

Pawlikowski, John. "*Nostra Aetate* Today: Reflections 40 Years After Its Call for a New Era of Interreligious Relations" (plenary address, Rome, Pontifical Gregorian University, September 25, 2005).

Pawlikowski, John T. and Jon Nilson. *Christ in the Light of the Christian-Jewish Dialogue.* New York: Paulist Press, 2001.

———. "Moving the Christian-Jewish Dialogue to a New Level: Can It Happen?" Stadt Heidelberg–ICCJ Agreement in Heidelberg, Germany, 3. 2008.

———. "The Papacy of Pius XII: The Known and the Unknown." In *Pope Pius XII and the Holocaust,* edited by Carol Rittner and John K. Roth, 56–69. New York: Leicester University Press, 2002.

———. *Restating the Catholic Church's Relationship with the Jewish People: The Challenge of Super-Sessionary Theology.* Lewiston, NY: The Edwin Mellen Press, 2013.

Perry, Marvin and Frederick M. Schweitzer. *Antisemitism: Myth and Hate from Antiquity to the Present.* New York: Palgrave Macmillan, 2002.

Phayer, Michael. *The Catholic Church and the Holocaust, 1930–1965* (Bloomington: Indiana University Press, 2000.

Pinker, Steven. *The Better Angels of Our Nature: Why Violence Has Declined.* New York: Penguin, 2011.

Pinnock, Sarah. *Beyond Theodicy: Jewish and Continental Thinkers Respond to the Holocaust.* Albany, NY: State University of New York Press, 2002.

Pontifical Biblical Commission. *The Jewish People and Their Sacred Scriptures in the Christian Bible*. Vatican City: Libreria Edifice Vaticana, 2002.

Pope Benedict XVI. "First Major Meeting with World Jewish Leaders." *Origins,* 35:6 (2005): 88–89;

———. "French Visit: Meeting with Jewish Leaders." *Origins* 38:16 (2008): 248.

———. "Meeting with American Jewish Leaders." *Origins* 38:38 (2009): 597–599.

———. "Message to Cardinal Kasper." www.bc.edu/research/cjl

———. "Visit to Cologne Synagogue." *Origins* 35:12 (2005): 205–207.

Ratzinger, Joseph. *Many Religions—One Covenant.* San Francisco: Ignatius Press, 2000.

———. "The Heritage of Abraham: The Gift of Christmas." *L'Osservatore Romano,* (December 29, 2001): 1.

Rhodes, Richard. *Masters of Death: The SS-Einsatzgruppen and the Invention of the Holocaust.* New York: Alfred A. Knopf, 2002

Riegner, Gerhart M. Letter to the editor, *SIDIC* (Rome), September 5, 2000.

———. *Never Despair—Sixty Years in the Service of the Jewish People and the Cause of Human Rights.* Chicago: Ivan Dee in association with the United States Holocaust Memorial Museum, 2006.

Rittner, Carol and Stephen D. Smith. *No Going Back. Letters to Pope Benedict XVI on the Holocaust, Jewish-Christian Relations & Israel.* London: Quill Press in association with The Holocaust Centre, 2009.

Roth, John K. *Ethics during and after the Holocaust: The Shadow of Birkenau.* London: Palgrave Macmillan, 2005.

———. "The Holocaust's Impact on Christian-Jewish Relations in the United States: Looking Back and Forward from 2011." *Organization of American Historians,* (March 19, 2011): 36–37.

Rubenstein, Richard L. "The Exposed Fault Line." In *After the Passion is Gone: American Religious Consequences*, edited by J. Shawn Landres and Michael Berenbaum, 207. Walnut Creek, CA: Altamira Press, 2004.

———. *Jihad and Genocide*. Lanham, MD: Rowan and Littlefield,2010.

Rudin, James A. *The Baptizing of America: The Religious Right's Plans for the Rest of Us.* New York: Thunder Mouth's Press, 2006.

———. *Christians & Jews Faith to Faith: Tragfic History, Promising Present, Fragile Future.* Woodstock: VT., Jewish Lights, 2011.

Sacks, Jonathan. *The Dignity of Difference: How to Avoid the Clash of Civilizations.* New York: Continuum, 2003.

Sanders, Theresa. *Tenebrae: Holy Week after the Holocaust.* Maryknoll, NY: Orbis Books, 2006.

Scherer-Edmunds, Meinrad. "Never Again! The Pope's Visit to the Cologne Synagogue Was Both a Milestone and a Missed Opportunity." *U.S. Catholic* 70:11 (2005): 50.

Sister Rose's Passion directed by Oren Jacoby (New Jersey Studios, LLC, 2004), DVD.

Small, Joseph D. and Gilbert S. Rosenthal, eds. *Let Us Reason Together: Christians and Jews in Conversation.* Louisville, KY: Witherspoon Press, 2010.

Spector, Stephen. *Evangelicals and Israel: the Story of American Christian Zionism.* Oxford: Oxford University Press, 2008.

Stassen, Glenn and David P. Gushee. *Kingdom Ethics: Following Jesus in Contemporary Context*. Downers Grove, IL: InterVarsity Press, 2003.

Swidler, Leonard, Reuven Firestone, and Khalid Duran. *Trialogue: Jews, Christians, and Muslims*. New London: Twenty-Third Publications, 2007.

The Jerusalem Fund. "Selected Documents Regarding Palestine: Hamas Charter (1988)." http://www.thejerusalemfund.org/www.thejerusalemfund.org/carryover/documents/charter.html.

Vatican Web site. "The Holy See Press Office, English Edition." http://www.vatican.va/news_services/press/sinodo/documents/bollettino_24_speciale-medio-oriente-2010/02_inglese/b11_02.html

Wegner, Gregory Paul. *Anti-Semitism and Schooling Under the Third Reich.* New York: Routledge Falmer, 2002.

Wiesel, Eva. "Honoring All Who Saved Jews." In *New York Times,* December 28, 2011, A21.

Wolfe, Alan. "Evil Intent." *Boston College Magazine*, 71:3, 2011, 22–26.
Wyschogrod, Michael. *Abraham's Promise: Judaism and Jewish-Christian Relations*. Grand Rapids: Eedrmans Publishing Company, 2004.

Index

About the Contributors

Alan L. Berger is the Raddock Family Eminent Scholar Chair of Holocaust Studies at Florida Atlantic University where he also directs the Center for the Study of Values and Violence After Auschwitz. Among the dozen books he has authored, co-authored, and edited are *Jewish-Christian Dialogue: Drawing Honey from the Rock* (co-authored with David Patterson); *Second Generation Voices: Reflections by Children of Holocaust Survivors and Perpetrators* (with his wife Naomi, winner of the B'nai Zion National Media Award); *Children of Job: American Second Generation Witnesses to the Holocaust*; and *Trialogue & Terror: Judaism/Christian/Islam After 9/11*. He edits the series Studies in Genocide: Religion, History, and Human Rights (Rowman & Littlefield). Berger holds a Doctor of Letters, *Honoris Causa* from Luther College.

Mary C. Boys is the Dean of Academic Affairs and Skinner and McAlpin Professor of Practical Theology at Union Theological Seminary in the City of New York. Among her many publications is her recently released *Redeeming Our Sacred Story: The Death of Jesus and Relations between Jews and Christians*. A Roman Catholic, she is a member of the Sisters of the Holy Names.

James Carroll is the author of eleven novels and seven works of non-fiction, including the National Book Award–winning *An American Requiem*; the New York Times bestselling *Constantine's Sword*, now an acclaimed documentary; *House of War*, which won the first PEN-Galbraith Award; and *Jerusalem, Jerusalem: How the Ancient City Ignited Our Modern World*, which was named a 2011 Best Book by Publishers Weekly. He lectures widely, both in the United States and abroad. Houghton Mifflin Harcourt published his eleventh novel, *Warburg in Rome,* and Viking will publish *Christ Actually: The Son of God for The Secular Age*, his eighth work of non-fiction. He is Distinguished Scholar-in-Residence at Suffolk University in Boston, where he lives with his wife, the novelist Alexandra Marshall. His *Boston Globe* columns won the 2012 Scripps Howard National Journalism Award for Commentary. The Judges' comment: "James Carroll's elegant style and historical depth of knowledge combine with his thoughtful, moral point of view to consistently provide his readers with a unique voice." He has also been termed "one of the most adept and versatile writers on the American scene today" (Denver Post).

Donald J. Dietrich (OBM) was Chair of and Professor in the Department of Theology at Boston College. He focused his research and publications on German Catholic experiences ranging from the Tübingen School of Theology to the Third Reich. Among his books are *Christian Responses to the Holocaust: Moral and Ethical Issues*. Editor, (Syracuse University Press), *Human Rights and the Catholic Tradition, God and Humanity in Auschwitz: Jewish-Christian Relations*, and *Sanctioned Murder* (Transaction Publishers), and *Catholic Citizens in the Third Reich: Psycho-Social Principles and Moral Reasoning* (Rutgers University Press). He was a member of the committee on Church Relations and the Holocaust and the Center for Advanced Studies at the United States Holocaust Memorial Museum.

Irving Greenberg has served in the Rabbinate (Orthodox) academia (associate professor of History, Yeshiva University; Professor of Jewish Studies at City College City University of New York), and Jewish communal life (Founding President, CLAL: The National Jewish Center for Learning and Leadership; Founding President Jewish Life Network/ Steinhardt Foundation). A pioneer in Holocaust education and commemoration as well as in the Jewish–Christian dialogue which sought to revise theology in the light of the Shoah, he has written extensively on Jewish theology, the ethics of Jewish power, Jewish–Christian relations, and religious and cultural pluralism.

Amy-Jill Levine is University Professor of New Testament and Jewish Studies, E. Rhodes and Leona B. Carpenter Professor of New Testament Studies, and Professor of Jewish Studies at Vanderbilt Divinity School and College of Arts and Science; she is also Affiliated Professor, Centre for the Study of Jewish-Christian Relations, Cambridge UK. Her books include *The Misunderstood Jew: The Church and the Scandal of the Jewish Jesus; Short Stories by Jesus: The Enigmatic Parables of a Controversial Rabbi; The Meaning of the Bible: What the Jewish Scriptures and the Christian Old Testament Can Teach Us* (co-authored with Douglas Knight); and *The New Testament, Methods and Meanings* (co-authored with Warren Carter). Dr.

Levine is also the editor of the *Jewish Annotated New Testament* (with Marc Z. Brettler). Holding the B.A. from Smith College, and the M.A. and Ph.D. from Duke University, she has honorary doctorates from the University of Richmond, the Episcopal Theological Seminary of the Southwest, the University of South Carolina-Upstate, Drury University, and Christian Theological Seminary. A self-described Yankee Jewish feminist, Professor Levine is a member of Congregation Sherith Israel, an Orthodox Synagogue in Nashville, TN, although she is often quite unorthodox.

David Patterson holds the Hillel Feinberg Chair in Holocaust Studies in the Ackerman Center for Holocaust Stduies at the University of Texas at Dallas. A winner of the National Jewish Book Award and the Koret Jewish Book Award, he has published more than 30 books and 150 articles and book chapters. His most recent books include *Anti-Semitism and Its Evil: Anti-Semitism from Nazism to Islamic Jihad* (2011), *Emil L. Fackenheim: A Jewish Philosopher's Response to the Holocaust* (2008), *Open Wounds: The Crisis of Jewish Thought in the Aftermath of Auschwitz* (2006), *Wrestling with the Angel* (2006), *Along the Edge of Annihilation* (1999), *Sun Turned to Darkness* (1998), and others. He is the editor and translator of *The Complete Black Book of Russian Jewry* (2002) and co-editor (with Alan L. Berger) of the *Encyclopedia of Holocaust Literature* (2002).

John T. Pawlikowski is a priest of the Servite Order. He serves as Professor of Social Ethics at the Catholic Theological Union in Chicago where he also directs the Catholic–Jewish Studies program. He has been associated with United States Holocaust Memorial Museum since its inception with Presidential appointments by Jimmy Carter, the senior George Bush and Bill Clinton. He currently serves on the Museum's Academic Committee and its Committee on Ethics, Religion and the Holocaust. Governor Pat Quinn of Illinois appointed him to the state's Holocaust and Genocide Commission. He is the author/editor of some ten books including *Ethics in the Shadow of the Holocaust*.

John K. Roth is the Edward J. Sexton Professor Emeritus of Philosophy and the Founding Director of the Center for the Study of the Holocaust, Genocide, and Human Rights (now the Center for Human Rights) at Claremont McKenna College, where he taught from 1966 through 2006. In 2007–2008, he served as the Robert and Carolyn Frederick Distinguished Visiting Professor of Ethics at DePauw University in Greencastle, Indiana. In addition to service on the United States Holocaust Memorial Council and on the editorial board for the journal *Holocaust and Genocide Studies*, he has published hundreds of articles and reviews and authored, co-authored, or edited more than fifty books, including *Approaches to Auschwitz; Ethics During and*

After the Holocaust; The Oxford Handbook of Holocaust Studies; *Rape: Weapon of War and Genocide;* and *Encountering the Stranger: A Jewish-Christian-Muslim Trialogue*. Roth has been Visiting Professor of Holocaust studies at the University of Haifa, Israel, and his Holocaust-related research appointments have included a Koerner Visiting Fellowship at the Oxford Centre for Hebrew and Jewish Studies in England as well as an appointment as the Ina Levine Invitational Scholar at the Center for Advanced Holocaust Studies, United States Holocaust Memorial Museum. From 2011 to 2013, he chaired the national board of the Federation of State Humanities Councils. In addition to holding several honorary degrees, Roth was named the 1988 U.S. National Professor of the Year by the Council for Advancement and Support of Education and the Carnegie Foundation for the Advancement of Teaching, and in 2012, he received the Holocaust Educational Foundation's Distinguished Achievement Award for Holocaust Studies and Research.

Elie Wiesel is the author of over fifty books, both fiction and nonfiction, including his international best-selling Holocaust memoir *Night*, which recounts his experience during the Shoah and the novel *A Beggar in Jerusalem*, winner of the *Prix Médicis*. He is the recipient of the United States Congressional Gold Medal, the Presidential Medal of Freedom, the French Legion of Honor's Grand Cross, an honorary knighthood of the British Empire and, in 1986, the Nobel Peace Prize.